Sultan Ahmed III's calligraphy of the *Basmala*:
"In the Name of God, the All-Merciful, the All-Compassionate"

The Ottoman Sultans

Mighty Guests of the Throne

Note on Transliteration

In this work, words in Ottoman Turkish, including the Turkish names of people and their written works, as well as place-names within the boundaries of present-day Turkey, have been transcribed according to official Turkish orthography. Accordingly, *c* is read as *j*, *ç* is *ch*, and *ş* is *sh*. The *ğ* is silent, but it lengthens the preceding vowel. *ı* is pronounced like the "*o*" in "atom," and *ö* is the same as the German letter in Köln or the French "*eu*" as in "peu." Finally, *ü* is the same as the German letter in Düsseldorf or the French "*u*" in "lune." The anglicized forms, however, are used for some well-known Turkish words, such as Turcoman, Seljuk, vizier, sheikh, and pasha as well as place-names, such as Anatolia, Gallipoli, and Rumelia.

The Ottoman Sultans

Mighty Guests of the Throne

SALİH GÜLEN

Translated by
EMRAH ŞAHİN

BLUE DOME

Originally published in Turkish as *Tahtın Kudretli Misafirleri: Osmanlı Padişahları*

13 12 11 10   1 2 3 4

Published by Blue Dome Press
535 Fifth Avenue, 6th Fl
New York, NY, 10017

www.bluedomepress.com

Library of Congress Cataloging-in-Publication Data Available

ISBN 978-1-935295-04-4

Front cover: An 1867 painting of the Ottoman sultans from Osman Gazi to Sultan Abdülaziz by Stanislaw Chlebowski

Front flap: Rosewater flask, encrusted with precious stones

Title page: Ottoman Coat of Arms

Back flap: Sultan Mehmed IV's edict on the land grants that were deeded to the mosque erected by the Mother Sultan in Bahçekapı, Istanbul (*Bottom*: 16th century Ottoman parade helmet, encrusted with gems).

Back cover: 18th century throne of Sultan Mahmud I given as a gift by Nadir Shah, embellished with emeralds, rubies, and pearls

Photographs: Mustafa Yılmaz, Bahadır Taşkın, Halit Ömer Camcı, Ahmet Özdemir, Salih Gülen, Ekrem Tez, Özer Akpınar, Harun Gülsül, and www.thinkstockphotos.com

Art Director: Engin Çiftçi
Graphic Design: Murat Arabacı

Printed by
Çağlayan A.Ş., Izmir - Turkey

Contents

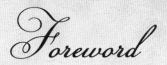

Foreword

The Ottoman Dynasty is unique in that it is the only male line dynasty ever to have continued uninterrupted for over 600 years. Humbly sharing the honor of being a member of this dynasty, I believe it is very important that people today are accurately informed as to the important part it played in the history not only of the Turks and of Islam, but also in that of the world as a whole. Among the thirty-six sultans who ruled over the Ottoman Empire, there were military commanders of exceptional ability, statesmen of genius, men of great athletic prowess, expert musicians, gifted composers and poets, and calligraphers of note. For many centuries, these rulers made it their primary goal to protect and defend their subject peoples, to sustain their welfare, to safeguard the Abode of Islam, and to further the development of Ottoman civilization.

Reflective of the Ottoman sultans' governmentality, all subjects belonging to different religions and of different ethnicities and speaking various languages were given, under their multi-century rule, the means and opportunity to co-exist happily. In my view, it is largely thanks to this "humane" method of administration that the Ottoman sultans are still revered in Turkey today, just as they are still remembered with affection in many parts of the Islamic world and are widely known in the Balkans, the Middle East, Africa, the Far East and Central Asia. It is perhaps also their humanitarianism that helps vindicate the Ottoman legacy while other comparable empires and kingdoms are doomed to be vilified after their demise.

In the fifteenth, sixteenth, and seventeenth centuries, the empire over which the Ottoman sultans ruled was the most powerful state in the world. But although the Ottomans held sway over countless peoples in territories that spanned three continents, they never set out to exploit their subjects either in material or in non-material ways. The fact that today, Turkish is a language known to very few in the Balkans or in the Middle East—both of which were under Ottoman rule for more than four hundred years—clearly demonstrates the lack of any attempt at cultural domination. In contrast, the languages of the West are as widely spoken, for instance, in Southern Asia and in Africa as are the native languages of these regions—further evidence of the marked difference in approach between the Ottomans and the European colonial powers, and of the comparative tolerance enjoyed by subjects of the Ottoman Empire.

The structure of Ottoman administration allowed several different legal systems to exist side by side, each community with its own courts in which judgments were given according to that community's laws. This system permitted different languages, religions, and sects to coexist successfully for hundreds of years—a record equaled by very few of the "advanced" democracies of our times. The cultural and legal synthesis achieved by the Ottomans also surpassed the systems in force in the countries of many of their contemporaries.

The Ottoman method of administration embodied the ideals of social harmony, social justice, and environmental awareness. Many of the charitable foundations established by the sultans and other members of the dynasty have survived until the present time. The complex of buildings called *külliye*s, which are centered around the mosques with schools, colleges, libraries, healthcare facilities, public water fountains, public baths, almshouses, and soup kitchens for the poor as well as caravanserais, which offered accommodation and stabling for travelers, built in every corner of the Ottoman territories, especially those in the Holy Cities of Mecca and Medina, were financed by charitable foundations of this kind, providing an example of how a state should ideally fulfill its social responsibilities. All these institutions rendered services to the poor, to travelers and to students free of charge for centuries. Benevolent services and good works of this kind, performed for religious reasons, show how the requirements of Islam were perceived by the Ottoman dynasty and how religious belief was put into practice in the Ottoman world at the time.

When the rulers of the Ottoman Empire were laying down the groundwork for their own civilization in the territories they had conquered, they behaved with respect towards those civilizations that had come before them, always trying to adapt and build onto whatever had been left behind in an effort to preserve the "common inheritance" of humanity that is only now recognized and appreciated. The contemporary survival of many buildings from the Roman and Byzantine periods is indebted to the respect the Ottomans afforded these civilizations.

A comparison of the Ottoman imperial palaces with their European and Asian counterparts makes it solidly clear that the Ottoman sultans lived their lives far more modestly. Even so, they cracked the mystery of ruling from their smaller Imperial Council Chamber (the *Kubbealtı*) over a much larger track of territory that stretched millions of square miles. And in fact, no greater peace has ever prevailed in the lands of the vast transcontinental Empire stretching from the Balkans to the Caucasus and from the Sahara to the Middle East. Those studying today's unrest in these lands should look further into the Ottomans' peaceful governing of the territories for centuries.

Contrary to what some argue, no sultan turned on his state, people, or the religion he believed in. This tradition of faithfulness continued even after the forced migration of the Ottoman dynasty that followed the abolition of the sultanate. Finally, not a single member of the dynasty engaged in any activity which might have caused difficulties for the newly-founded Turkish Republic.

A number of the members of the Ottoman dynasty live outside of Turkey today, while some of them reside in the homeland; indeed, a significant number of them are citizens of the Republic of Turkey. It is the common wish of every member of the Ottoman family that the Republic of Turkey, which resuscitated from the ashes of the Ottoman Empire, should be a powerful state, having its voice heard on a global stage.

This book, *The Ottoman Sultans: Mighty Guests of the Throne*, is an important work in that it sets forth the contributions made by the sultans to the development of the Turkish nation, as well as to that of the Islamic world as a whole. I hereby appreciate and thank very much the author Salih Gülen and the publisher, Tughra Books.

Finally, I would like to commemorate, with grace and sincere gratitude, my ancestors and grandfathers who "guested" on the Ottoman throne for the period spanning from 1299 to 1922.

Osman Osmanoğlu
Beylerbeyi, May 29, 2009

Preface

"Throning" an empire like the Ottoman Empire, whose territory rested on three continents and stretched for more than 7.7 million square miles (20 million square kilometers) at the height of its power, was a tremendous responsibility that impacted of the entire world of that time. No one would know the responsibilities of this great power better than the members of the Ottoman dynasty, the sultans in particular.

The question comes to mind: why hasn't such a research project been hitherto conducted, while many other works on the Ottoman Empire were published time and again? This work aims to examine not only the political work of the sultans, but the efforts they made in enriching Turkish culture, and most importantly, the contributions they made to the common legacy of human civilization.

The difficulty of introducing all the sultans within the limited scope of this study inhibited the discussion of many significant details. In particular, our research team had to sum up some of the facts, in a nutshell, about those sultans who ruled the empire for more than two decades.

The information in this book was cross-referenced with the most recent scholarship in the field. Furthermore, we applied the interpretations emerging from the authentic sources; understandably, however, the work could not reflect all available perspectives. Ultimately, this text intends to canvass a broader picture of Ottoman history and to identify the place of sultans in it.

Distinguished from other works which underscore the sultans' political sovereignty, this work analyzes the sultans' various responsibilities as champions of the Muslim world, and highlights their achievements as caliphs.

The visuals included in the work come from a wide array of original sources. The selections give more emphasis to the arts and the sultans' contributions and less to the battle specters. In this respect, various historical photographs, miniatures, and gravures are also published here for the first time. Some contemporarily remnant works of art were photographed and added to them, which together illustrate their details of elegance and appeal, perhaps not possible to grip at first sight.

Finally, I would like to recognize the many people who worked to make this book possible. Apparently, they do not receive well-deserved acknowledgment, for it is only my name that appears in the credits. I would like to express my gratitude particularly to Professor İlber Ortaylı, the director of the Topkapı Palace, who taught me many unknown details about the palace and the relations between the sultans and their households; Şehzade Osman Osmanoğlu Efendi, a descendant of the Ottoman lineage, who kindly offered his family collection and generously shared his informed expertise on the imperial traditions and unknown aspects of sultans of the later periods, especially of his paternal grandfather Sultan Murad V and his maternal grandfather Sultan Mehmed Reşad; Dr. Reşit Haylamaz, the editor-in-chief of the Kaynak Publishing Group, who continuously supported the project for over two years so that it grew into the publication of this book; the Topkapı Palace staff for their generous and rich visual contributions; Istanbul University; and the photographers whose perspectives and shots brought color and spirit into this book.

Salih Gülen
Istanbul, January 2009

Ottoman family tree from Osman Gazi to Abdülhamid I

THE OTTOMAN DYNASTY

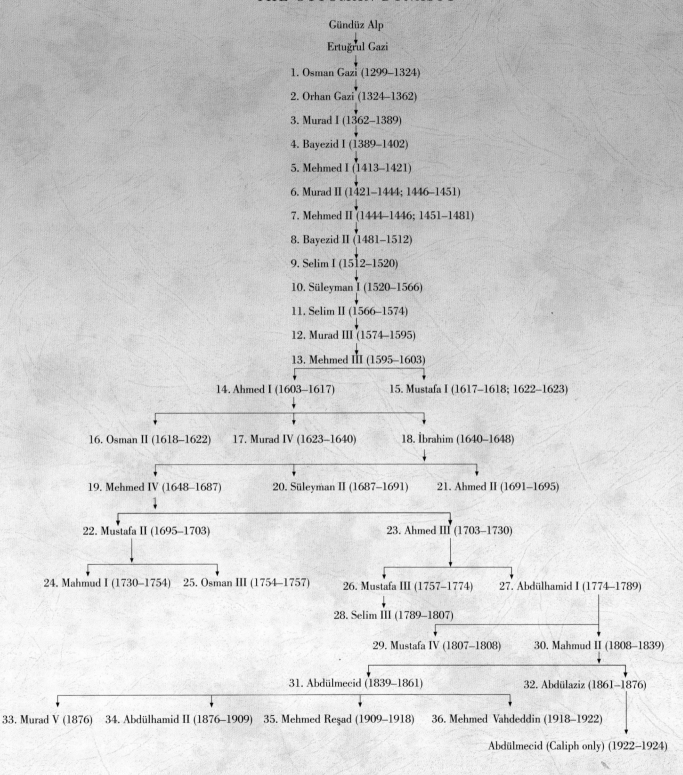

Gündüz Alp

Ertuğrul Gazi

1. Osman Gazi (1299–1324)

2. Orhan Gazi (1324–1362)

3. Murad I (1362–1389)

4. Bayezid I (1389–1402)

5. Mehmed I (1413–1421)

6. Murad II (1421–1444; 1446–1451)

7. Mehmed II (1444–1446; 1451–1481)

8. Bayezid II (1481–1512)

9. Selim I (1512–1520)

10. Süleyman I (1520–1566)

11. Selim II (1566–1574)

12. Murad III (1574–1595)

13. Mehmed III (1595–1603)

14. Ahmed I (1603–1617)　　　15. Mustafa I (1617–1618; 1622–1623)

16. Osman II (1618–1622)　　17. Murad IV (1623–1640)　　18. İbrahim (1640–1648)

19. Mehmed IV (1648–1687)　　20. Süleyman II (1687–1691)　　21. Ahmed II (1691–1695)

22. Mustafa II (1695–1703)　　　　　23. Ahmed III (1703–1730)

24. Mahmud I (1730–1754)　25. Osman III (1754–1757)　　26. Mustafa III (1757–1774)　27. Abdülhamid I (1774–1789)

28. Selim III (1789–1807)

29. Mustafa IV (1807–1808)　　30. Mahmud II (1808–1839)

31. Abdülmecid (1839–1861)　　　　　32. Abdülaziz (1861–1876)

33. Murad V (1876)　34. Abdülhamid II (1876–1909)　35. Mehmed Reşad (1909–1918)　36. Mehmed Vahdeddin (1918–1922)

Abdülmecid (Caliph only) (1922–1924)

The first Ottoman Sultan

Osman Gazi

Reign: 1299—1324

Honorifics and Aliases: Gazi [Warrior for the Faith], Fahreddin [the Pride of the Faith], Osmancık [literally "Little Osman," the diminutive of "Osman" in Turkish to express endearment and affection], and Kara [Both his gallantry and the jet black color of his hair, his beard, and eyebrows earned him in his youth the title of Kara ("Black") Osman.]

Father's Name: Ertuğrul Gazi
Mother's Name: Hayme Ana
Place and Date of Birth: Söğüt in northwestern Anatolia, 1258
Age at Accession to the Throne: 41
Cause and Date of Death: Gout, 1324
Place of Death and Burial Site: Söğüt – his tomb is in Bursa
Male Heirs: Orhan, Çoban, Melik, Hamid, and Pazarlu
Female Heir: Fatma Melek

Osman Gazi,[1] whose name would inspire the title of the Ottoman Empire,[2] is the Ottoman sultan to have bequeathed the fewest of records, inasmuch as nobody presumed that his insignificant principality would eventually swell into a state of such magnificence. A considerable part of the Turkish sources on him are not contemporary, but are formed out of oral history pieces, which were put together later on. The conventional accounts state that Alaeddin

Miniature of Osman Gazi by Levni[3] in his *Kebir Musavver Silsilenâme* (The Great Envisaged Portraiture Geneology)

Keykubat, the sultan of the Anatolian Seljuk Turks,[4] bestowed on the Kayı tribe of the Oghuz Turks the regions of Karacadağ and Söğüt as its homeland, and Domaniç as a pasture—a reward for Ertuğrul Gazi, the leader of the tribe and father of Osman Gazi, and his men's courage on the battlefield.

Osman Gazi established his frontier principality in Söğüt in northwestern Anatolia, which neighbored Byzantium. This frontier territory was closest to Byzantium and gave him a tremendous opportunity for rapid territorial expansion. Another great achievement of Osman Gazi was his commandership that welcomed the masses of Turcoman refugees known as *garip*s, who had been stripped of their homeland. He trained these Turcoman *garip*s streaming into his territory and banded them under the same flag.

From one narration, which the sources relate to Osman's ascendancy to the reign, emerges the following anecdote. The Turcomans who had moved toward the western frontiers proclaimed that sovereignty over the region could go to no other tribe but the Kayı tribe of the Oghuz Turks after the weakening of the Anatolian Seljuk state that lost its power as a result of the devastating Mongol invasions from the east. They further told Osman Gazi, "The Khan thou shall be and engaged with *gaza*s we your subjects shall thus be." Osman Bey[5] accepted this offer.

A lack of consensus in the contemporary sources notwithstanding, the genealogy of Osman Gazi is acknowledged as in the following order of succession: Oğuz, Gökalp, Kızıl Boğa, Kayaalp, Mir Süleyman Alp, Şahmelik, Gündüz Alp, Ertuğrul Gazi, and Osman Gazi. According to the historical accounts, Ertuğrul Gazi had three heirs named Gündüz Alp, Sarubatu, and Osman. On his deathbed, Ertuğrul Gazi declared that he wished his youngest son Osman to succeed him as the new *bey*, the Turkish title for the chief sovereign. Osman's older brothers consented and did not refrain from serving under their youngest brother.

During the formative years of the Ottoman *beylik*—the territorial domain ruled by the Turkish chief sovereign who was called *bey*, Osman Gazi's most notable companions were such *alperen*s ("hero-saints") as Turgut Alp, Aykut Alp, Saltuk Alp, Hasan Alp, Konur Alp, Abdurrahman Gazi, and

Akçakoca. Later, the sons and grandsons of these *gazi*s would reach preeminence in the Ottoman administration and army.

Osman Gazi adopted two primary methods of conquest against Byzantium: *gaza* and *istimalah*, or "warming" hearts to Islam. The objective of the *gaza* was to conquer new lands; *istimalah* was used to win the support of the newly conquered.

Contrary to common mythical assumptions, the native peoples of the conquered regions were not subject to forced conversion. In fact, the Ottomans did not consider those who converted to Islam under coercion to be Muslim. For them, the only method of conversion was to gain the goodwill of the conquered, embellish their cities, facilitate their commercial activities, and provide their welfare while allowing them to practice their respective religions. In this way they showed the conquered the excellence of Islam. It is thus that many people embraced Islam by will.

The Bosnian and Albanian Muslims of today are the descendants of those who became Muslims following the Ottoman conquests in the Balkans. In their conquests, the Ottomans utterly respected the important motto, "thou that oppress evermore shall expect a good end no more."

Osman Gazi often consulted Sheikh Edebali and Faqih Dursun, Islamic scholars of his time, on the matters of conquest and administrative affairs, and sought their advice regarding his policies conformity to Islam. Overall, he was very careful to govern his principality in compliance with the Islamic law.

The greatest military achievement of Osman Gazi was perhaps the fact that he successfully united under a single flag all his soldiers regardless of their diverse background. The Byzantine sources introduce Osman Gazi as the most gallant commander that ever made incursions to the lands of Byzantium. Expectedly, the *gazi*s and *alp*s ("heroes") united under the flag of Osman Gazi, the most successful commander among them. Not only the Muslims but also the *tekfur*s, or the old Christian lords of the conquered lands, turned into Osman's new companions-in-arms as soldier servants.

Clemency, dialogue, and compromise played as profound a role in the success of his leadership as did the idea of engaging *gaza*s. But the ideal of *gaza* was an important factor in the development of the Ottoman state. This method would later become so sophisticated as to generate new military units like the Janissaries[6] and the Sipahis.[7]

Osman Gazi fortified the physical strength of his *beylik*, or principality, thanks to military might, economic opportunities, and the diplomacy he pursued. In addition, he strengthened the religious foundations of his principality by winning the support of *ahi dervish*es, who were the spiritual leaders of semi-religious fraternities for the tradesmen and artisans, and Islamic jurists and by accepting as his spiritual master Sheikh Edebali, one of the most acclaimed contemporary religious leaders. Jurists like Faqih Dursun, who excelled in Islamic law and the Sunni principles, were personally involved in the founding and institutionalizing of the Ottoman principality on the principles of Islam. Then they served as *imam*s, or religious leaders, in the newly conquered cities, towns, and villages. They also played a tremendous role in enlightening the public. In order to provide them with the means to keep their services, both Osman Gazi and his son Orhan Gazi granted them lands for their religious foundations. The imperial registers (*tahrir defter*s) that survive to this day provide evidence for various endowment lands granted by them. In fact, the first ministers, or viziers, of the principality were chosen among those Islamic jurisprudents.

Miniature of Osman Gazi with Akçakoca Bey on his left and Konur Alp on his right

5

It was during the formative years of the Ottomans that the Ilkhanid Moguls had defeated the Anatolian Seljukid state and had become the dominant force in Anatolia (Asia Minor). The Mogul domination in Anatolia resulted in massive discontent. In alliance with the Turcomans, the Mamluks[8] supported a series of revolts led by the local Mogul governors in Anatolia against the Ilkhanids. Such a chaotic situation gave Osman Gazi a golden opportunity to advance toward Byzantium without a serious Mogul threat in Anatolia.

In the first decades, Osman Gazi was busy mainly with pulling his bands together and disciplining them. In his first combat against the local Christian lords, he faced off against the lord of İnegöl in the area called Ermenibeli en route between Söğüt and Domaniç. Osman Gazi's troops lost this battle, and his nephew fell a martyr.

This was Osman Gazi's first battle against the Byzantium lords. In order to conquer İnegöl, he first captured Kulaca Hisar near İnegöl in 1285. This forced the lords of İnegöl and Karacahisar to combine their forces against the Ottomans. A bitter battle broke out near İkizce in 1286. The Ottomans won the battle; however Sarubatu Savcı, the brother of Osman Gazi, died a martyr. A couple of years later, Osman Gazi conquered Karacahisar and occupied the surrounding region. The Friday sermons acknowledged his sovereignty and announced the independence of his *beylik* (principality) in 1299. Karacahisar eventually turned into a Muslim fortress-city, accommodating the immigrants from the regions nearby as well as other Anatolian Turkish principalities.[9]

Osman Gazi soon moved on to a new conquest on the eastern side of the Sakarya River. The support of Köse Mihal and Samsa Çavuş, his local allies, earned him the keys to numerous towns in the region. His conquests further brought the local Christian rulers to submission.

With the rapid territorial expansion of his principality came Osman Gazi's retirement. Osman Gazi split the newly conquered lands among his dynasty and companions who made it possible, and entrusted the throne to them. In 1299, Osman Gazi gave İnönü to Orhan Bey, Yarhisar to Hasan Alp, and İnegöl to Turgut Alp. Over the course of time, granting particular lands to the commanders who conquered them would be applied in the Rumelia region as the chief method of conquests.

In the early years of his principality, Osman Gazi relied not only on warfare but also diplomacy. For instance, the dialogue and alliance that the Gazi made with Mihael, the lord of Harmankaya who would later be known as Gazi Köse Mihal, afforded him both an ally who proved to be a worthy source of intelligence on Byzantium and a fighter at his side. Mihael would soon be an early Muslim convert and a devout warrior fighting for Islam.

Osman Gazi, who had resided in Yenişehir, chose İznik (Nicaea) as his next area of conquest. He besieged İznik following a series of initial incursions. Upon hearing about the siege of the city, Byzantium mobilized troops for a rescue mission. Moreover, the local Byzantium lords of Bursa, Kestel, and Orhaneli began an attack against the Kayıs. Osman Gazi, informed of the enemy's collective rescue efforts, waged full charge at the Battle of Koyunhisar to declare a final victory on July 27, 1302. The Greek survivors took emergency refuge at the fortress of İzmit. Despite the fact that Osman Gazi continued the siege and patiently waited for the eventual surrender of the city, İznik would not count to his credit. Orhan Gazi would collect the city in 1331.

The victory at Koyunhisar gave recognition and fame to Osman Gazi and his Kayı tribe and brought other Gazis around under his flag. Furthermore, the Byzantine domination in southern Marmara came under jeopardy. Now that the Ottomans captured the environs, the city of Bursa became the *Kızıl Elma* (literally "Red Apple"), or the new Promised Land. The city came under blockade following the war in 1303. Indeed, the Byzantine registers show that the Turks had already been visible everywhere up to the straits of Constantinople even before the year of 1304.

An old photograph of the Tomb of Osman Gazi taken after its renovation by Sultan Abdülhamid II

Osman and Orhan, father and son, were laid to rest in tombs high up on the Tophane hill, Abdullah Brothers

General view of 19th century Bursa from the Tophane section of the city by the Abdullah Brothers

7

Osman Gazi ruled his principality with other members of his dynasty. This is quite exceptional as this system of governance was not applied to the later periods. On the contrary, the later convention dictated a monarchical structure, which was ruled by the sultan as the head of the central administration.

As a symbol of sovereignty, the Ottomans painted the Seal of Kayı (with three arrows and a bow) on their flags and minted it on their coins from the beginning of the establishment of their state.

Osman Gazi assigned his son Orhan as his *de facto* successor in the last years of his life when his illness did not allow him to rule. It is narrated that Osman Gazi looked forward to hearing from Orhan Gazi the good news that Bursa had been conquered. He then requested his tomb be built there. In 1324, after serving as the head of the Kayıs for twenty-seven years, he passed away.

Osman Gazi wished that his son always conform to Islamic law, protect and accommodate his subjects, seek consultation for state affairs, remain just, and defend his people at all costs.

Osman Gazi was a leader who had always been concerned with his principality and subjects. He lived a decent life and always took great pleasure in being among his people. He paid utmost attention to consultation in state affairs and applied the decisions that came from the deliberative body. His remaining assets included not more than a piece of cloth for his turban (*sarık*), which is about six-feet long, an armor set for his horse, a saddlebag, one single garment, a saltshaker, a spoon holder, a pair of boots, a prayer beads, an elegant sword, a shield and spear, a few horses, and several sheep grazed to sacrifice for his guests. Osman Gazi set a good example for future "guests of throne" of how an ideal sultan should live on a modest substance.

Century-old painting of the Tomb of Ertuğrul Gazi, the father of Osman Gazi, in Söğüt

The Second Ottoman Sultan

Orhan Gazi

Reign: 1324–1362

Honorifics and Aliases: *Gazi, İhtiyareddin, Seyfeddin,* and *Şücaeddin*
Father's Name: Osman Gazi
Mother's Name: Malhun Hatun
Place and Date of Birth: Söğüt, 1281
Age at Accession to the Throne: 43
Cause and Date of Death: Mental anguish – 1362
Place of Death and Burial Site: Bursa – his tomb was built in the new capital, Bursa.
Male Heirs: Süleyman, Murad, Halil, İbrahim, and Kasım
Female Heir: Fatima Hatun and Hadice Hatun

Orhan Gazi was raised and trained to be the future Bey. Osman Gazi, his father, sent him on a series of campaigns with experienced commanders like Akça Koca, Konuralp, and Köse Mihal so that he would be ready for his career. Then he handed over his principality to his son after his sufferings from gout made him unable to walk. Soon after his father's death, Orhan ascended to the throne with no competitor in sight. In fact, nobody impeached his rise to power despite the fact that he had other brothers.

Miniature of Orhan Gazi by Levni in his *Kebir Musavver Silsilenâme*, (The Great Envisaged Portraiture Geneology)

The great conquest of Bursa in 1324 marked the ascendancy of Orhan Gazi to the throne. Bursa, on the opposite side of the Marmara Sea from the Constantinople, became the new center of the Ottoman *beylik*. It is well known that many constructional projects undertaken in Bursa right after the conquest renovated the city. Orhan Gazi built merchantile establishments as well as open and covered bazaars in an effort to elevate the city of Bursa to a trade center. Upon his visit to Bursa ten years after the conquest, the famous contemporary traveler Ibn Battuta illustrated the city as "a big city with vivid bazaars and wide streets."

The Ottoman frontier principality was no more than one of many principalities during the formative period when Osman Gazi became the *bey*. However, the historic activities initiated during the reign of Orhan Gazi attributed the Ottoman principality a later structure that would enable it to find an expansive territory for conquest toward the Balkans and that would connect all other principalities to it in the coming thirty years.

After the conquest of Bursa, Ottoman *gazi*s conquered the forts on the northwest Anatolian coast, including Kocaeli, Kartal, and Aydos, reaching the Straits of Constantinople on the Anatolian side. Another Ottoman victory was sealed in 1329 at the Battle of Palekanon, which the Byzantine Emperor Adronikos III initiated near Darıca with the objective of breaking the siege around İznik and reclaiming the lands he lost to the Ottomans. This victory also showed how far the Ottomans had come up to that point in time. The Ottomans then conquered İznik in 1331, Gemlik in 1334, and İzmit in 1337. As a result, there remained "no territory in the vicinity to subjugate of the Byzantium lords." The Ottoman success personified in the character of Orhan Gazi came as a chain of interconnected events and granted him the access to many doors he perhaps would have never expected. The internal strife from which the Turcoman Karesid principality on the eastern side of the Dardanelles suffered provided Orhan Gazi with the opportunity to claim this principality. The acquisition of the Karesid principality, the first Anatolian principality to join the

The Green Mosque built in İznik (Nicaea) in the early Ottoman period is famous
for its green tiles, the oldest in Ottoman history, decorating the minaret.

Ottomans in 1345, launched the naval activities as the *gazi*s of the Karesids began to advocate a campaign across the Dardanelles.

In response to the request of Yohanniz Kantakouzenos, who wanted to be crowned Byzantium Emperor after the death of the Emperor Andronikos III Palaiologos, Orhan Gazi sent the army commanded by his son Süleyman Pasha to Edirne and helped Kantakouzenos subdue of Serbian and Bulgarian pressure in 1352. Through this relationship, the Ottomans crossed into Europe settling at the Fort of Çimpe (Tzympe) in Gallipoli in 1353. This was their first settlement in the Balkans across the Dardanelles where they obtained a military base to use for further conquests in the Balkans. Contrary to conventional assumptions, Kantakouzenos' continuous demands that the Ottomans evacuate the fort prove that this fort was not simply handed over by the Byzantium emperor. Later, Süleyman Pasha besieged the Gallipoli fortress and began to wait for its surrender. Quite extraordinarily, a severe earthquake that happened at night crumbled the walls of the fortress. The Ottomans captured the fortress much more easily than they would have ever expected, granted the usual reparations, and made themselves at home. This marked the first permanent settling of Muslims in the Balkans and thus the first sign of Islam in the region never to be eradicated.

The news reached Byzantium and the broader Christian world with tremendous anxiety. Europe was planning a crusade, this time not to reclaim Jerusalem but to save Constantinople from the Ottomans. Gregory Palamas, the archbishop of Salonica who had been taken as a prisoner of war during those years, reported the Ottomans having mentioned to him, "God is their greatest helper to constantly advance Islam from the East to the West and this is a clear proof that Islam is the true religion."

Orhan Gazi, who pursued a superb policy of settlement to ensure the conquests' permanency in the Balkans, settled many Muslim

The Orhaniye Camii (Orhan's Mosque) built by Orhan Gazi in Bursa

families from Anatolia in the newly conquered lands and established new Muslim towns in the Balkans. Those emigrants who made the sacrifice of moving from their permanent residences to a place unknown played a profound role in expanding Islam and in the growth of their principality.

Two events during this period interrupted the Ottoman headway into the Balkans. First, Şehzade[10] Halil was kidnapped at a young age in 1356 by Genovese pirates during a boat trip along the shores of İzmit. In 1359, Ioannes V, the Byzantine emperor sailed with his navy to Foça (near İzmir), paid 100.000 gold coins to rescue him, and turned him over to his father Orhan Gazi in İzmit. Second was the absence of Süleyman Pasha, who passed away in a miserable way when he fell from his horse during a hunting expedition. Orhan Gazi then

14

assigned his son Şehzade Murat to future conquests in the Balkans. In order for the absence of his elder brother not to be felt, Şehzade Murad did his best and carried on the conquests in Rumelia with his tutor Şahin Pasha.

The news that he had lost his great son whom he loved too much almost destroyed Orhan Gazi, now in his seventies. He asked Şehzade Murat to run the state, and then isolated himself only to pass away a few years later in 1362, most probably in Bursa.

Orhan Gazi conquered three major cities of the time: Bursa, İznik, and İzmit and thus played a primary role in the growth of the Ottoman principality. He carried the Muslims—boxed in Anatolia for three centuries—to the European continent thanks to his conquests in Rumelia.

In this respect, while Osman Gazi had provided the transition of his minor Kayı tribe to a great principality, his son Orhan Gazi began the process of turning the principality into a state. It was for the first time during his reign that the administration, military, and legislation were structured. The state council that assembled under his leadership would also be the point of departure for the later Ottoman Imperial Council. While the provinces that had been conquered were partitioned and distributed among the *gazi*s, which in a way constituted a feudal structure during his father's reign, Orhan Gazi constructed a centralist administration which assigned the officials to the newly conquered lands under the counseling of viziers from the elite-intellectual class.

Following the siege of İzmit, Orhan Gazi insisted that his principality have a professional army. Therefore, he established a regular army composed of infantry and cavalry units. In addition, the first *medrese*, or higher education institution, opened in İznik in 1331, and was headed by Davud of Kayseri, one of the contemporary leading scholars.

The sources narrate that Orhan Gazi had built two mosque complexes in Bursa and İznik for various benevolent services for the community. He sometimes served soup to the poor in the soup kitchen of the complexes. Orhan Gazi was a religious ruler. He was a smart commander as well; in fact, he was such a brave commander that he used to ride his horse and lead his army from the very front ranks. He ful-

This ownership brief, granted by Orhan Gazi, is the oldest Ottoman document still kept in the Ottoman central archives.

filled his father's will by always being among the people and for the people.

Famous for his unassuming character, Orhan Gazi was recommended by his brother Alaaddin Ali as his father's successor to the throne. The Ottoman sources show that he did not seek but accepted the throne only upon his brother's insistence to do so. The traveler Ibn Battuta, who met with Orhan Gazi in Bursa, regarded him as "the grandest of all Turcoman sultans" and recorded that he was always out there making conquests, spending no more than a month where he went.

Tomb of Orhan Gazi in Bursa

This fourteenth century almshouse, named after Nilüfer Hatun—wife of Orhan Gazi, serves today as a museum in İznik.

The Third Ottoman Sultan

Sultan Murad I

Reign: 1362–1389

Honorifics and Aliases: *Gazi Hünkar* [Combatant Sovereign], *Hüdavendigar* [the God-like One], *Emir-i Azam* [Great General], *Han* [Khan, ruler], *Padişah* [Great Monarch], and *Sultan'us-Selatin* [Sultan of Sultans]

Father's Name: Orhan Gazi

Mother's Name: Nilüfer Hatun

Place and Date of Birth: Bursa, 1326

Age at Accession to the Throne: 36

Cause and Date of Death: Martyr at the Kosovo Battlefield, 1389

Place of Death and Burial Site: Kosovo – his two tombs were built in Kosovo and in Bursa.

Male Heirs: Yakup Çelebi, Yıldırım Bayezid, Savcı Bey, and İbrahim Bey

Female Heir: Nilüfer Hatun and Melek Hatun

Sultan Murad I, who rose to power as the third Ottoman Sultan, had ruled as the governor of Bursa and then Sultanoyuğu (now Eskişehir) while he was a *şehzade*, or the heir to the throne. Upon the death of his brother Süleyman Pasha, "the Conqueror of Rumelia," he took up the cause and continued the conquests in Rumelia. Murad I obviated the landing of the Papacy and Byzantine troops on the Lapseki and Saros

Miniature of Sultan Murad I by Levni in his *Kebir Musavver Silsilenâme* (The Great Envisaged Portraiture Geneology)

gulfs, and mobilized the pioneer light cavalry units called *akıncıs*[11] all the way up to north near Istanbul to blockade the city during the conquest of Edirne (Adrianople), which would become the second Ottoman capital after Bursa. He also sent the army to Edirne under the leadership of Lala Şahin as a pioneer army. Once this army of Lala Şahin defeated the forces of the local Byzantium ruler of Edirne in the valley of Sazlıdere, Şehzade Murad marched to Edirne with his army on May 5, 1361. As he had prepared for further conquests from Edirne, he received the sad news of his father's death.

During the first years of his reign, Murad I led a series of combats against Karamanids and the Eretna state in Central Anatolia. Ankara went under the Ottoman domination during his time. In the western frontier, Murad I's conquests near Constantinople caused Byzantium to organize a crusade against the Ottomans. In 1366, a crusader army reclaimed and handed Gallipoli on the European side of the Dardanelles back to Byzantium. Sultan Murad I, who thought this would jeopardize the Ottoman presence in Rumelia, pressured Byzantium to return Gallipoli to him as a pre-condition for any terms of peace.

Although Byzantium had been sandwiched territorially by the Ottomans, the Byzantine emperor chose not to return Gallipoli but rather to establish an alliance with the Serbs to rid Rumelia of the Ottomans once and for all.

The Serbs, who had a strong army composed of the Serbian and other local Christian forces, assembled all the way from Thrace to Albania and marched on Lala Şahin. Sultan Murad I was in Bursa by then and mobilized his forces no sooner than he received his commander Lala Şahin's call for help. The Byzantines who held Gallipoli did not let the Ottoman army pass through. On another theater of war, the Serbian army advanced as far as Çirmen on the Meriç River and began to challenge the city of Edirne. Lala Şahin, the protector of Edirne, did not receive the help he requested from Anatolia. He knew that he was alone to fight against the Serbs. He decided to send his pioneer light cavalry (*akıncı*) units head-on to the Serbs on Sep-

قوس اوه ده شهید ولاﻦ سلطان مراد

Miniature of Sultan Murad I on horseback, painter unknown. The top of the miniature reads, "Sultan Murad martyred in Kosovo."

tember 26, 1371. The Ottoman pioneer units commanded by Hacı İlbeyi made a surprise attack when they caught the Serbian soldiers at night in a vulnerable state. In the ensuing chaos, the Serbs fell into confusion; some died in combat while others fell into the Meriç (Maritza) River. The result was a total defeat. Noted in Ottoman history as the Victory of *Sırpsındığı* (The Serbian Defeat), this event revealed the unbelievable truth that the blocked and unaided Ottoman forces had vanquished the Serbian army of 60,000 soldiers and further fed a sense of astonishment and dismay in the Christian World.

The Serbian princes and the Balkan dynasties recognized the superiority of Sultan Murad I and agreed to pay tributes. The Papacy was informed of the defeat of the Christian army six months later. In his letter to the Hungarian King, Pope Gregor XI stressed his fear that the Turks would proceed inside Hungary, Serbia, and Albania after vanquishing the Serbs and might regrettably advance toward the Adriatic Sea, and urged him to remove the Turks from the Christian lands.

While Sultan Murad I was in Rumelia, the *de facto* Byzantine emperor had supported him, most likely in person. During this time, the crown prince Andronikos in Istanbul announced himself as the Byzantine emperor, and Şehzade Savcı Bey in Bursa made a claim to the Ottoman sultanate. Both the Ottomans and Byzantines were caught in these simultaneously-emerging revolts. It is recorded that Murad I came down to the Biga region upon hearing of his son's rebellion. He feigned ignorance of the whole affair and invited his son to a hunting party. Manipulated by those around him, Savcı Bey distributed the state treasure, had his name mentioned at Friday prayers as a symbol of sovereignty, and rejected his father's invitation. In fact, he recruited an army and decided to fight his father. In return, Sultan Murad I marched to Bursa, captured the *şehzade* in an encounter near the Valley of Kite, and killed those who had provoked the *şehzade* to claim the throne. Although Murad I advised his young *şehzade* to confess and repent for his guilt, Savcı Bey responded to him with cruel and harsh words that ended with the blinding of Savcı Bey in 1374 so that he would not rebel again with such severity.

The sultan then gave priority back to the conquests in Rumelia. He led the campaigns from Edirne and the commanders, especially Candarid Kara Halil Hayreddin, Evrenos Gazi, and Lala Şahin Bey, participated in the ongoing conquests.

Murad I then marched on Ivan Shishman of Bulgaria and subjugated him. Ivan agreed to pay tribute to the Ottomans and promised to partake in every battle of the sultan.

At this point, Sultan Murad I assigned Kara Timurtaş Pasha as the *beylerbeyi* (governor general) of Rumelia.[12] This was an important step toward fortifying the Ottoman domination in Rumelia, and shows that Murad I's officers were consummate masters of their profession. Kara Timurtaş Pasha got the consent of the sultan in the years 1375–1381 to undertake in Rumelia the first distribution of *tımar*s (military fiefs) among the native Christian soldiers. He permitted them to live on some parts of the land they used to live on in return for serving in the Ottoman army. This act led to the establishment in the Balkans of an Ottoman army composed of Muslim and Christian soldiers.

Sultan Murad I used dynastic marriages as a means of diplomacy in foreign relations. He endeavored to establish a closely-knit web of connections through marriages between the Ottoman dynasty, the Anatolian Turkish principalities and the Balkan dynasties. The first marriage at this period was announced by the wedding ceremony of his son Şehzade Bayezid and Germiyanid Süleyman Bey's daughter Devlet Hatun. Following this wedding, Kütahya, Tavşanlı, Simav, and Emet were added to the Ottoman territories peacefully as the dowry gifted by the bride's father. The sultan also promised the hand of his daughter Nefise Hatun to Karamanid Alaeddin Ali Bey at the fore-mentioned wedding; they married at a later time. Furthermore, he bought the towns of Akşehir, Beyşehri, Seydişehri, Karaağaç, and Isparta from the Hamidis, who were present at Bayezid's wedding. In Turkish state tradition, the land for the sake of which lives are spared instead of surrendering it to the enemy cannot be given up for whatever reasons, neither as dowry nor a commercial commodity. The dowry and buying of lands during Murad I's reign are interpreted as a proof and professed excuse for the growing acceptance among the Anatolian Turkish principalities that the Ottomans had already become a major political power.

The objective of the sultan was to provide safety in Anatolia and engage in conquests in Rumelia. However, the Göller Yöresi (Lakes Region) in the southwest of Anatolia, which he had bought from the Hamidis, became estranged from the Ottomans and Karamanids. Therefore, Sultan Murad I was forced to march on the Karamanids, who had invaded the region when he was away in Rumelia in 1386. The Karamanids were defeated in the Battle of Frenkyazısı. Sultan Murad I further besieged the city of Konya, the Karamanid capital, but he lifted the siege out of his benign character when his daughter asked him for mercy, and his son-in-law Alaeddin Ali Bey kissed his hand as a sign of respect.

During this period, a blood relationship was formed with Süleyman, the son of the Kastamonu Bey: Murad I wedded his niece Sultan Hanım with Süleyman Bey. In doing so, Kastamonu expressed its allegiance to the Ottomans. Meanwhile, the combats against the Kadı Burhan al-Din state in the East continued. Benevolent relations had been established between the Ottomans and the Mamluks during Murad I's reign, and they supported each other against the crusades. The benevolence between them continued until the death of the sultan.

As a result of the defeat that came after Albania's Frontier-Commander Şahin Bey was ambushed in Pločnik, the Balkan states ventured to attack the Ottomans. Leading a composite army with soldiers from Serbia, Kosovo, Bosnia, Bulgaria, Catalan, Hungary, Czech, Albania, and Wallachia, the Serbian Knez Lazar refused to pay tribute, massacred the innocent Muslim frontier villagers, and was declared by the Serbian Church as "the grand imperator." Therefore, Sultan Murad felt obliged to make a sixth expedition toward Rumelia. The armies of those states that had continued to pay tribute to the Ottomans also joined the Ottoman army.

As part of his divide and conquer strategy to reduce the sheer number of enemy fighters, Sultan Murad first mobilized an army against the Bulgarians and detached Bulgaria from the greater Balkan League. The sultan prepared his military camp in the Kosovo valley to march against the crusader army. However, he not only had to fight the enemy, but he also had to deal with the cloud of dust that descended on his camp. Aware of the fact that a reverse wind that could blow from the enemy side would limit the visibility range of his soldiers, the sultan prayed all night long. Following his prayers, it started to rain, dispelling the cloud of dust. In another prayer, the sultan said: "O my God, sacrifice me in the name of all the Muslims that are and are not here on this battlefield. Take my soul but make us victorious! You made me a veteran on your path and then shall I be a martyr, my Lord."

The first pitched battle of the Ottomans started at dawn and continued for eight uninterrupted hours. Both sides used a new weapon in this war, the canons engineered by the craftsmen in Dubrovnik on the Adriatic Sea. The two wings of the Ottoman army were commanded by Şehzade Bayezid and Şehzade Yakup Bey. When the left wing began to collapse, the Ottoman army would have suffered a miserable defeat if the right wing led by Şehzade Bayezid had not arrived to reinforce Yakup Bey's soldiers. The scattering of the kings that allied with

An old postcard picturing the remnants of the Eski Saray (Old Palace) built by Sultan Murad I in Edirne, which became the new Ottoman capital in 1365

Lazar disbanded the Balkan League, and the Ottomans reached a glorious victory in Kosovo.

Milosh Kobilovich, a wounded veteran lying next to the enemy corpses wanted to be distinguished as the killer of Sultan Murad, who was now inspecting the battle field. Kobilovich leaped forward to the legs of the sultan. Before the sergeants could step in, he kneeled down as if he would kiss the coattail of the sultan, and stabbed the dagger he pulled out of his boots right into the heart of the sultan. The Ottoman chronicler Hoja Saadeddin Efendi in his *Tacü't-Tevarih*[13] depicts the scene in the following way: "To the Shah he flank attacked and the wound carved up by his stabbing / With blood everywhere tulip gardens flourished / The whole world was surrounded and submitted to such wailing." Milosh tried to escape but was caught and executed.

Sultan Murad I must have been happy to see all his prayers answered, calling his wound as a debt his soul should pay. Sultan Murad's son Yıldırım Bayezid was rather shocked and cried with grief at the sight of his seeing his heavily-wounded and semi-conscious father. The sultan asked Şehzade Bayezid to succeed him to the throne. Meanwhile, Şehzade Yakup Bey was chasing the enemy away, uninformed of his father's assassination and its aftermath.

The state high officials and *beys* discussed the Savcı Bey Incident, which almost had brought the state to chaos and unanimously agreed that the fledgling state could not bear another *şehzade* contest. Therefore, they agreed that "sedition is more dangerous than death," which meant that the other *şehzade* would have to be sacrificed for the sake of religion and the state; that is, in order to avoid countrywide disorder and thus cause a civil war as well as for the greater good of the state, which had been incessantly engaged in *gaza*s. This decision was carried out in Kosovo, and Yakup Bey's coffin was sent to Bursa with his father's. This was the first fratricide in Ottoman history that resulted from the greater notion of protecting and ensuring the survival of the Islamic state. It enabled the state to continue engaging in *gaza*s and to remain unified. Contrary to some assumptions, these decisions did not please the Ottoman sultans at all. The ensuing bitter events like those during *Fetret Devri*, or the Era of Interregnum, caused this application to recur at times. However, fratricide was not the norm throughout Ottoman history.

The Christian world welcomed the death of Murad I in Kosovo. The news that the sultan who had proved unbeatable at battlefields was a danger no more raised a wave of joy and celebration in Paris and Byzantine Istanbul. The assassination of the Ottoman sultan also brought about a series of false news in Europe. In the news, the Turks were reported to have suffered a total defeat, and the Ottoman sultan, one of his sons, and the greater portion of his army eliminated. Another myth was spread of twelve heroes who cut through the Ottoman lines, moved to the tent of Sultan Murad I, and annihilated him!

The Battle of Kosovo, which represents the last great defense of the Serbs, is regarded as the national epic of the Serbs. The Serbian histories initially narrated on "the great achievement of Knez Lazar" and "the victory of Serbs!," but subsequent sources give credit to the defeat by the Ottomans. Oddly enough, Bosnian King Tvrtko I, who sent Vlatko Vukovic to the battle, assumed in his letters that the claimed victory belonged to him!

Sultan Murad I, who was the first and only sultan in the Ottoman history to be martyred by the enemy at the battlefield, was a middle-sized, square-built man with a round face, hook-nose, thick eyebrows, and a thick mustache. His shoulders were straight, his arms muscled and strong. He had fair skin with a light brown-haired beard.

Tomb of Sultan Murad I in Bursa

This old photograph taken around 1895 shows the Tomb of Sultan Murad I in Kosovo Polje, where his innards were buried following his martyrdom on the battlefield in the First Kosovo War in 1389. When Sultan Mehmed Reşad (ruled 1909–1918) visited the tomb in 1911, tens of thousands of Kosovans and Albanians welcomed him, and together they performed the Friday Prayer.

Sultan Murad I gave the *gazas* such high priority that he made six campaigns during his reign to Rumelia and carried Islam to the Balkans. He never wanted to quarrel with the Anatolian Turkish principalities, which he knew originated from the same ancestry and preferred to negotiate and establish marriage alliances with them instead.

Ottoman sources regard him as an observant Muslim blessed with sainthood. He was calm, caring, philanthropic, and righteous. He reflected the affection of Islam on his Christian subjects and was loved by them in return so much that many Christians converted to Islam thanks to his good behavior and attitude. He respected the intellectuals and artisans. He was a smart commander and an organizing statesman. He spoke very little and spoke in sage expressions when he did so. He had a balanced character and good presence.

Anatolia and the surrounding regions generally sympathized with Sultan Murad I as the great *gazi* sultan fighting against the crusaders. The Turks, Arabs, and Persians and other ethnicities who came from the Turkish-Islamic world and wanted to fight in the Ottoman service were recruited to the *Sipahi* units in the palace; thereby the institution of the *Kapıkulu Sipahi*s (Cavalry of the Porte) was established, and it would become the imperial army to guard and provide security for the sultan and Ottoman statesmen.

Sultan Murad I constructed the Hüdavendigar *külliye*, or complex of buildings constructed around the mosque for public good, the Hüdavendigar Mosque, and the Hisar Mosque in Bursa, the Hüdavendigar Mosque in Ayvacık, and one mosque in both Bilecik and Yenişehir. He also had a modest palace in Edirne and an almshouse in İznik built in the name of his mother Nilufer Hatun. After the conquest of Edirne, he converted one church located inside the fortress and another in Plovdiv into mosques. Sultan Murad I's tomb stood outside of the Ottoman territory after the Balkan Wars (1912–1913) and was turned into ruins after the war. In recent years, the Turkish state has restored the tomb and made it accessible to visitors.

The Fourth Ottoman Sultan

Sultan Bayezid I

Reign: 1389–1402 — The Thunderbolt

Honorifics and Aliases: *Yıldırım* ("the Thunderbolt," from the energy and bravery he displayed in battle and the quickness of his movements in action.)
Father's Name: Murad I
Mother's Name: Gülçiçek Hatun

Place and Date of Birth: Edirne (then-capital city), 1354
Age at Accession to the Throne: 35
Cause and Date of Death: Mental anguish, March 8, 1403
Place of Death and Burial Site: Akşehir – his tomb was built in Bursa
Male Heirs: Musa Çelebi, Süleyman Çelebi, Mustafa Çelebi, İsa Çelebi, Mehmed Çelebi, Ertuğrul Çelebi, and Kasım Çelebi
Female Heir: Hundi Hatun, Oruz Hatun, Fatma Hatun, and Erhondu Hatun

The title *Yıldırım*, or Thunderbolt, was given to Sultan Bayezid, the first and only sultan in Ottoman history to assume this honorific during his *şehzade* years for the bravery he displayed at the Battle of Frenkyazısı against the Karamanid Alaeddin Bey in 1386.

Bayezid was a distinguished sultan not only because he was very brave, venturesome, and quite skillful at using weapons and horse riding, but also be-

Miniature of Sultan Bayezid I by Levni in his *Kebir Musavver Silsilenâme* (The Great Envisaged Portraiture Geneology)

cause he was a smart and efficient commander in chief who knew how to maneuver and dispatch the soldiers under his command. While he was still a *şehzade*, he obtained a great deal of experience as the governor of the lands given to the Ottomans by the Germiyanid Süleyman Çelebi as dowry of his daughter Sultan Hatun, who had married Bayezid. His experience and great skills paid off at the first Battle of Kosova, where he played a major role in the Ottoman victory.

Sultan Murad I's greatest reason for recommending his older son Bayezid as his successor to the throne was not his position as the eldest son but his extraordinary talents. The *beys* of Western Anatolian principalities rose up in revolt upon the news of the assassination of Sultan Murad I; thus, during the first months of his reign, Bayezid had to grapple with these principalities in Western Anatolia.

Bayezid was the first Ottoman sultan to besiege Istanbul. The city failed to fall although he tried four times. Hungarians and Venetians established an alliance to launch a new crusade as a result of both their will to lift the siege of Istanbul in 1396 and their common discontent at the Ottoman conquests in Greece, Bulgaria, and Albania. No sooner had the Hungarian King Sigismund blockaded the Nikopol Fort than Yıldırım Bayezid reached Nikopol from near Istanbul and gave a fatal blow to the crusaders in front of the Nikopol Fort on September 25, 1396.

Bayezid put great effort into establishing political unity in Anatolia and became successful especially in Western Anatolia. He was engaged in combats against the Kadı Burhan'al-Din state in the East. When the Karamanids formed an alliance with this state, Bayezid could do nothing but lift his ongoing siege of Konya and eventually come to terms with the Karamanids. His campaign on the Candarids in the North gave the Ottomans the entire Candarid territory except Sinop. Although the Ottomans had lost in combats against the Kadı Burhan'al-Din state and although this defeat unbalanced the status quo in the East, the ensuing period attached the Amasya region of the Kadi Burhan'al-Din state to the Ottoman domain. In addition, the local governors turned pro-Ottoman, which shifted the balance in favor of Sultan Bayezid.

Anatolian Fortress, the first Ottoman structure Sultan Bayezid I erected on the Anatolian shores of Istanbul to conquer the city

The sultan then occupied himself with fighting the West. He pressured Byzantium even more, and mobilized the raiders in the frontiers to chase conquests inside the Balkans. During this period, the Hungarian and Venetian threat still survived; however, the Bulgarians remained subordinate to the Ottomans. Yıldırım Bayezid, who ventured to subjugate the Balkans, marched to Greece that sought allegiance with the Venetians and recaptured Salonica to the Ottomans' credit in 1394. Having crushed the crusaders in the Battle of Nikopol on September 25, 1396, he took Vidin on the southern bank of the Danube from the Bulgarians and refocused on blockading Istanbul. Upon the increasing demands from Sultan Bayezid, the Byzantine Emperor Manuel had to accept the establishment of a Turkish quarter, the construction of a mosque, and the assignment of a Muslim judge in Istanbul. During the next year, Athens was added to the Ottoman lands, and the Karamanid Alaeddin Bey, who had acted as a political hack during the Battle of Nikopol, was confronted and defeated in the Battle of Akçay, never to endanger the Ottomans from behind again. Moreover, this battle with the Karamanids registered Konya and Karaman to the Ottoman realm.

The Ottomans seized Malatya in the East from the Mamluks, which disrupted Ottoman-Mamluk relations. Even though the Ottomans were in dire need of an alliance with the Mamluks against the Timurids, Yıldırım Bayezid turned hostile to the Mamluks, a decision which has been interpreted by historians as a great mistake on the part of Bayezid. Tamerlane, also

The tomb, mosque, and college of Yıldırım Bayezid I

Sultan Bayezid I's architectural masterpiece, the Ulu (Great) Mosque in Bursa, is a monumental edifice, standing out from the modest single-dome mosques of the early Ottoman era.

Above and right: The Ulu (Great) Mosque in Bursa with splendid large-scale calligraphic works on its walls and massive pillars

known as Timur the Lame (1370–1405), marched toward eastern Anatolia in late 1399 intending to capture the western lands. In fact, Tamerlane, who regarded himself as the heir to the Seljukids and Ilkhanids, wanted to occupy all of Anatolia, but he hesitated to fight Bayezid, who was in constant warfare in the name of God. The benevolent relations between these two Turko-Muslim rulers became murky when some notables who had challenged Yıldırım Bayezid sought refuge from Tamerlane and still others who had opposed Tamerlane chose to ask for Bayezid's protection. The invasion and plundering of Sivas by Tamerlane and the exchange of harsh letters between the two rulers eventually brought the two states face-to-face against each other in the Valley of Çubuk, Ankara on July 28, 1402. In the Battle of Ankara, Sultan Bayezid lost his army, the political unity he had worked hard to establish in Anatolia, and his title. It was only seven months later on March 8, 1403 that Bayezid passed away, under captivity in Akşehir, on account of a severe mental anguish resulting from sorrow and despair.

The Battle of Ankara almost brought the Ottoman Empire to the brink of collapse. Both the Anatolian notables who reclaimed their old lands and the Ottoman *şehzade*s who had begun to challenge each other for the remaining territories recognized Tamerlane's domination. This period, known as the Interregnum Era, ended with the rising of Sultan Bayezid's son Mehmed I to the throne; in addition, the Anatolian political unity like in the days of Yıldırım Bayezid would be established, once again, during his reign. Yıldırım Bayezid aimed to control the Anatolian principalities and the Balkan dynasties, and wanted to centralize the entire Ottoman state based on Islamic principles. In doing so, he seemed successful in turning the Ottoman state into a major center of international diplomacy in a region where the lands of the ancient world merged. However, this central state was almost strangled by Tamerlane and retreated all the way back to the borders drawn in Anatolia by Murad I. Despite all, the lands in Rumelia did not split from the Ottoman center, which helped to relax the Interregnum Era and made an Ottoman renaissance possible.

Sultan Bayezid spent almost all his life on the battlefields and in combats. He was an extremely brave, active, and successful commander and a righteous ruler. He had a brazen character; in particular, he did not recoil from severely punishing those who had received bribery and committed injustices.

Bayezid was tall, fair-skinned and hook-nosed with a thick mustache. His round lower chin was circled by his beard, which was lighter in color than his mustache; his voice was rotund. His frowning brows and big black eyes were said to be his weapons, strong enough to consternate his enemies at sight.

Of his six sons, Süleyman, İsa, Musa, and Mehmed Çelebis had joined in the competition for the throne during the Interregnum Era, while Mustafa Çelebi, nicknamed "Mustafa the Pretender," emerged during the reign of Murad II as a claimant of the throne.

In the course of his reign, Bayezid constructed numerous dervish lodges, *medrese*s, almshouses, and travelers' and medical hospices, as well as Ulu Camii (the Grand Mosque) in Bursa in 1400, which is, simply put, a prestigious exhibition of a distinct Ottoman calligraphy.[14] A wide array of these charitable constructions still remains in most of the cities across Anatolia and Rumelia. The Anatolian Fortress, also known as Güzelhisar, is also one of his heritages, which was particularly used during the siege of Istanbul between 1396 –1397.

An old photograph of the Mevlevi dervishes in Damascus visiting the Imperial Gifts Caravan en route from Istanbul to the Haramayn

Sultan Bayezid I also had initiated the later tradition of the annual procession (*sürre alayı*) to meet the needs of the Haramayn, the combined name of the blessed cities of Mecca and Medina, and to pay the salaries of the officials there. Bayezid sent the first procession from Edirne in 1389. The processions with the caravan of imperial gifts for the Haramayn would continue until the reign of Mehmed Vahdeddin, the last Ottoman sultan, as a sign of the Ottomans' attachment to the Prophet's legacy.

Tomb of Sultan Bayezid I a century ago by the Abdullah Brothers

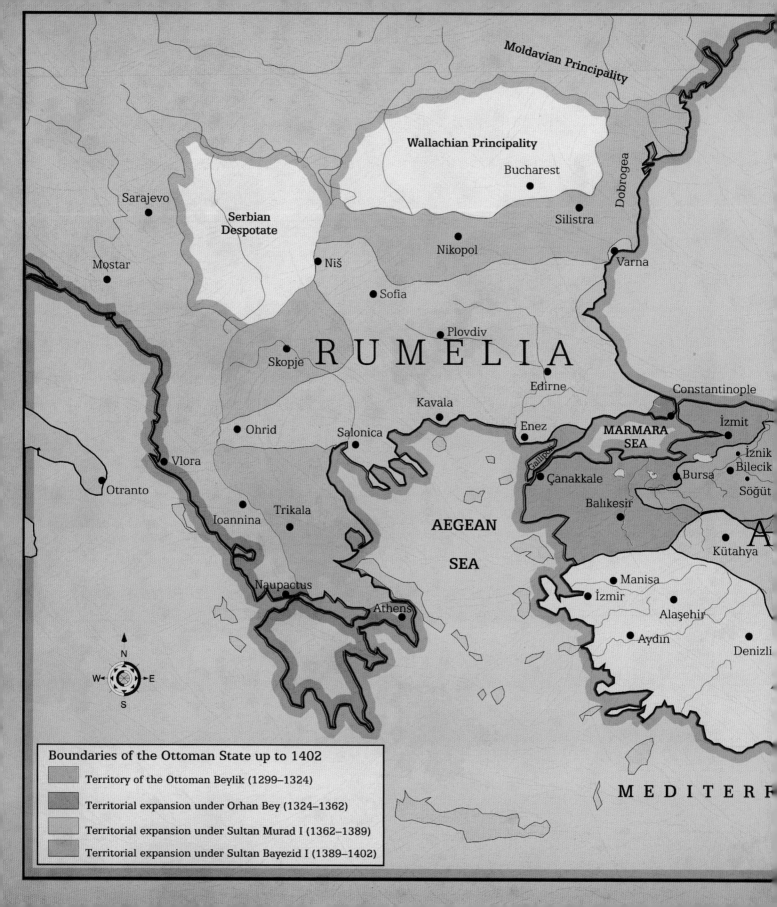

Moldavian Principality

Wallachian Principality

Bucharest

Sarajevo

Serbian
Despotate

Silistra

Dobrogea

Mostar

Niš

Nikopol

Varna

Sofia

Plovdiv

R U M E L I A

Skopje

Edirne

Constantinople

Kavala

İzmit

Ohrid

Salonica

Enez

MARMARA
SEA

İznik

Gallipoli

Bilecik

Vlora

Çanakkale

Bursa

Söğüt

Otranto

Balıkesir

AEGEAN

Ioannina

Trikala

SEA

Kütahya

A

Naupactus

Manisa

İzmir

Athens

Alaşehir

Aydın

Denizli

N
W ← → E
S

M E D I T E R R

Boundaries of the Ottoman State up to 1402

Territory of the Ottoman Beylik (1299–1324)

Territorial expansion under Orhan Bey (1324–1362)

Territorial expansion under Sultan Murad I (1362–1389)

Territorial expansion under Sultan Bayezid I (1389–1402)

BLACK SEA

Sinop

Amasra

Kastamonu

Samsun

Giresun   Trabzon

EMPIRE OF TREBIZOND

Tokat

Yozgat   Erzurum

Ankara   Erzincan

ATOLIA   Sivas

Kemah

Kayseri

Harput

Maraş

Dulkadirids

Konya

TIMURID
STATE

Adana   Ramazanids

Şilifke

Antakya

EAN SEA

Aleppo   Rakka

MAMLUK STATE

Sultan Mehmed I

Reign: 1413—1421

Honorifics and Aliases: Çelebi [Courteous and gentleman] and Kirişçi [An archer with extraordinary strength in cording the ends of the bow]
Father's Name: Sultan Bayezid I
Mother's Name: Devlet Hatun
Place and Date of Birth: Edirne, 1387
Posts Prior to Reign: Governorship of Tokat, Sivas and Ankara regions in Central Anatolia as well as Amasya in the north
Age at Accession to the Throne: 26
Date of Death: May, 1421
Place of Death and Burial Site: Edirne – his tomb was built in Bursa
Male Heirs: Murad II, Mustafa, Kasım, Ahmed, Yusuf, and Mahmud
Female Heir: Selçuk Hatun, Hafsa Hatun, Ayşe Hatun, Sultan Hatun, and İlaldı Hatun

The defeat of Sultan Bayezid I in the Battle of Ankara destroyed the Anatolian unity and instigated contests for the throne between the şehzades. Tamerlane, who had besieged İzmir, granted Süleyman Çelebi a certificate that assured his sovereignty in Rumelia. Although he also had called Sultan Bayezid's other son Mehmed Çelebi to Kütahya, Mehmed Çelebi left his call unanswered.

Miniature of Sultan Mehmed Çelebi by Levni in his *Kebir Musavver Silsilenâme* (The Great Envisaged Portraiture Geneology)

The *şehzade*s began an intensive struggle for the control of the Ottoman territory. Mehmed Çelebi fought against the principalities of Tokat and Amasya and subordinated them, which gave him more military strength. His first confrontation with the other *şehzade*s was against İsa Çelebi, who succeeded in capturing Bursa from Musa Çelebi. As the third *şehzade* to seize Bursa at the Battle of Ulubat, Mehmed Çelebi declared his rulership. Later in the contest, Musa Çelebi sided with Mehmed Çelebi while İsa Çelebi supported Süleyman Çelebi. Mehmed Çelebi successfully withstood the onset of the army of İsa Çelebi, who allied with the Anatolian principalities; thus the danger to be inflicted by İsa Çelebi was eliminated in 1403. Rule over Bursa changed hands for the fourth time when Süleyman Çelebi, the ruler of Rumelia, seized the city along with Ankara from Mehmed Çelebi in 1404. Meanwhile, Mehmed Çelebi retreated near Amasya and mobilized an army commanded by Musa Çelebi to Rumelia to fight against Süleyman Çelebi. The success of Musa Çelebi in the Eastern Balkans forced Süleyman Çelebi to relinquish Bursa and resulted in a combat between the two brothers. Musa Çelebi captured Edirne, where he proclaimed his own regality. Soon after Musa and Mehmed Çelebis confronted each other; although Mehmed Çelebi was defeated in the first round of combats, he won the war near Sofia on July 5, 1413, eventually ending the eleven-year Interregnum Era.

The Ottoman chronicler Neşri records that, following the Battle of Ankara in 1402, Süleyman Çelebi ruled for eight years, ten months, and seventeen days; Musa Çelebi for two years, seven months, and twenty days; and Mehmed Çelebi for seven years and eleven months. The main reason for the long duration of the Interregnum Era was that the Balkan states, primarily Byzantium, and Anatolian principalities incited, polarized, and supported the *şehzade*s against one another.

Following his ascendancy to the throne, Sultan Mehmed Çelebi first made alliances with Byzantium, the Wallachian principality, and the despotate of the Morea to secure the western borders. Second, Mehmed Çelebi embarked on reestablish-

Eskicami (Old Mosque) built by Sultan Mehmed Çelebi in Edirne

ing the political unity in Anatolia, which had long been severed. This policy served the function of lowering the risk of fighting concurrent wars in the east and west.

Tamerlane, having captured İzmir from the Knights Hospitaller after the Battle of Ankara, bestowed the city to the Aydınids and returned to the Central Asia. The greatest service of Tamerlane in Anatolia was that he added İzmir to the Abode of Islam in 1403. The first thing that Sultan Mehmed Çelebi did in Anatolia was to incorporate İzmir, under the control of the Aydınid Cüneyd Bey, to the Ottoman lands. The sultan appointed Cüneyd Bey to the frontier governorship of Nikopol after he asked for the sultans' mercy.

During this period, the Western Anatolian principalities pledged their allegiance to the Ottoman sultan. Furthermore, the Ottomans confronted the Karamanids for the first time. The Karamids had assaulted the Ottoman lands during the contests of reign engaged against Musa Çelebi in which Mehmed Çelebi acquired the lands of Beyşehir and Akşehir. The sultan also made an incursion to the Candarids and attached their principality to the Ottoman lands, appointing the Candarid Kasım Bey as the local governor of the region conquered from the Candarids.

Another incident that confronted Mehmed Çelebi was the mutiny led by Sheikh Bedreddin, the son of the judge of Simavna in the west of the Meriç River. Mehmed Çelebi would not tolerate the spread of "a fire of sedition" ignited with superstitious beliefs. He had Sheikh Bedreddin caught, brought to the court, and executed according to the court's decision in 1416. Then in 1420, Grand Vizier[15] Bayezid Pasha soon after instigated a counter-insurgency against the Karamanids and quelled a series of revolts that Bedreddin's mutiny had inspired in Anatolia.

Tamerlane captured Mustafa Çelebi, the son of Yıldırım Bayezid, and took him to Samarkand after the Battle of Ankara. Upon assuming control over the administration after the death of his father, Tamerlane's son Shahrukh perceived the consolidation of the Otto-

The octagonal shaped Yeşil (Green) Tomb of Sultan Mehmed I on top of a hill in Bursa is a unique architectural structure with its green-blue tile adornments, crowned with a high hemispherical dome.

Copper candle hanger with gilding, late 15th century

man unity in Anatolia by Mehmed Çelebi as a challenge to the Timurid State. Therefore, he released Mustafa Çelebi in an effort to ignite diplomatic chaos. In response to Shahrukh's actions, Mehmed Çelebi wrote him a letter in which he stated that the partition of the Ottoman Empire would not serve any other but the enemies of Islam. Nevertheless, Mustafa Çelebi made a sudden appearance in Anatolia and entered Wallachia, claiming the throne. Byzantium also became involved in the *şehzade*'s contest for throne, which would be called the "Mustafa the Pretender Incident" in Ottoman chronicles. Mustafa Çelebi organized a rebellion near Salonica and Tessalia and received the support of the Aydınid Cüneyd Bey, the frontier-governor of Nikopol. The appearance of Mustafa Çelebi became reason enough to encourage the states in Anatolia and Rumelia, which had been looking forward to a regenerated internal strife in the Ottoman Empire.

Mustafa Çelebi and Cüneyd felt stronger with the military support that Mirce, the Voivode of Wallachia, had provided them, but they could not win the Ottoman frontier forces to their side. They returned to Istanbul. When Byzantium sent the *şehzade* to Salonica this time in 1416, Mehmed Çelebi had to declare war against Byzantium. Mehmed Çelebi requested that the rebels be delivered to him;

Prayer hall of the Eskicami (Old Mosque) in Edirne with splendid calligraphy on the walls and pillars

43

An Ottoman child waiting at the gate of the Yeşil (Green) Mosque,
the great contribution of Sultan Mehmed Çelebi to the city of Bursa.
Taken by the Abdullah Brothers (circa 1895).

however, Byzantine Emperor Manuel, who planned to exploit the situation to the fullest, rejected the idea. At last, the Byzantine emperor promised to keep Mustafa Çelebi in prison as long as Sultan Mehmed Çelebi was alive. The compensation for this favor would cost the Ottomans 300,000 *akçe* (10,000 ducats) in gold, to be paid annually to Byzantium.

Mehmed Çelebi assured the loyalty of the Saruhan, Aydın, and Menteşe principalities to the Ottoman Empire and thereby established a solid Ottoman presence along the eastern coast of the Aegean Sea. In the maritime war between the Ottomans and Venetians in 1416, the Ottoman navy under Çalı Bey suffered a defeat near Gallipoli. This defeat was indicative of the fact that the Ottomans had not yet formed a strong naval force. As a result of this war, an agreement was reached with the mediation of Byzantium. The agreement stipulated that the belligerent states would liberate the captives in their reserves, and the Ottomans would allow the Venetians free exportation from the Ottoman realm.

Mehmed Çelebi led a campaign against the Wallachian Voivode Mirce, who interfered with the contests of throne during the Era of Interregnum, and bound Wallachia to pay tribute to the Ottoman Empire. In addition, Mehmed Çelebi organized a successful expedition on behalf of the Bosnians, who called the Ottomans for protection against the Hungarian oppression, and acquired the allegiance of the Bosnians in return.

Sultan Mehmed Çelebi was worried that Byzantium would release Mustafa Çelebi in order to benefit from a possible inner strife in the Ottoman Empire and was terrified by the possibility that the Ottomans would suffer another Era of Interregnum. Mehmed Çelebi wanted his eldest son Şehzade Murad to access the throne with peace of mind, so he disguised his illness and ordered his death be kept a secret until Şehzade Murad arrived from Amasya. This made him the first Ottoman sultan the news of whose death had not been immediately conveyed. Meanwhile, those supporting Şehzade Murad undertook the public responsibility of quickly spreading a rumor that Mustafa Çelebi had died and the person in Byzantium claiming the throne was Mustafa the Pretender, no more than a puppet.

Mehmed Çelebi saved the Ottoman Empire from disintegration once again; therefore, he is regarded as a second founder of the Ottoman imperial state. During the period of his reign, his priority lay in recovering Ottoman Anatolia and Rumelia from the traumatic effects of the Battle of Ankara. Successfully he fortified his empire back to a sovereign power in the region despite a cumulative of opposing efforts in Anatolia and Rumelia.

Mehmed Çelebi knew well how to control his anger, and had the character of a calm, serious, and determined person, qualities that gave confidence to his statesmen and army. He was very good at using weapons and bold enough to fight in the front lines. The chronicles narrate that he had more than forty concrete wounds on his body as a reminder of twenty-four major battles he fought in.

Mehmed Çelebi was philanthropist: he undertook vast building projects in Bursa, including mosques, *medrese*s, almshouses, and his own tomb. In addition, the Eskicami (the Old Mosque) constructed in Edirne and the Yeşil (Green) Mosque in Bursa were completed during his reign. He treated his subjects, Muslims and non-Muslims, fairly.

Mehmed Çelebi, a wrestling-lover stalwart with a large chest, was strong enough to strike a bow with a string with his bare hands. He had a relieving face, thin and long frowning brows with dark hazel eyes, and he was hook-nosed. His chin was balanced, and his hands were muscular and strong.

He preferred to wear a high-collared caftan made from shiny textures and with fur on the inside. His *sarık*, the long single-piece turban wound around an inner headgear, was made from plain joint cloth. And it went with his gold-embroidered *kavuk*, or quilted headgear.

Mehmed Çelebi followed the tradition of the *surre* procession, which began with his father, and sent the caravans of imperial donations in cash and kind to the Haramayn.

The Sixth Ottoman Sultan
Sultan Murad II

Reign: 1421—1444 (first term)
1446-1451 (Second term)

Honorifics and Aliases: *Ebu'l-hayrat* [the Father of charity works]
Father's Name: Mehmed Çelebi
Mother's Name: Emine Hatun (of the Dulkadirids)
Place and Date of Birth: Amasya – July, 1404
Post Prior to Reign: Governorship of Amasya
Age at Accession to the Throne: 17
Date of Death: February 3, 1451
Place of Death and Burial Site: Edirne – his tomb is in Bursa
Male Heirs: Mehmed II, Ahmed, Alaeddin, Orhan, Hasan, and Ahmed
Female Heir: Şehzade Sultan and Fatma Sultan

Sultan Mehmed Çelebi had already passed away in Edirne by the time his eldest son Şehzade Murad reached Bursa in accordance with his father's dying wish. The death of the sultan was kept as *arcanum imperii* to avert potential internal upheavals and the release of Mustafa Çelebi by Byzantium. When he ascended the throne as his father's successor, Murad II undertook the greatest challenge of his life at the young age of seventeen.

Miniature of Sultan Murad II by Levni in his *Kebir Musavver Silsilenâme* (The Great Envisaged Portraiture Geneology)

Of Sultan Murad's brothers, Şehzade Mustafa was twelve years old and had been located at Hamidili, a frontier principality. Şehzade Yusuf was eight, and Şehzade Mahmud was seven years old. Mehmed Çelebi had known too well about the fraternal disputes to let his sons fight and fratricide, so he concluded an agreement with the Byzantine Emperor to prohibit the incident of Mustafa the Pretender from occurring again. The agreement stipulated that Şehzade Murad would be his successor, and Şehzade Mustafa would administer Anatolia. Furthermore, Byzantium would not free Mustafa Çelebi, and in return the younger brothers Yusuf and Mahmud would be sent to the Byzantine Emperor with inclusive expenses to be paid by the Ottomans. Sultan Murad II, however, rejected to send his younger brothers to Byzantium. Thus Byzantium sent Yıldırım Bayezid's son Mustafa Çelebi, who the Byzantine Empire argued was the legitimate sultan to Gallipoli along with Cüneyd Bey of the Aydınids, so that he could contest the throne. Mustafa Çelebi agreed to return such a favor of Manuel, the Byzantine emperor, by handing over the region of Thessaly and Gallipoli no sooner than he assumed the reign.

Murad II's uncle, Mustafa Çelebi, who was supported by Byzantium and sent to Gallipoli with a naval fleet, was not the only difficulty he would cope with. At this time, the principalities in Anatolia joined in the opposition. The Germiyanids claimed that they would not respect Sultan Murad II's authority and supported Mustafa Çelebi. The Karamanids occupied the lands of the Hamidis, and the Menteşeoğlus occupied the lands of Aydınids and Saruhanids. When the Candarid İsfendiyar Bey recaptured the lands that Mehmed Çelebi had given to İsfendiyar's son Kasım, the Ottoman Empire made its way into a civil strife.

Having landed on Gallipoli, Mustafa Çelebi left the Aydınid Cüneyd Bey to capture the Gallipoli Fort and moved on to Edirne. Although Sultan Murad II had placed his hopes on the Rumeli *Beylerbeyi* Bayezid Pasha, whom he directed toward his uncle, the forces of Bayezid Pasha unexpectedly joined the ranks of Mustafa Çelebi. The young sultan had been stranded. Mustafa Çelebi entered the city of Edirne and proclaimed his regency. The Gallipoli Fort, which was

An old photograph of the Üç Şerefeli (Three-Gallery) Mosque taken around 1895

under siege, followed suit. Bayezid Pasha, who betrayed and fought for Mustafa Çelebi, was executed, and the masses readily accepted Mustafa Çelebi as their sultan.

Mustafa Çelebi had not kept his promise to hand over Gallipoli to Byzantine Emperor Manuel, which caused Byzantium to rescind its support for him. Meanwhile, Murad II cancelled the debts of the Genoese; in return, Genoa offered him naval support and a score of soldiers. As a result, a balance of power was maintained in the face of Mustafa Çelebi, who held the Ottoman navy, the Rumelian forces, and the routes from Gallipoli.

Regardless, Mustafa Çelebi marched to Bursa and reached as far as Ulubat, forcing Sultan Murad II into a quagmire. This time, Murad II was well prepared, in diplomatic terms, for his paternal uncle. First, he promised to bestow the provinces of İzmir and Aydın to Cüneyd Bey, the greatest supporter of Mustafa Çelebi, which dissociated Cüneyd Bey from Mustafa Çelebi. He then dispatched his commanders to meet up with the frontier *bey*s and soldiers in Rumelia. His strategy succeeded in winning them to his side. Thus, Mustafa Çelebi's forces diminished all at once, resulting in an even greater psychological ebb in Mustafa Çelebi's camp. Mustafa Çelebi's army had weakened, but it could still annihilate Sultan Murad II's army. With the help of the Genoese, the sultan was able to chase Mustafa Çelebi, who had retreated to Edirne, and to capture him. Mus-

The Edirne Dar'ül Hadis (Daru'l Hadith) Mosque the construction of which Sultan Murad II worked in person

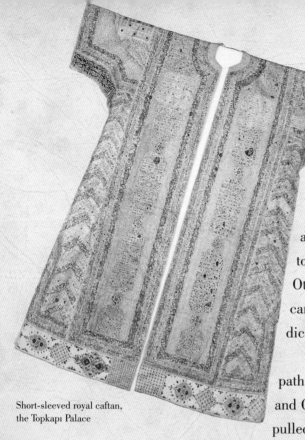

Short-sleeved royal caftan,
the Topkapı Palace

tafa Çelebi organized a notorious rebellion with the Byzantine support and had many Muslims killed to no avail, the penalty for which he paid with his life in 1422.

Soon after, the sultan laid a siege to Istanbul to make Byzantium suffer, for it had continuously agitated Mustafa Çelebi to contest for the throne, caused bloodshed, and prevented the Ottomans from further conducting *gaza*s in the form of military campaigns. In the course of the siege in 1422, another major predicament, the Şehzade Mustafa incident, arose.

This time, the thirteen year-old Şehzade Mustafa, following the path of his paternal uncle, acquired the support of the Karamanid and Germiyanid principalities and besieged Bursa. Sultan Murad II pulled the remarkable division of his army off the siege of Istanbul and marched with it to Edirne. Murad II's soldiers led by Mihaloğlu successfully disbanded the forces of Şehzade Mustafa. The young *şehzade* first took refuge with the Byzantine emperor; then he moved to İznik with the emperor's support. After learning about the Byzantine support given to the *şehzade*, Murad II marched on İznik. As a result of bitter combats, Şehzade Mustafa and his associates were executed, which inhibited the rate of such sedition likely to spread in 1423.

Having crushed his rebellious paternal uncle Mustafa Çelebi and his brother Şehzade Mustafa, Sultan Murad II continued to work on achieving unity in Anatolia. To begin with, he regained the loyalty of the Candarid İsfendiyar Bey to his empire. The Aydınid Cüneyd Bey had supported Şehzade Mustafa Çelebi and challenged the Ottoman Empire time and again; therefore, Murad II sent to the region Hamza Pasha, the *beylerbeyi* of Anatolia, to eventually capture İzmir. The principalities of Aydın, Menteşe, and Teke were captured. The Germiyanids were reintegrated into the Ottoman Empire, for its ruler the Germiyanid Yakup Bey had so wished after his death with no male heir in 1429. Thus, the security of the Aegean shores was confirmed.

A contest for the throne in the Karamanid principality brought about the death of the Karamanid Mehmed Bey. Amidst the competition, Sultan Murad II had helped İbrahim Bey

Muradiye Külliye in Bursa

to become head of the Karamanids. Even so, and despite the fact that Murad II had married his sister to İbrahim Bey to create a family kinship with the Karamanids, as the new Karamanid ruler, İbrahim Bey, maintained his attitude of hostility against the Ottoman Empire and even allied with the Hungarians. Murad II became obliged to march on the Karamanids. In the course of this campaign, İbrahim Bey was beaten and asked for mercy; Murad II forgave him, kept him at the head of his principality, and returned to Edirne.

During the reign of Murad II, the Ottoman domain had spanned from Macedonia to the Adriatic and as far as the eastern and western shores of the Aegean. This expansion completely disconcerted the Venetians, the major naval power in the region. The very fact that the Venetians held a strong naval power and a greater part of the Aegean islands had been under their possession pointed to a possibility that the Venetians could detach the Ottoman connections between Anatolia and Rumelia—the Ottoman lands in Europe.

Sultan Murad II positioned his entire army on the Rumelian side: in 1430, he occupied Salonica, the strategically vital Macedonian port city, and took it back from the Venetians, to whom Byzantium had formerly given the city. The following year, the conquests of Ioannina and Serres in the Northern Greece provided the Ottomans with a solid grip of the Southern Albania.

The Serbs handed Belgrade over to the Hungarians after the Ottoman-Venetian wars. Moreover, the Wallachians and Bosnians refused to subjugate to the Ottomans; therefore, the Hungarians, Serbs, Bosnians, and Wallachians formed an alliance against the Ottoman Empire, which would pave the way to the crusade alliance that would later emerge.

During the throne-contest in Hungary that resulted from the death of the Hungarian King Sigismund, the Ottoman forces captured Semendria, the pivotal Serbian center in the Balkans in 1439. They thereby ended Serbian despotism in the region, pressured Bosnia and Herzegovina, and made a failed attempt to capture Belgrade.

In fact, the failure in the siege of Belgrade was the harbinger of a losing streak that followed. Hunyadi Janos, the new Voivode of Transylvania appointed by the King Ladislas, who had ascended to the Hungarian throne, proceeded to attack the Ottomans, and successfully reclaimed Semendria on the Danube, signaling for the Ottomans that more territorial losses would ensue. Venice enthusiastically welcomed the news of an Ottoman defeat, and the Venetians celebrated it for days. Worse, the defeat encouraged the Karamanids back in Anatolia to move against the Ottomans, and they marched on Akşehir and Beyşehir. The chain of disasters was followed by the martyrdom of Mezid Bey, the frontier *bey* of Serbia, in an ambush in 1441, and in 1442 the defeat of the Ottoman army commanded by Şehabeddin Şahin Pasha, the *beylerbeyi* of Rumelia. Meanwhile, Sultan Murad II marched toward the Karamanids. Reinforced by the forces of Şehzade Alaeddin from Amasya, he defeated the Karamanids. As a result, the Ottomans captured Konya and Larende from the Karamanids. Sultan Murad II, who had to face the volatile situation of Rumelia, signed a peace treaty with the Karamanids and returned to Edirne.

The series of defeats that the Ottomans suffered in Europe gave Europeans tremendous joy and excitement. The idea of removing the Muslims from the Balkans with the help of a new crusade resurged. Likewise, Byzantium agreed on a crusade as the only way to get rid of the Ottomans. In 1437, Byzantine aided in the signing of a pact, which stipulated the collaboration of the Orthodox and Catholic Church and the origination of a crusade. Finally, the crusade army, led by the Transylvanian Voivode Hunyadi Janos, the Hungarian King

The Muradiye Camii (Murad's Mosque) in Edirne built by Sultan Murad II

Ladislas, the Serbian Despot, and the Wallachian Prince, passed through the Danube to the Ottoman lands. The first battle broke out near Niš between the Ottoman pioneer squads and the crusaders. The Ottomans suffered another defeat, losing Niš and Sofia in 1443.

Murad II confronted this crusader army at the Izladi (Zlatitsa) Passage and put it to a partial halt. The crusaders retreated because of the harsh winter conditions. However, the advance of the Hungarians inside of the Balkans brought about new developments. The Albanian Iskender Bey (also known as Skanderbeg) escaped the battlefield during the war against the Hungarians and revolted in his country. Then Sultan Murad II received a piece of news that crushed him: his favorite eldest son Alaeddin Ali Çelebi had passed away in Amasya unexpectedly. For the sultan, the horrible events did not stop there. This time, the Karamanids had exploited the situation to attack the Ottoman lands.

In the face of all that was transpiring in the Balkans, Murad II approached the Hungarians for peace. The two parties signed the Treaty of Edirne-Segedin in 1444, which outlined the conditions of a perpetual peace for ten years. The treaty gave the conquered lands back to the Serbian Despot Djuradj Brankovic (known also as Vılkoğlu in Turkish historical records), acknowledged the Danube as the frontier in-between, acknowledged the sultan's sovereignty in Bulgaria, sealed the allegiance of the Wallachian Prince and his continuing tribute to the sultan. And Sultan Murad II believed at heart that this treaty would afford the peace he desired.

After achieving stability in the Balkans thanks to the peace treaty, Sultan Murad II marched on the Karamanids. However, he chose this time not to invade the Karamanid principality but to sign an accord (*sevgendname*) with the Karamanid ambassadors in Yenişehir, Bursa. It was thus agreed that the Karamanids would donate a military force to the Ottomans every year in return for the restoration of Beyşehir, Seydişehir, Oklukhisarı, and Akşehir to the Karamanid principality.

The subsequent defeats, the death of his oldest son, and opposition of the frontier *bey*s to his authority are likely to have made the sultan apply these policies. As a result of the treaties he signed, Sultan Murad II had to retreat from strategically vital territories he had conquered in the east and west. With these treaties he also believed that he had brought peace to Anatolia and the Balkans. It was this belief and such sense that led him, in Mihaliç in August of 1444, to relinquish his throne before *bey*s and his army so that his son Şehzade Mehmed would receive progression. This act made him the first sultan to ever give up the throne at will, which was followed by his better devotion to practicing his prayers in Bursa.

European rival states translated the rise of a youngster as the new Ottoman sultan into an incredible opportunity. The Papacy urged the rejection of the Treaty of Edirne-Segedin. The Hungarian King Ladislas broke his promise of a mutual peace and prepared himself to lead a crusader army composed of Hungarians, Polish, and Venetians. The crusaders passed through the Danube and invaded the Ottoman territory in the Balkans. The Venetians closed the Dardanelles to passage of the Ottoman ships. Moreover, the advance of the crusaders through the borders next to Varna, on the Black Sea in Rumelia, had instilled anxiety among the statesmen, and a migration from Edirne to Anatolia followed. Amidst all these, Murad II was called back to duty by his son Sultan Mehmed II, Grand Vizier Candarid Halil Pasha and other eminent statesmen. He rushed to Edirne and got ready to face off the crusaders as the head of the Ottoman army.

During the confrontation, which history would later record as the Battle of Varna, the Hungarian heavy-cavalry units first scattered the Ottoman flanks in a fierce assault. When the crusaders neared Sultan Murad II's camp, he considered withdrawing. In this decisive moment, Karaca Bey stepped in, rejected the idea of a withdrawal, and energized the soldiers to recollect around their sultan. The encirclement and execution of the Hungarian King Ladislas by the Janissaries aroused a sense of panic among the crusaders, and Hunyadi Janos barely escaped for his life.

The victory of Varna reached Edirne, the broader Ottoman lands, and the Abode of Islam, receiving a joyful reception. This victory was interpreted as a sign that Byzantium would fall; in fact, it sealed the Ottoman supremacy in the Balkans in 1444.

Murad II had retired to Manisa following the victory at Varna, which provided another proper season for the Hungarians and Wallachians to reawaken. In addition, a mutiny led by the Janissaries in Edirne erupted, forcing the old sultan to return to the throne for a third term.

Soon after, Sultan Murad marched on the Morea and then against the Albanian Iskender Bey. The Morea acknowledged the Ottoman suzerainty once more.

Composed of the Hungarian, Wallachian, Polish, and German soldiers, the crusaders invaded Serbia and moved in the Ottoman domain with the idea of reversing the ill-effects of the defeat they suffered at Varna on the western coast of the Black Sea. Sultan

Murad II confronted them in Kosovo. After a three-day long war, the Ottoman Empire gave the crusaders another crushing defeat in 1448. As a result of this victory, the Ottoman authority was confirmed in the Balkans, Wallachia was subordinated once again to the Ottomans, and the crusaders became too dismayed to attack the Ottomans. After this war, the Muslims took the offensive in the Balkans, and the crusaders turned defensive. What is also striking about this war was that the Karamanids had sent military reinforcement to Sultan Murad II as promised.

Sultan Murad II turned ill in Edirne after the wedding ceremony of Şehzade Mehmed and Sitti Hatun, the daughter of the Dulkadirid Süleyman Bey. He passed away within a few months at the age of forty-eight on February 10, 1451.

In his letter of will that he had written five years prior to his death, he announced his wish "to be buried in an open-top grave in Bursa next to his long-gone son Alaeddin and that no other from his dynasty should be buried in the same yard."

Murad II established his reputation as a sultan who never abstained from engaging in *gaza* for the cause of Islam regardless of time or overwhelming circumstances. He was generous and good-tempered and treated his subjects fairly. He did not take risk in state affairs, just as he never fought simultaneous combats in Anatolia and Rumelia. When the situation was calm in Anatolia, he campaigned to the Balkans, and vice-versa.

The traveler Broquiere had wanted to see the Muslims in person to collect further intelligence for crusades, so he visited the Ottoman lands on the way back from Jerusalem. In his *Le Voyage d'outremer*, Broquiere emphasized that the sultan was very strong and said: "Among the rulers that I know of, this Ottoman sultan is the one who receives the greatest respect by his people." In his visit to Edirne in 1432, Broquiere described the strength of the sultan in the following way: "Based on what I have been told, he (the sultan) is not keen on wars. The impression I got from him is the same; he could easily conquer a greater part of Europe only if he wished to put his forces and vast income to use, considering the lame resistance he faced from the Christian world."

The Ottoman life of knowledge gained considerable momentum during the reign of Sultan Murad II: Molla Gürani, Ataeddin et-Tusi, Şerefeddin Kırımi, Şeydi Ahmed Kırımi et al. came from Arabia, Turkistan and Crimea. Many scholars and intellectuals of the time of Sultan Mehmed the Conqueror were educated during this period, which would, in other words, lay groundwork for the scholarly formation so essential to the conquest of Istanbul.

In addition, it was during this time that the Sufi orders expanded. The orders of Zeyniyye, Mevleviyye, and Bayramiyye spread amongst the official ranks and the public. In particular, Sultan Murad II did not tax the disciples of Hacı Bayram-ı Veli of Ankara. Murad II had a *medrese* and small dervish lodge constructed in Bursa near the mosque in his name. This quarter of the city called "Muradiye" also hosts the tombs of Sultan Murad II and his son Alaeddin.

Murad II had his greater works built in Edirne, at the top of the list is the Daru'l-Hadith (school for teaching hadith) near the Tunca River and the Yeni ("New") Mosque, also known as the Üç Şerefeli ("Three Galleried") Mosque. The latter is regarded among scholars of the field as the archetype of the huge Ottoman mosques. Sultan Murad II had laid the foundation of the mosque on the way to his campaign against Hungary in 1438, and the mosque came into service in 1447. We also find mosques and fountains in his name in Salonica, Skopje, Alacahisar, and Merzifon. Indeed such great charity works earned him one of his nickname *ebu'l hayrat*, "the father of charity works."

Along the lines of his grandfather Sultan Bayezid I and his father Sultan Mehmed I, Sultan Murad II kept the tradition of sending *surre*—annual procession of carrying royal gifts to the Haramayn during the *hajj* season; additionally, he made it a habit to annually distribute gold to the descendants of the Prophet Muhammad, peace and blessings be upon him, living in his empire.

Sultan Mehmed II

Reign: 1444–1446 (first term)
1451–1481 (Second term)

The Conqueror

Honorifics and Aliases: *Fatih* [the Conqueror], *Avni* [pertaining to Divine Aid], *Ebu'l Feth* [the Father of Conquest], and *Gazi Hünkar* [Combatant Sovereign]
Father's Name: Murad II
Mother's Name: Hüma Hatun
Place and Date of Birth: Edirne, March 30, 1432
Age at Accession to the Throne: 13 (First term) and 19 (Second term)
Cause and Date of Death: Gout, Poison; May 3, 1481
Place of Death and Burial Site: Hünkarçayırı near Maltepe, Istanbul – his tomb is near the Fatih Mosque which he had built in the Fatih district of Istanbul
Male Heirs: Bayezid, Cem, and Mustafa
Female Heir: Ayşe Sultan and Gevherhan Sultan

Succeeding Sultan Murad II to the throne after his death in 1451, Sultan Mehmed II is regarded in world history as well as in Turkish-Islamic history as the ruler whose conquest of Istanbul marked the end of the Middle Ages and the beginning of the Modern Era.

From governor of Manisa in western Anatolia as a young *şehzade*, Mehmed II became the only surviving heir to the throne after the sudden death of Alaeddin, his older brother.

Miniature of Sultan Mehmed the Conqueror by Levni in his *Kebir Musavver Silsilenâme* (The Great Envisaged Portraiture Geneology)

In 1444, he was physically present in the Ottoman capital of Edirne where his father signed the peace treaty with the Hungarian king, the Serbian despot, and the ambassadors of the Wallachian prince. He occupied the throne for the first time in the year 1444 when his father decided to retire into solitude in Bursa, only to return to command the Ottoman army at the Battle of Varna on the western coast of the Black Sea against the newly-formed crusaders. He returned the throne to his father a second time as the struggles between the pashas and the Janissaries' mutiny became too overwhelming for him. It turned out that the two sultanate years between 1444 and 1446 had given this young sultan a ruling experience so profound that he would master his diplomatic skills, learn to command his soldiers, and successfully uphold the state authority. For this reason, he was able to put in practice the sophisticated plans of conquering Istanbul once he eventually settled to the throne for life. During his *şehzade* years, he fought naval battles with the Venetians, marched on rebellious İskender Bey, and personally fought on the army's left wing during the Battle of Kosovo II, all of which vested the young *şehzade* with the tremendous experience he would efficiently employ in his vigorous *gaza*s for the cause of Islam.

Mehmed II's second accession to the throne happened after his father passed away, making him a nineteen year-old Ottoman sultan on February 18, 1451. During the first years of his reign, he confronted the Karamanids, who had allied with the Venetians and agitated other *bey*s in Anatolia against the Ottomans as part of their broader objective of benefiting from the immediate succession of the Ottoman throne. At the end of the march on the Karamanids, a peace treaty was signed, as requested by the Karamanid İbrahim Bey.

Prior to embarking on his conquest of Istanbul, Sultan Mehmed II wanted to attain safety in Anatolia: he first made peace with the Karamanids and then established benevolent relations with the Mamluks. He further exploited, to the fullest extent, a range of conflicts among the Venetian, Neapolitan, and Sicilian states in Italy. Brilliantly enough, he granted commercial privileges to the Venetians and Genoese, and as a result they sided with the Ottomans just as he had predicted.

Miniature of the young sultan on horseback, by Özcan Özcan

Miniature of the historic peninsula, by Hatice Ünal

First among the main reasons why Sultan Mehmed II desired to conquer Istanbul comes his idea that he truly wanted to be the conqueror professed and praised by Prophet Muhammad, peace and blessings be upon him, in his following hadith: "Surely, Constantinople (Istanbul) will be conquered; how blessed the commander who will conquer it, and how blessed his army." The Ottomans knew where the soldiers blessed by the Prophet would have gone if they had died; thus they exerted great force to conquer Istanbul. Sultan Bayezid I, Musa Çelebi, and Sultan Murad II had previously made failed attempts to conquer it.

Strategically speaking, the conquest of Istanbul meant the unification of the Ottoman lands in two adjacent continents, Anatolia (Asia Minor) and Rumelia in Europe. Furthermore, the obstacles that Byzantium presented to the Ottomans' military mobilization from Anatolia to Rumelia would be eliminated.

Awakener of the crusading spirit of Christian Europe at every turn and instigator of organizing the crusades, Byzantium would dissolve with the Ottoman conquest of Istanbul. Worse, Byzantium had ignited the *bey*s of the neighboring Anatolian principalities to rise up against the Ottomans. It also supported the *şehzade*s to later flame up contests for the Ottoman throne, which led to fraternal bloodshed and exacerbated the situation of the Ottoman Empire. In the longer run, the rebellions that Byzantium spearheaded using the Ottoman *şehzade*s hindered the Ottoman conquests and spoiled the spirit in Anatolia.

Sultan Mehmed II, a far-sighted planner in the conquest of Istanbul, rushed on the preparations to conquer the city soon after he returned from his march on the Karamanids. The preparatory process was illustrative of the fact that the young sultan had learned his lessons from his past experiences. An obvious example is his construction of Boğazkesen, also known as Rumeli Hisarı (Rumelian Fortress) in 1452 on the European side of the Bosphorous at the opposite shore of Anadolu Hisarı (Anatolian Fortress) in an informed attempt to cut off the reinforcements from the Genoese colonies on the Black Sea ports to Byzantium.

Just as he made an agreement with the Karamanids in Anatolia, Sultan Mehmed II signed several treaties (through Çandarid Halil Pasha) with the Venetians and Hungarians in Europe. Mehmed II then convinced the Serbian despot and the Bosnian king to side with the Ottomans. In addition, he captured Vize and Silivri as well as other territories outside of the inner city of Istanbul, which ultimately disconnected Byzantium from the west side. Now that the Ottoman Empire was confidently safe from all sides, the sultan spelled out his plan

Miniature of the Rumelian Fortress that Sultan Mehmed the Conqueror had constructed across the Anatolian Fortress, by Ersan Perçem

Miniature depicting the story of the conquest of Istanbul, by Özcan Özcan

for conquest. At the same time, he strongly invested in sending atypical reserve troops to the Morea and the Balkans in case of need, confirming the value of the lessons he learned from the experiences of his grandfather Bayezid I and his father.

In addition to the preparations for the siege by land, Mehmed II had a navy assembled, particularly to support the siege of Istanbul from the sea. He also had massive cannonballs crafted in Edirne, strong enough to tear down the walls of Byzantium; the biggest of those came to be called *shahi* (imperial) which were larger than any that had been seen before. In addition, he prepared long-range mortars that would leap over the city walls. Mehmed II opened up the issue of conquest in a meeting with his advisory council. Seeing that the majority of statesmen opted for the conquest and despite the pessimistic approach several officials took justifying a more ambivalent strategy, he moved from the capital city of Edirne in a venture to siege Istanbul on April 6, 1453. Byzantium's response to the suggestion that Mehmed II's ambassador carried to the Byzantine emperor directly from the Imperial camp established behind the defensive Byzantine walls between the gates of Edirnekapı and Topkapı was negative: they would not surrender the city in peaceful terms. With cannons rumbling around the city walls, the Ottoman offensive began.

The greatest setback that the Ottomans faced in the siege of Istanbul came when the emperor shut down the Golden Horn with veteran ships and sets of chains. In addition, what the Byzantines called the *grejuva* (Greek fire), an element inflammable even in the water, caused the Ottoman army great difficulty.

Two different *millets* lived in contemporary Istanbul: the Greeks and Latins. The local Greeks, who detested the Latin settlers,[16] rejected and protested in the presence of the emperor the first ritual conducted by the principles of the ecclesiastical unification as signed previously with the Pope in the church of Ayasofya (Hagia Sophia) in order to mobilize Christian Europe against a common enemy. In the city, the prevalent idea was "better the turban of the Turk than the Latin mitre."

During the fifty-four day siege between April 6, 1453 and May 29, 1453, the Ottoman army mounted attacks not only by land but also by sea. The Golden Horn was impassable thanks to the great chain barrage stretched across the mouth of the Golden Horn to prevent vessels entering this Bosphorous inlet bisecting the European side of the city. But the Byzantines had not anticipated the young sultan's plan to transport the Ottoman warships overland on greased runners into the northern shore of the Golden Horn to bypass both the chain barrage and fortresses blocking the entrance to the city. The Ottomans conquered Istanbul on Tuesday, May 29, 1453. Mehmed II, known as Sultan Mehmed the Conqueror from that point on, entered the city by the Edirnekapı (Edirne Porte). He performed his ritual prayer in Ayasofya and announced that the lives and property of the Byzantines who flowed into the church of Ayasofya from every part of the city would be provided with security. The Conqueror confirmed that the local people who paid their ransom could stay in Istanbul; those who had fled the city began to return, and the sultan provided them with housing and exempted them from taxes.

Sultan Mehmed II, who made Istanbul the third and last Ottoman capital after Bursa and Edirne, was not only a conqueror but also a builder. Indeed, the Conqueror's new imperial capital was destined to become the new center of the Abode of Islam as well as the capital of a great civilization. By the time the Ottomans conquered the city, the imperial glory of Istanbul was almost gone, and it was already largely depopulated since the Latin occupation period. Thus the ensuing policies of Sultan Mehmed the Conqueror focused on reconstructing and repopulating the exhausted city, reflecting the multi-ethnic character of the empire. The multi-national and multi-religious *millet* system[17] of the Ottomans was indeed initiated by the Conqueror after the conquest of Istanbul. He granted the Christian and Jewish communities freedom of religion and beliefs, which won over their hearts. The Conqueror did not disband the Orthodox Patriarchate, which was without a patriarch at the time, but

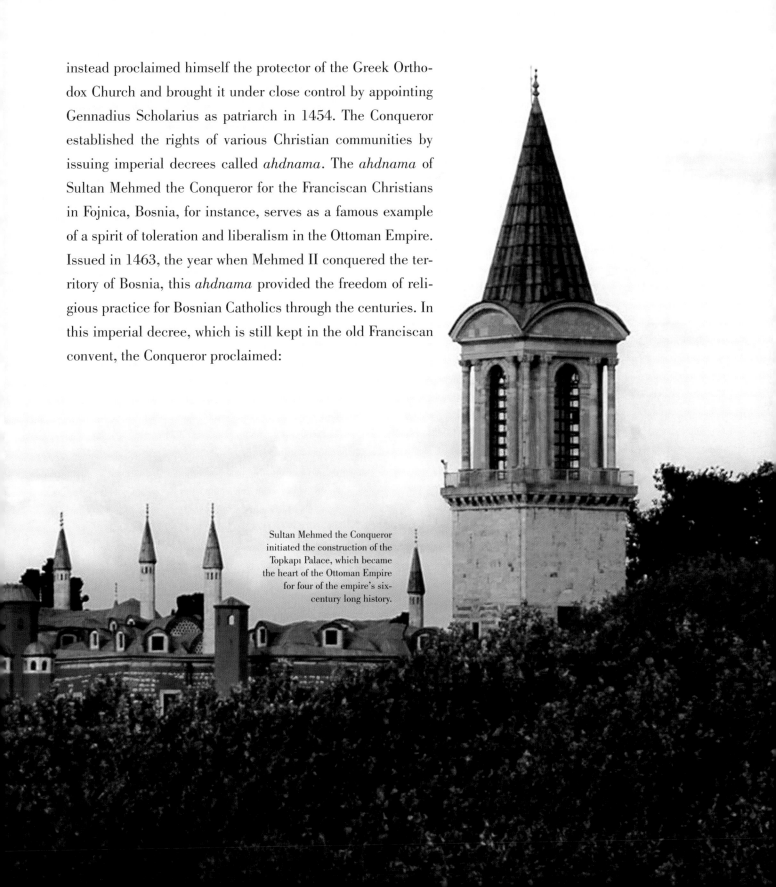

instead proclaimed himself the protector of the Greek Orthodox Church and brought it under close control by appointing Gennadius Scholarius as patriarch in 1454. The Conqueror established the rights of various Christian communities by issuing imperial decrees called *ahdnama*. The *ahdnama* of Sultan Mehmed the Conqueror for the Franciscan Christians in Fojnica, Bosnia, for instance, serves as a famous example of a spirit of toleration and liberalism in the Ottoman Empire. Issued in 1463, the year when Mehmed II conquered the territory of Bosnia, this *ahdnama* provided the freedom of religious practice for Bosnian Catholics through the centuries. In this imperial decree, which is still kept in the old Franciscan convent, the Conqueror proclaimed:

Sultan Mehmed the Conqueror initiated the construction of the Topkapı Palace, which became the heart of the Ottoman Empire for four of the empire's six-century long history.

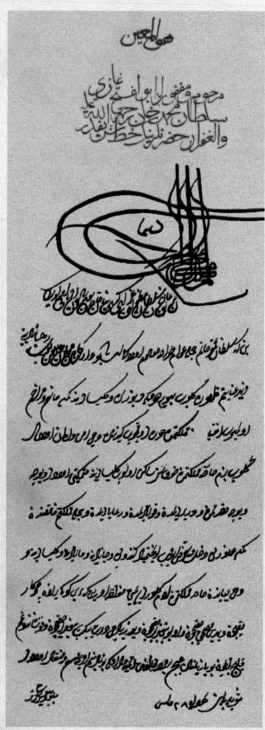

The original of this *ahdnama* (solemn charter) above is still kept in the Franciscan Catholic Monastery in Fojnica, Bosnia. It is one of the oldest documents in the history of human rights and freedom that entered into force in 1463, granting legal guarantees 326 years before the French Revolution in 1789 and 485 years before the International Human Rights Declaration in 1948.

I, Sultan Mehmed Khan,

hereby declare to the whole world that,

the ones who possess this imperial decree, the Bosnian Franciscans, are under my protection. And I command that:

No one shall disturb or give harm to these people and their churches! They shall live in peace in my state. These people who have become emigrants shall have security and liberty. They may return to their monasteries located in the borders of my state.

No one from my royal highness or my viziers or clerks, or my servants, or any of the citizens of my state shall disturb, insult or give any harm to the lives, properties, and churches of these people! And anybody they bring from abroad into my country will have the same rights.

By declaring this decree, I hereby take my great oath in the name of the Creator of the heavens and the earth, in the name of God's Messenger Muhammad and 124,000 former Prophets, and in the name of sword I gird that nobody shall do contrary to what has been written in this decree!

Indeed, there are many examples of such imperial decrees proclaiming religious freedom in the Ottoman Empire and displaying the famous permissiveness and tolerance of Ottoman administrative practice. Toleration as the chief component of Ottoman identity found its expression both on the level of state rule and in everyday cultural life.

Soon after the conquest of Istanbul, the Conqueror began a wide scale reconstruction plan for the new imperial capital with a Turkish Islamic outlook. He ordered the construction of the Eyüp Sultan Mosque, which is named after a Companion of the Prophet, Abu Ayyub al-Ansari, who had died outside the city walls while besieging the city back in 669. Paying special attention to improve its economy, the Conqueror gave instructions for the construction of a grand bazaar and other buildings. By adding three larger towers to the four pre-existing Byzantium towers on the inner city walls, the Conqueror formed the Fortress of Seven Towers, called *Yedikule*, which was used as state treasury during most of the Ottoman period.

The Ottoman conquest of Istanbul caused the Europeans to feel more profoundly the severe threat imposed by the Ottomans against them, and initiatives were taken to establish a unified crusade front with solid encouragement of the Pope. Sultan Mehmed the Conqueror wanted to forestall the unification of the Christians against his empire, so he settled with Venetians in 1454, allowing them to place a *balyos*,[18] or ambassador, in Istanbul and to trade with the Ottomans on favorable commercial and customs terms. In the East, the conquest of Istanbul raised the reputation of the Ottoman Empire in the eyes of the Muslim World.

The Conqueror's next step was to engage a series of *gaza*s to reinstall the Ottoman supremacy in the Balkans, which had shattered during the reign of his father, and to make sure that it would be permanent. All the Serbian lands but Belgrade were added to the Ottoman domain in 1459. The Conqueror then marched on the Morea and Trabzon, both of

The Eyüp Sultan Mosque in Istanbul

67

which could claim their Byzantine affinity and desire to resurrect Byzantium, and conquered the Morea on the southern end of the Balkans in 1460. This victory secured a strategic base to supply his future campaigns to Italy. During the next year, he marched on the Empire of Trebizond (Trabzon) on the Black Sea cost of northern Anatolia. The fact that the Empire of Trebizond asked the Pope for help against the Ottomans and allied with Uzun Hasan, the ruler of the Akkoyunids (the White Sheep Turcomans) in eastern Anatolia, forced the Ottomans to rush their campaign on Trabzon. After a difficult and burdensome military excursion in Trabzon, the young sultan dissolved another empire in 1461.

Ottoman parade helmet, encrusted with gems, the Topkapı Palace

The Conqueror had to shift his route back to the Balkans for another campaign in response to an alliance the Prince of Wallachia Vlad Dracula, also known as Vlad the Impaler, forged with the Hungarians as well as his assault on the Ottoman lands in the Balkans. His first campaign on Wallachia reclaimed Wallachia to the Ottoman domain in 1462. Sultan Bayezid I(ruled 1389–1402) had forced Bosnia to pay annual tributes, but now it challenged the Ottoman authority and supported the Wallachian prince against the Ottomans. Being the sultan's second target in the region, Bosnia became an Ottoman territory, and the Ottoman frontier institutions were established there in 1463. In a relatively short term, Islam spread in the land. Meanwhile, the Herzegovina Duchy proclaimed its allegiance to the Ottomans in 1465. Later in 1476, Moldavia in the north of Wallachia would become a province of the Ottoman Empire. Following the death of Iskender Bey, Albania too began to wave the Ottoman flag in 1479. This latest addition indeed sealed the successful series of conquests in the Balkan Peninsula.

After the Balkans were added to the Ottoman domains, the Conqueror decided to pursue the objectives of enforcing unity in Anatolia and controlling the profitable Black Sea trade. In line with this objective, he captured Amasra from the Genoese in 1460, and secured Kastamonu and its vicinity after putting an end to the Turkcoman İsfendiyarid Principality in 1461. Finally, the conquest of Trabzon established the Ottoman control of the Anatolian shores of the Black Sea.

In Central Anatolia, the Karamanids allied with the Venetians against the Ottomans causing Sultan Mehmed the Conqueror to pursue a campaign against the Karamanids. He

Mehmed the Conqueror entering Istanbul through the Edirnekapı (Edirne Porte), by the Ottoman court painter Fausto Zonaro, 1908

captured Konya and Karaman and put most of the principality under direct Ottoman control in 1466. Pir Ahmed, the Karamanid Bey, had taken refuge with Uzun Hasan of the Ak-koyunids and caused the Ottoman-Akkoyunid relations to deteriorate.

The Akkoyunid Turcomans, who had established a powerful state in eastern Anatolia in the wake of the 15th century, were determined to expand their boundaries at the expense of the Ottoman Empire, which soon brought the two states in a clash. Uzun Hasan allied against the Ottomans with the Karamanids, the Empire of Trebizond, and Venice. The Conqueror marched on Uzun Hasan, whose ambitions led the Akkoyunids to reach an agreement with the Christian states at the expense of another Muslim country. The Ottomans won this Battle of Otlukbeli in eastern Anatolia in 1473, and the Akkoyunid State lost its power to challenge the Ottomans anymore. In addition, the Ottoman decisive victory at Otlukbeli enabled the Conqueror to secure the eastern side of his empire.

Initially, the Conqueror pursued benevolent relations with the Mamluks who ruled Egypt, Syria, and the Hijaz region of the western Arabian Peninsula. Later on, he captured the lands of the Karamanids. The Ottoman Empire, then, became a neighboring state to the Dulkadirids who ruled the Maraş region in southeastern Anatolia and were loyal to the Mam-luks. This territorial proximity changed the course of Ottoman-Mamluk relations into one of belligerence. The news that the Mamluks wanted to take possession of the Dulkadirid lands received a reactive response from the Ottomans who had a dynastic relationship with the Dulkadirids. As a result, Ottoman-Mamluk relations staggered.

An important portion of the Middle East belonged to the Mamluks, including the Hijaz region, the site of Islam's holy cities of Mecca and Medina. When the pilgrims complained about the lack of potable water en route to Hijaz, the Conqueror sent a team of craftsmen from Istanbul to open wells on the road and fix the existing but inefficiently running wells. The already staggering relations worsened when the Mamluks, the guardians of the pilgrimage route, obstructed the craftsmen from doing the work the Conqueror assigned them.

Sultan Mehmed the Conqueror wanted to have control over Europe economically by dominating the trade networks extending from the Mediterranean through the Aegean to the Black Sea; therefore, he established naval yards in Gelibolu (Gallipoli), İzmit, Gemlik, and Istanbul. Thanks to the naval power that the yards provided, an Ottoman navy emerged strong enough to brave the Venetians and Genoese on the sea.

The miniature of the Conqueror by Şiblizade Ahmed painted in 1475

71

The eastern trade of Venice had taken a serious blow when the Conqueror took complete possession of the Morea, Serbia, Bosnia, and Albania. For this reason, Venice forged an alliance with the Hungarian Kingdom and the Albanian principality. During the sixteen-year war that the Ottoman Empire fought (in intervals) against this alliance, which the Karamanids and the Akkoyunids also supported, many of the Aegean islands including the Eğriboz (Euboea) island, one of the most valuable of Venetian dependencies, waved the Ottoman flag. Venice could do nothing but ask for peace in 1479. The ensuing treaty stipulated that the Ottomans would keep Kruja and Shkodra in the northwest of the Balkans; the Venetians would pay war indemnity and annual tributes, and maintain the presence of an ambassador (*balyos*) in Istanbul along with the right to carry duty-free commerce on the Ottoman seas.

Having established the Ottoman authority on the Anatolian shores of the Black Sea, the Conqueror dispatched Gedik Ahmed Pasha to the north of the Black Sea; in return, Gedik Ahmed Pasha won to the Ottomans' credit the Genoese colonies of Kaffa, Azov, and Mangup in the Crimean Peninsula in 1475. Following the death of Hacı Giray, the Khan of Crimea, his sons tumbled into a struggle for the throne, and the march of the ruler of the Golden Horde to Crimea doubled the political turmoil in the region. Gedik Ahmed Pasha, who was watchful of the situation, made an expedition and attached Crimea to the Ottoman State in 1477. This conquest marked the Ottoman dominance in the Black Sea and expelled the Genoese from the Black Sea region.

When the Kingdom of Naples in Italy began to pursue hostile diplomacy against the Ottomans in the Aegean and Mediterranean, the Conqueror assigned Gedik Ahmed Pasha as the commander of campaign to Italy. The ensuing series of expeditions gave the Ottomans the islands of Zante, Kefalonia, and Lefkada on the Ionian Sea as well as Otranto of the Kingdom of Naples on the Adriatic coast of Southern Italy in 1480. The sudden death of the Conqueror in 1481 left the campaign to Italy incomplete; furthermore, the Kingdom of Naples reclaimed Otranto as soon as Gedik Ahmed Pasha departed Italy.

Sultan Mehmed the Conqueror died on May 3, 1481 in Hünkarçayırı near present-day Maltepe on the Anatolian side of Istanbul as he departed Istanbul through Üsküdar for a new campaign. Although common knowledge suggests that the Conqueror was leading an expedition toward the East, chronicles narrate that he was either poisoned by a Venetian doctor on his way to Rome or fell dead as a result of the gout he suffered from.

Inner domes of the Fatih (Conqueror's) Mosque built by Mehmed II in the Fatih district of Istanbul

Sultan Mehmed the Conqueror was a tough-built, tall man and with a hook-nose and full lips. He was the sultan of a smart and rough character, distasteful of fun and pleasure. He respected the scholars and men of knowledge. He enjoyed meeting with them and provided full-fledged support to all kinds of scientific research. The Conqueror, who had a commanding knowledge of at least five languages, including Turkish, Arabic, Persian, Old Slavonic, and Greek, enriched his library with a great number of scientific books written in various languages. From the personal library of the Conqueror fifty books on the Western cultures survived, forty-two of which were written in Greek. Out of these forty-two books, eight are related to history, six to mathematics and astronomy. The books on history and geography make up more than one third of the entire collection that is still kept in the Topkapı Palace Museum Library.

As well as having foresight, and cultural literacy, Mehmed the Conqueror was an extraordinary commander whose objective was to spread to "the known world" the religion he believed in, and this was reflected in his presence in twenty-five military campaigns. He tried relentlessly to make the *Devlet-i Aliyye* (the Sublime Ottoman State) a world power in all respects.

During his reign, the Conqueror opined a completely centralist approach in state matters; he not only appeased notable families willing to wield influence on administration but also promoted viziers among those faithful to him. He gave them more authority, and his strategy resulted in the formation of an efficient and successful team of statesmen, which had included advisors from Florence, Genoa, and Ragusa.

The sultan had studied well the results of the Janissary mutiny during his first tenure of reign; thus, his second period of reign witnessed the reconstruction of the Janissaries and the march lords, called *uç bey*s, so that they were forced to give up their self-interest and pledge their allegiance to him. In the end, he succeeded in commanding the army in a real sense.

The Conqueror was a fan of history; for instance, he was the student of Italian historians on Roman history during his *şehzade* years, and had Greek scholar Georgios

Sultan Mehmed the Conqueror's sword en detail

Amirutzes prepare a world map in 1456. Illustrative of the Islamic spirit of tolerance, he further allowed the Greek Orthodox and Armenian *millet*s to have their respective patriarchs as well as the Jewish *millet* their chief rabbi in Istanbul, coexisting peacefully in his new imperial capital. All of these decisions can be understood as a sign that he intended to make the Ottoman Empire the dominant world power. But having a great power and influence in the world was nothing more than the means. For him, more essential than becoming a world power was the protection of the Abode of Islam against any attacks; therefore, the *gaza*s took the lead in his policy making. He gave the permission for fratricide because he wanted more than anything to maintain the unity of the Ottoman Empire and get rid of those who would drift into bloody contests to claim the throne; hence, the state would not struggle with internal deadly throne contests but use its full-force for *gaza*s beyond its borders.[19]

The Conqueror was a master of poetry and wrote many poems under the pseudonym *Avni* ("of the Divine aid"). His poems applied lucid expressions and fluidity of language; in fact, they are regarded as one of the best examples of Ottoman Turkish poetry.

Along with religious knowledge, he was interested in geography, mathematics, and astronomy. He invited quite a number of scholars to teach him these sciences. His lessons took place on a regular basis; certain hours were assigned for certain classes every day. Among his teachers were the contemporary distinguished scholars like Molla Gürani, Hocazade Muslihuddin, Molla İlyas,

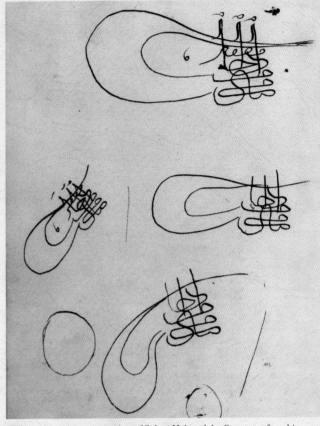

Calligraphic signature exercises of Sultan Mehmed the Conqueror from his notebook during his early childhood. Every Ottoman sultan had his own splendid stylized signature, called *tughra*, written in elegant, expressive calligraphy. Indeed, the earliest surviving tughra of the Ottoman sultans belong to the second Ottoman Sultan Orhan Gazi, and every Ottoman sultan after him created his own individual tughra from the beginning of his reign. The tughras, which were initially used in official documents and correspondence to give formality, were later seen on sultanic seals, standards, monuments, mosques, palaces, coins, stamps, and passports as a symbol of sovereignty.

The thirty-five tughras of all Ottoman sultans from Orhan Gazi to the last Ottoman Sultan Mehmed Vahdeddin are given next to the name of each sultan throughout this book. It is noticeable that the calligraphic style of the names of the Sultan [Orhan] and his father in the expression, "Orhan—the son of Osman," are written out in the bottom section of the tughra and formed the skeleton and the main text for subsequent tughras, which later evolved, including the expression of *muzaffer daima* ("ever victorious") as well as the sultans' honorific titles. It is possible to view in this book how the tughras developed slowly from the time of Orhan Gazi to later times. The calligraphic design of tughra achieved its standards under Sultan Mehmed the Conqueror and reached its classic, lavish form during the reign of Sultan Süleyman the Magnificent in the sixteenth century. From the period of Sultan Mehmed the Conqueror on, the spaces between the letters were illuminated, a practice that continued until the mid-nineteenth century. In addition, the court calligraphers used black, red, green, and blue inks, as well as gold, to write the tughras. The choice of colors was not arbitrary as each had a specific meaning in Ottoman protocol.

Following pages: Aerial view of the 1500 year-old Ayasofya, Istanbul. This colossal edifice with a central dome 108 feet (33 meters) in diameter and flanking domes has survived up until our time thanks to the Ottoman palace protocol giving priority to this great heritage of the city.

View of the historic peninsula of Istanbul and the Galata region with the portraits of sultans from Osman Gazi to Sultan Murad III

Siraceddin Halebi, Molla Abdülkadir, Hasan Samsuni, and Molla Hayreddin. In addition, his tutor and counselor Akşemseddin played a profound role in the education of the Conqueror.

Sultan Mehmed the Conqueror placed a tremendous priority on education. After the conquest of Istanbul, eight churches in the city were turned into *medrese*s, or higher education institutions, including the Ayasofya Medrese. He further established the famous *medrese*s named Sahn-ı Seman (present-day University of Istanbul) near the Fatih Mosque, which is one of the largest examples of Turkish-Islamic architecture. He used to inspect schools in person, participate in seminars, and award remarkable students. His intellectual background in philosophy was proven comprehensive and strong enough to conduct inspiring discussions with philosophers of the West. In his presence, the great thinkers, representative of both the East and West, such as Amirutzes, Ali Kuşçu, Georgios Trapezuntios, and Hocazade Muslihiddin, found a respected common ground to explain and discuss their views.

Mehmed the Conqueror left behind many legacies. He had two daughters named Ayşe and Gevherhan, and the latter married Mehmed Bey, the son of Uzun Hasan. Göde Ahmed, who would later rise to the Akkoyunlu throne, was the son of Gevherhan and the grandson of the Conqueror. In addition, it was the Conqueror who ordered the initial construction of the Topkapı Palace, the official and primary residence of the Ottoman Sultans in Istanbul for four of their six-century long reign. Istanbul is the most remarkable legacy the Conqueror left behind. It was here that he undertook a profound project in constructing some of the most sublime contributions to Islamic and human civilization, such as the Fatih Mosque and numerous *medrese*s. Within a century after the conquest, Istanbul was to become the largest city in Europe.

Interior of the Ayasofya Museum with enormous medallions on the massive pillars supporting the dome

A portrait of Sultan Mehmed the Conqueror on canvas by Gentile Bellini, November, 24, 1480. On the bottom left it reads, "Victor Orbis" in Latin, meaning "the Conqueror of the World." It seems that Bellini painted the three crowns on both sides of the arch to symbolize the six Ottoman sultans preceding Mehmed II. The seventh crown, that of the reigning Sultan Mehmed II, is found on the embroidered cover in the portrait.

81

Sultan Bayezid II

Reign: 1481–1512

Honorifics and Aliases: *Veli*, *Adli*, and *Sofu*
Father's Name: Sultan Mehmed the Conqueror
Mother's Name: Gülbahar Valide Sultan
Place and Date of Birth: Didymoteicho on the western banks of the Meriç River, December 3, 1448
Age at Accession to the Throne: 33
Cause and Date of Death: Gout, Poison; May 21, 1512
Place of Death and Burial Site: Çorlu on the east of Istanbul – his tomb is located near the Bayezid Mosque which he had built in the Bayezid Square, Istanbul
Male Heirs: Mahmud, Ahmed, Şahinşah, Sultan Selim I, Mehmed, Korkud, Abdullah, and Alimşah
Female Heir: Aynişah Sultan, Gevher Sultan, Müluk Sultan, Hadice Sultan, Selçuk Sultan, and Hüma Sultan

*I*n accordance with the usual and practical assignment of the young *şehzade*s as governors to one of the *sancak*s, which were second-order administrative units as part of the largest divisions called *beylerbeyilik*, Bayezid II was assigned as the governor of Amasya at the age of seven years old. He was guided by a tutor and advisors, and received an impressive education as the son of a science-and-arts loving father. Later in his mid twenties, he commanded the right wing of the Ottoman army during the Battle

Miniature of Sultan Bayezid II by Levni in his *Kebir Musavver Silsilenâme* (The Great Envisaged Portraiture Geneology)

of Otlukbeli in eastern Anatolia in 1473. When his father Sultan Mehmed the Conqueror passed away, his brother Şehzade Cem was also assigned as the governor of Karaman. The statesmen polarized among Bayezid and Cem on the matter of who would succeed their father. Meanwhile, the Janissaries in Istanbul had organized demonstrations in favor of Bayezid as the next sultan. İshak Pasha, the guardian of Istanbul, brought Korkud, the son of Bayezid II, to the throne by proxy so that there would be no gap in the dynastic rule of succession until Bayezid II came to Istanbul to be the de facto ruler. Once Bayezid II reached Istanbul, Korkud relinquished the throne to his father.

Cem did not give up his right to the throne, however. He garnered support from the statesmen of Turcoman origin and engaged in a throne-contest against his elder brother. With his supporters from Anatolia, he marched to Bursa and captured the city. Having defeated his older brother's troops, Cem had his name minted on the coins and mentioned at the sermon of the Friday Prayer to commence the acknowledgment of his authority. He further recommended that Bayezid II split the empire, in which case he would be the sultan in Anatolia, the Asian half of the state, and Bayezid II in Rumelia, the European half; however, Bayezid II rejected this idea and declared war on Cem. Bayezid II won the ensuing battle in Yenişehir, forcing him to retreat to Karaman. Cem Sultan would later take refuge with the Mamluks in Egypt in 1481 and complete his pilgrimage to Mecca while there. The Karamanid Kasım Bey provoked his return, and Cem came back to Anatolia to lose against his older brother once again. He then took refuge on Rhodes Island, which had never failed his father even after long naval battles. The knights of St. John in Rhodes took the young şehzade to France in order to bargain with the Ottomans; the young şehzade was then taken from France to Rome, where the knights handed him over to the Pope. Bayezid II's efforts to secretly re-snatch his brother from the papacy did not yield any results. Meanwhile, Charles VIII, the French King, took Cem Sultan with him following the French expedition to Italy; however, Şehzade Cem died in 1495 on the way to France most probably because he had been poisoned. His dead body returned home to Bursa four years later.

Short-sleeved royal caftan,
the Topkapı Palace

Cem Sultan played into the hands of the European powers causing disputes with the Ottomans, which in fact deprived the conquests of momentum. The efforts of Bayezid II in preserving domestic order rather than external territorial expansion further impeded the conquests. The Karamanid state was ultimately abolished during this time because of the chaos it incited in Anatolia; and this time the Karamids also got involved with the Cem Sultan incident and Ottoman internal affairs in 1487.

Herzegovina had acknowledged the Ottoman sovereignty in the land and was eventually attached to the Ottoman territory in 1483. Then the Kilia and Akkerman forts, which had obstructed the Ottoman land route from Crimea and obviated the trade on the Black Sea, were conquered in 1484 by Bayezid II as a result of his expedition in response to the alliance of the Wallachian prince with the Hungarians against the Ottomans. This conquest marked the establishment of Ottoman dominance along the western shores of the Black Sea.

The Venetian-held ports and forts in the Morea continuously obstructed Ottoman navigation in the Mediterranean. Strengthened during the reign of Bayezid II, the Ottoman navy was ready to challenge Venice on the sea. After a host of naval battles against Venice, the Ottomans conquered Naupactus, Methoni, Koroni, and Navarino. The conquest of Naupactus, situated on a bay on the north side of the straits of Lepanto, provided the Ottoman fleet with a strategically vital base in the Adriatic.

The Andalusian Muslims turned to the Ottomans as the most powerful Islamic state of the time when the Catholic inquisition courts pressured, oppressed, and tortured the Muslims and Jews in Spain. Although Bayezid II wanted to help them, he could not quite do so as he was too busy with the Cem Sultan incident; however, he sent Captain Kemal Reis to Spain to save them from the persecution and torture of the Inquisition,[20] and in 1505 Kemal Reis moved the Muslims of Spain down to North Africa, and the Jews eastward to Istanbul and Salonica.

The Mamluks protected Cem, increased their pressure on the Dulkadirid principality, and taxed the Turkish pilgrims, all of which exacerbated the already fragile Ottoman-Mamluk relations. The problems between the Ottomans and Mamluks had begun during the reign of the Mehmed the Conqueror because of the problems with the Hijaz waterways. A series of battles began in 1485 between the Ottomans and Mamluks and lasted about six years. In 1491, the Tunisian sultan arbitrated and helped end the war between the belligerent parties, neither of which had been able to win any major victory on the field. According to the truce that followed, the Ottomans returned the captured Adana and Tarsus regions, for they had been endowments registered to the Haramayn.

The Akkoyunid state entered the year 1490 with contests to the throne. This was followed by the domination of greater Azerbaijan by Shah Ismail in 1502 and the establishment of the Safavid state. The Safavids recognized Shi'a Islam as their official state policy and thus ventured to spread Shi'a Islam in Anatolia shortly thereafter. The main objective of Shah Ismail was to capture the Ottoman lands in Anatolia. To this end, he dispatched his eminent disciples to Anatolia to propagate Shi'ism and undermine the Ottoman authority in Anatolia. While the Shah's methods proved impactful and his followers began to mushroom in Anatolia, the young Şehzade Selim, then the governor of Trabzon, became the first Ottoman statesman to recognize of the Shah's dangerous infiltration into Anatolia and applied preventive measures to counter it.

The opening page of the Qur'an manuscript written in the *nesih* script by the young Şehzade Korkud, Sultan Bayezid II's son

Interior of the Bayezid Mosque built by Sultan Bayezid II

The silhouette of the Bayezid Mosque in the Bayezid Square is one of the defining features of the historic peninsula of Istanbul (circa 1870).

Some peddlers and groups of people gathering in the courtyard of the Bayezid Mosque in around 1905. Historically, the Bayezid Square surrounding the mosque had been a traditional fairground, especially during the month of Ramadan.

Courtyard of the Bayezid Mosque

The 1511 civil unrest that broke in the Teke region in southwestern Anatolia generated a struggle between the Sunnis and Shiites in Anatolia. Nureddin Ali, nicknamed "Shah Kulu," had been sent by Shah Ismail to Anatolia along with other propagators. Shah Kulu defeated the military forces sent to catch him, moved through the vicinity of Bursa up to Sivas and took refuge with the Safavids. It seems that Şehzade Ahmed's failure in thwarting this revolt became one of the main reasons that Şehzade Selim would become the next Sultan. In Tokat, even *khutba*s were read in reference to Shah Ismail during the revolt; despite all, the revolt was able to be quelled. The rising unrest played a profound role in Bayezid's loss of the throne, and the following period saw a contest for the throne among his sons.

Şehzade Selim, the governor of Trabzon, went to Kaffa in Crimea, where his son Şehzade Süleyman (later Sultan Süleyman the Magnificent) was the governor, and asked his father Sultan Bayezid II to transfer him to Silistra on the southern banks of the lower Danube river—for it was closer to Istanbul—but his father did not accept the proposal. When Şehzade Selim moved with his forces through Kilia to Edirne, Sultan Bayezid II announced that he transferred Selim to Semendria and would not let Şehzade Ahmed access the throne. However, the agreement did not gain permanent ground. Şehzade Selim eventually confronted his father militarily, but he was defeated in the Battle of Uğraşköy and returned to Kaffa. Then the Janissaries revolted when Şehzade Ahmed was called to Istanbul in September, 1511. Instead of Şehzade Ahmed, they wanted Şehzade Selim to be their commander. Şehzade Selim came to Istanbul and kissed his father's hand in the Topkapı Palace. Here Bayezid abdicated the throne in his favor. Oddly enough, Bayezid II, who had come to the throne in response to the Janissary pressure, relinquished the throne again for the same reason on April 24, 1512 – thirty-one years later.

When Bayezid II was departing Istanbul for retirement in his native Didymoteicho, Sultan Selim accompanied him until he had left the city walls. Bayezid II felt under the weather when he reached the Abalar village near Çorlu and passed away on May 21, 1512. In spite of contradictory speculations on the causes of his death, many sources agree that he was poisoned.

Bayezid II was a tall man with hazel eyes, a wide chest, and swarthy visage; and he was clement in nature. He was a devout Muslim; in fact, he came to be called as Bayezid-i Veli (God's Friend Bayezid), for he was extraordinarily concerned with his religious duties and charities. He was for peace and engaged wars only when necessary, consolidating successfully the conquests of his father's reign.

Bayezid II gathered famous scholars around him from his *şehzade* years to increase his wisdom and knowledge. He was a man of poetry: he composed a sizeable *divan* (collection) comprised mainly of *ghazal*s (lyrical poems) under the penname "Adli." In addition, he was quite a talented calligrapher, and he knew the Uyghur Turkic and Italian languages.

When his father's spiritual guide and tutor Molla Gürani died, Bayezid II participated in his funeral and paid the expenses from his treasury. Bayezid patronized and supported all kinds of scientific and literary research; as a result, his period of reign witnessed the rise of many distinguished scholars and artists such as Molla Lütfi, Müeyyedzade Abdurrahman, İbn Kemal, İdris-i Bitlisi, Tacizade Cafer Çelebi, Zenbilli Ali Efendi, Necati, Zati, Visali, and Firdevsi. He also made contact with artists in Europe. A letter from Leonardo da Vinci, still available in the archives of the Topkapı Palace, states that da Vinci had been interested in constructing a bridge to the Golden Horne and the Bosphorus. Michelangelo too wanted to visit Istanbul when he heard this news; unfortunately, these projects never materialized.

Sultan Bayezid II built many social works in Istanbul, Amasya, Edirne, Osmancık, Geyve, and Saruhan; some examples of these are the *külliye*s in Istanbul and Edirne and the Pirinç Han, the inn in Bursa rented out to support various charitable organizations.

Sultan Selim I

The Brave

Reign: 1512–1520

Honorifics and Aliases: *Yavuz* [the Brave, for his great courage and martial prowess]
Father's Name: Bayezid II
Mother's Name: Ayşe Hatun
Place and Date of Birth: Amasya, October 10, 1470
Age at Accession to the Throne: 42
Cause and Date of Death: Cancer, September 21, 1520
Place of Death and Burial Site: Çorlu – his tomb is located near the Yavuz Selim Mosque in Istanbul
Male Heirs: Süleyman the Magnificent
Female Heir: Hadice Sultan, Fatma Sultan, Hafsa Sultan, and Şah Sultan

Prior to his ascendancy to the throne, Şehzade Selim, one of the youngest sons of Bayezid II, was the governor of Trabzon, which was quite far from Istanbul. His successful campaigns against the Georgians and Safavids distinguished him from his brothers. Seeing that his father did not take necessary measures to face the Safavid threat, Yavuz turned against and competed with his father, which gave him the respect and support of the Janissaries, and eventually the throne.

Miniature of Sultan Selim I by Levni in his *Kebir Musavver Silsilenâme* (The Great Envisaged Portraiture Geneology)

The main objective of Sultan Selim I was to maintain unity in the Turkish and Muslim world. He made peace agreements with European powers and directed his full force toward the East during his initial years of reign. To solidify his aims, he had geographers draw a world map just as his grandfather Sultan Mehmed the Conqueror had done and pinpointed on the map the spots he would conquer.

In reply to the arising Safavid threat in Anatolia, Sultan Selim I first closed the Ottoman border gates to the Safavid state. With this act, he disrupted the Safavid commercial relations with Anatolia. The fact that the Safavid Shah Ismail allied with the Mamluks and Venice against the Ottomans further aggravated relations between the two polities. Finally, the Ottoman army departed Istanbul on a march against Safavid Persia.

Sultan Selim I predicted that a revolt was likely and that the army could be exposed to severe dangers en route. Thus he settled a reserve troop of forty-thousand soldiers between Sivas and Kayseri. The soldiers became exhausted and complained that the campaign would take too long and supplies would not last; the Janissaries even attempted to charge a mutiny at one point. The sultan reacted to all by severely punishing Dukakinzade Ahmed Pasha, who secretly backed up the Janissaries in their attempts to rebel and did clandestine talks with the Dulkadirids. As a result, the Janissaries could do nothing but continue to obey him. In fact, Selim I was one of the most competent sultans in Ottoman history in commanding the army.

The Ottoman army confronted the Safavids on the Çaldıran prairies and inflicted a major defeat on the Safavid army in 1514. As Shah Ismail escaped from the battlefield, leaving all of his belongings behind, the Ottoman victors paraded through the Safavid capital of Tabriz. Although the campaign did not lead to the conquest of the Safavid Persia, Sultan Selim the Brave eliminated the Safavid threat targeting Anatolia. The east side of Anatolia was now safe and clear. The sultan, well-aware of the discontent among his soldiers, gave up his broader plans of reaching all the way up to Turkistan and returned westward, spending the winter back in Amasya. After this decisive

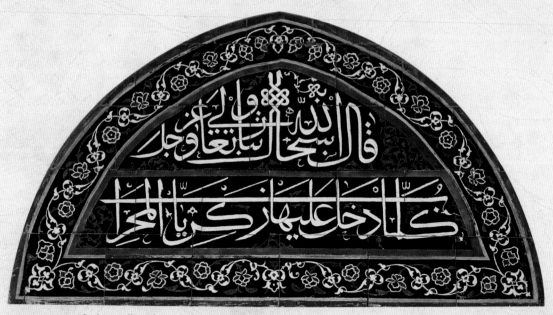

Qur'anic calligraphy on the top of a façade window of the Sultan Selim Mosque, Istanbul. It reads:
"God Almighty, may His Glory be exalted, said, '*Whenever Zachariah entered the sanctuary to see her (Mary)…*'" (3:37).

victory against the Safavids, the stations of the Silk Road[21] between Tabriz-Aleppo and Tabriz-Bursa were brought under Ottoman control.

Sultan Selim I attached the Dulkadirids to the Ottomans as a result of the Battle of Turnadağ, which the Ottoman army fought in the following spring after the expedition to Safavid Persia; thereby the Ottomans came to border the Mamluks territorially. The Ottoman-Mamluk relations had been staggering since the reign of Sultan Mehmed the Conqueror. But after the Mamluk ruler Qansuh al-Ghawri allied with the Safavids against the Ottomans at the time the Ottomans annexed the Dulkadirid principality, war became a possibility. The Sherif of Mecca, who was charged with protecting the Holy Lands and ensuring the safety of pilgrims, proposed that Qansuh al-Ghawri request the assistance of Selim the Brave, the sultan of the most powerful force of Islam, in defending the Arab world from the Portuguese attacks in the Red Sea. Qansuh al-Ghawri strongly disagreed with this proposal; however, the Arabs rested their hopes on Sultan Selim the Brave to save the holy cities of Mecca and Medina. Sultan Selim the Brave aimed to alleviate the damage inflicted on the Muslims and their holy cities by the Portuguese, who were on the Red Sea and the Indian Ocean, and to control the Spice Road if his campaign to Egypt proved successful. Another goal of the campaign was to establish Turkish-Islamic unity.

The Mamluks held Malatya and Divriği and stopped Grand Vizier[22] Sinan Pasha from passing over the Euphrates on his way to Safavid Persia. Furthermore, Qansuh al-Ghawri cast an alliance with Shah Ismail of the Safavids. In a final analysis of the situation, Sultan Selim the Brave consulted the Islamic scholars on what to do in face of the Mamluk sultan. Sultan Selim, having obtained their authoritative consent to engage war on the Mamluks, mobilized his army against another Muslim state.

The Holy Mantle of the Prophet was brought to Istanbul by Sultan Selim I and was later placed by Sultan Abdülaziz in a large golden chest on a high four-legged table in the Throne Room of the Topkapı Palace.

Sultan Selim the Brave sent his navy to the shores of Syria to reinforce his march on land. While the army was in Adana, the Ramazanid principality too waved the Ottoman flag. The Ottoman and Mamluk armies confronted each other in Marj Dabik (or Mercidabık) to the north of Aleppo on August 24, 1516, and the Ottomans crushed the Mamluks thanks to their superior military techniques. At the end of the day, Sultan Selim the Brave annexed Syria, Lebanon, and Palestine and paved the way open to Egypt. The humble character of Sultan Selim is illustrated in his meeting with the Abbasid Caliph al-Mutawakkil (d.1543) in the Ulu Mosque in Aleppo. When the caliph called him as *Hakimu'l Haramayn* (the Ruler of the holy cities of Mecca and Medina), he stated that he'd rather be called *Khadimu'l Haramayn* (the Servant of the Holy Cities). The Mamluk sultans, on the other hand, used to be addressed as *Hamiu'l Haramayn* (the Guardian of the Holy Cities).

Sultan Selim sent his messenger to the Mamluk Sultan Tomanbay, who succeeded Qansuh al-Ghawri, and urged him to recognize the Ottoman domination; however, Tomanbay opposed his call. For Sultan Selim the Brave, the victory of Marj Dabik (Mercidabık) would have been void unless Egypt fell to the Ottomans; therefore, he marched into Egypt head-on. He announced to the Egyptians, both city dwellers and peasants, that the Ottomans would not be hostile to them as the ongoing war was not against them but against the Mamluk army.

93

The Sultan Selim Mosque-complex built at the order of Sultan Süleyman the Magnificent in honor of his late father Sultan Selim I on a hilltop overlooking the Golden Horn.

94

Meanwhile, Tomanbay believed that the Ottoman sultan would follow the path of Genghis Khan and Tamerlane and lead his army back from Palestine, never daring to march on Egypt. The Ottoman army under the leadership of Sultan Selim the Brave, however, passed through the impassable Sinai Desert thanks to pleasantly surprising divine grace, rain falling on the desert! The army finally reached the gates of Cairo in January 16, 1517.

Sultan Selim the Brave learned that Tomanbay had dug ditches and trenches, and the front lines of his army were positioned with the stationary cannons he bought from Venice. Thus Sultan Selim circled the Mount of Al-Muqaddam and attacked the Mamluk army from the southeast at Ridanieh near Cairo. The Mamluks were not even able to fire their cannons. While the Ottoman right flank momentarily lost discipline, the grand vizier Hadım Sinan Pasha risked a severe injury and stepped in to pull the flank together. The war ended with a remarkable and certain Ottoman triumph, but a wounded Sinan Pasha secured his martyrdom.

Barakat ibn Muhammad al-Hasani, the Sherif of Mecca, sent an emissary delegate headed by his twelve year-old son Sherif Abu Numayy to Sultan Selim the Brave while the sultan was in Egypt in order to proclaim his allegiance to the Ottoman sultan. The delegate further presented the keys of Mecca, a symbolic gesture acknowledging the leadership of the sultan over the Muslim world, as well as some of the sacred trusts, including the holy mantle and banner of Prophet Muhammad, peace and blessings be upon him. As he sent the delegate off, Sultan Selim granted Sherif Barakat an

Inner dome of the Privy Chamber built by Sultan Selim I in the Topkapı Palace

edict, making him the Emir of Mecca. He also donated 200,000 golden duchies to be distributed to the residents of the holy cities and shipped with them abundant provisions. The two *surre* officials and two judges who accompanied the delegate back home partook in the distribution of donations and provisions.

During this period, the Portuguese had penetrated into the Red Sea, and the news that the Portuguese would strike Mecca and Medina caused a score of anxiety among the Muslims. From Cairo, Sultan Selim ordered the construction of an enormous fleet in the Suez to face this possible threat and dispatched Admiral Selman Reis to that location. Later at a time when even the Sherif of Mecca hopelessly fled Mecca for his life, Selman Reis would heroically protect Mecca from the Portuguese as they attacked Jiddah, the principal gateway to Mecca on the coast of the Red Sea.

Before setting out to Istanbul, the sultan sent the Abbasid Caliph and his family as well as the Muslim scholars and sheikhs from Cairo to Istanbul as a precaution; the latter would become teachers and scholars in the Ottoman *medrese*s in Istanbul. The first pieces in the collection of the sacred trusts were placed in the Topkapı Palace. The arrival of the sacred trusts in the palace inspired the beginning of a five-century old and still practiced tradition of reciting the Qur'an twenty four hours everyday in the Throne Room [*Has Oda*] of the Topkapı Palace in front the holy mantle of the Prophet like a spiritual watch by forty *hafiz*es, those who have memorized the Qur'an—the fortieth of which is said to have been Sultan Selim himself.

Sarcophagus of Sultan Selim I inside the tomb built in his name

Tomb of Sultan Selim I in the garden of the Sultan Selim Mosque by the Abdullah Brothers

The Fountain Hall in the Pavilion of the Sacred Trusts was used as the sultan's working room. Sultan Selim I would work long hours at night and mostly have some rest here on a simple cushion sofa rather than in his Privy Chamber in the palace.

The bodies of deceased sultans were put on the marble platform to be washed next to this incense mortar where the dusts from the cleaning of the Pavilion of Sacred Relics were placed out of respect shown to the Sacred Trusts.

Now that the Ottoman sultan received the Caliphate, Islamic law began to play an even more profound role in state affairs. The annual *surre* procession, which had been sent to meet the needs of the Haramayn since the reign of Sultan Bayezid I, took place on a more regular basis, and the Ottoman rulers took on the responsibility of the protection of the Muslims of the entire world.

Sultan Selim the Brave abolished the Mamluk state with his expedition to Egypt, bringing Syria, Palestine, Hijaz, and Egypt under direct Ottoman administration. Thereby, a large portion of the Muslim world came under Ottoman rule. In addition, the Spice Road passing

Funeral of Süleyman the Magnificent, from *Lokman Tarih-i Sultan Süleyman*. While it is said that the chest in front of the sultan's coffin contained his innards, it is most likely the golden chest that contained the Prophet's Holy Mantle.

99

through the Red Sea came under Ottoman control. The financial gains to be secured from the Spice Road coupled with the gains of war would fill up the Ottoman treasury. An extra income would come from Cyprus, as the Ottomans began to receive the tribute from Venice for Cyprus, which previously had been paid to the Mamluks. The gains of war during the reign of Sultan Selim the Brave were too many to store in the Topkapı Palace Chamber of Treasure. Thus, the surplus was shipped to repositories located in Yedikule (Fortress of Seven Towers) in Istanbul. In accordance with Sultan Selim the Brave's order that said, "the treasury that I filled up with gold be sealed with the cachet of whoever from my successors will refill it with money; or else my cachet should stay in effect," the outer gate of the Imperial Treasury continued to be sealed with Sultan Selim's cachet until the Topkapı Palace was turned into a museum four centuries later. The center of the seal displays the name of the sultan around which this expression is written, "In God I put unshakable trust and reliance." As a matter of fact, the immense treasury that Sultan Selim left behind provided his succeeding son Şehzade Süleyman with the tremendous financial security he would need to conquer the known world.

Sultan Selim the Brave ordered the preparation of his navy for a new campaign on his way back from Egypt to Istanbul. His men hurried to maximize the Ottoman naval capacity. The naval yard expanded, more nautical engineers were brought in, and the admiral of the fleet on the Red Sea was called to Istanbul. In a short span of time, an enormous naval fleet comprised of about 250 ships emerged ready to set sail to war.

Two obstacles aborted the commencement of the campaign, the destination of which was known only by the sultan himself. First was the revolt that Celal of Bozok launched in Anatolia but was quelled in a short time. Nevertheless, the revolts that would later strike in Anatolia came to be called "the Celali Revolts." Second was the furuncle that had appeared on the sultan's back before his departure from Edirne and had been diagnosed as anthrax. The furuncle, which was touched off by Hasan Can, one of his aides, grew into a substantial lesion. Eventually, the sultan died, like his father, near Çorlu on September 21, 1520 while being transferred to Istanbul. The sources narrate that he read the Surah Ya Sin from the Qur'an during the last minutes of his life.

The scholars predict that Sultan Selim the Brave would have made his last campaign to Sicily, Italy, or the Rhodes Island in the Aegean Sea.

Sultan Selim the Brave was an extraordinary sultan who successfully implemented eighty years of work into his seven-and-a-half-year reign; thus, he is regarded as one of the astonishingly universal sultans in Turkish and Islamic history. He further preserved his exceptional status in the history of the Ottoman dynasty as a sultan to be envied by the late Ottoman sultans. Like his father and grandfather before him, Sultan Selim was a distinguished poet who wrote many poems in Arabic and Persian under the pseudonym Selimi. It is well known that he was very supportive of scientific research and highly respectful of the scholars. His period of reign coincided with the rising to eminence of scholars like Zenbilli Ali Efendi, and Ibn Kemal. Whereas Sultan Selim the Brave was simple and quiet in his private life, he was quite fierce and authoritative in state affairs.

The sultan espoused freedom of expression no matter how contrary the ideas were to his; and he attentively listened to all available ideas. Sometimes, he changed his opinion after contemplation that lasted days; however, he always recognized the rule of majority in state matters, and severely punished those who clandestinely lobbied against the decision that had already been approved and taken in effect. Despite his rigor and fiery temper, he was appreciative of merits. It was usually difficult to work with him, but those who did knew that they were highly valued in his eyes. He hated and refrained from wastefulness, luxury, and ostentation; he preferred to have one dish at a meal and liked to use wooden objects. He was very concerned with the strength of the Imperial Treasury. He constructed no *köşk* (Turkish style summer palace) or *yalı* (mansion on the Bosphorus) for himself. He spoke little and smiled little, and when he spoke, he articulated and repeated words as necessary. It is known that The sultan loved to read; he even took many books on his campaigns. On the way back from Cairo to Istanbul, he commissioned İbn Kemal to translate İbn Tağrıberdi's *An-Nujum az-Zahira*, and read the translation made on the road piece by piece. İbn Kemal, who gained the sultan's favor, was travelling in front of the sultan during their return from the victory of Marj Dabik, and his horse splashed mud on the sultan's robes. Always being respectful to his teachers and scholars, the sultan smiled and, saying that the mud was an ornament to his robes, ordered that they be saved—unwashed—and used to cover his coffin. Selim I, a poet, philosopher, and scholar sultan, is considered as one of the most intellectual and wise Ottoman sultans. The fact that he did not allow a triumph demonstration on his way back from Egypt and waited until midnight to quietly enter the Topkapı Palace is illustrative of his humble character.

Sultan Süleyman I
The Magnificent

Reign: 1520–1566

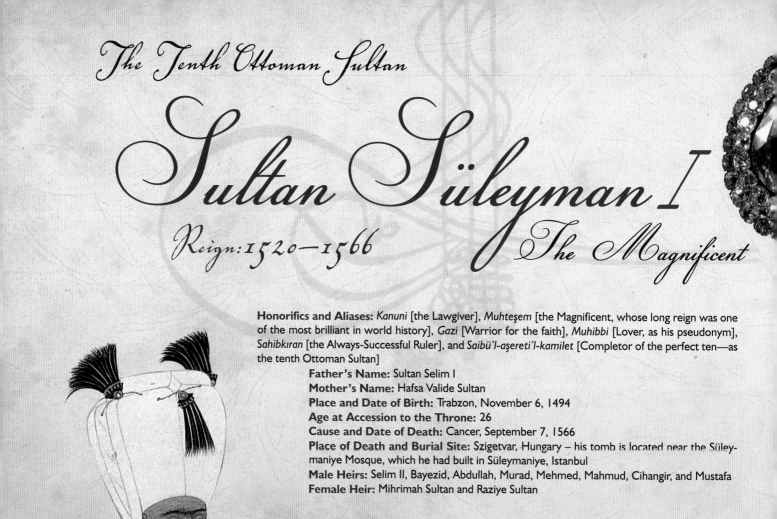

Honorifics and Aliases: *Kanuni* [the Lawgiver], *Muhteşem* [the Magnificent, whose long reign was one of the most brilliant in world history], *Gazi* [Warrior for the faith], *Muhibbi* [Lover, as his pseudonym], *Sahibkıran* [the Always-Successful Ruler], and *Saibü'l-aşereti'l-kamilet* [Completor of the perfect ten—as the tenth Ottoman Sultan]

Father's Name: Sultan Selim I
Mother's Name: Hafsa Valide Sultan
Place and Date of Birth: Trabzon, November 6, 1494
Age at Accession to the Throne: 26
Cause and Date of Death: Cancer, September 7, 1566
Place of Death and Burial Site: Szigetvar, Hungary – his tomb is located near the Süleymaniye Mosque, which he had built in Süleymaniye, Istanbul
Male Heirs: Selim II, Bayezid, Abdullah, Murad, Mehmed, Mahmud, Cihangir, and Mustafa
Female Heir: Mihrimah Sultan and Raziye Sultan

Born as the only son of Sultan Selim I in Trabzon, where his father spent his *şehzade* years as the governor, Süleyman I received a very good education from his childhood and was raised meticulously. The emphasis of his education was on state and military administration and Islamic sciences. At thirteen years old, he moved to

Miniature of Sultan Süleyman the Magnificent by Levni in his *Kebir Musavver Silsilenâme* (The Great Envisaged Portraiture Geneology)

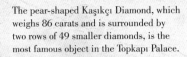

The pear-shaped Kaşıkçı Diamond, which weighs 86 carats and is surrounded by two rows of 49 smaller diamonds, is the most famous object in the Topkapı Palace.

Şebinkarahisar and to Bolu the following year where he was assigned to the post of governor of Kaffa. Süleyman supported his father and participated in his father's march from Trabzon to Istanbul.

Süleyman lived in Istanbul and Edirne during the time that his father was contesting his uncles for the throne, and he was residing in Istanbul when Sultan Selim I ascended to the throne in 1512. He then remained governor of Saruhan (now Manisa) in western Anatolia until his father's death. On September 30, 1520, eight days after the sad news of his father's death reached him, he arrived in Istanbul and rose to the throne following the accession ceremony in the Topkapı Palace.

Süleyman was a lucky new sultan: his father had left him an Imperial Treasury filled to the brink, a loyal and strong military both on land and at sea, and no other male heir to challenge him for the throne. The first law of Süleyman I, who would later be known as "the Lawgiver," or *Kanuni* in Turkish, was the lifting of the ban on the import of silk threads.

Although his reign started with tremendous opportunities, Süleyman I was forced in early years to deal with the revolts that mushroomed in Anatolia and Egypt. Most importantly, he remained occupied with the pro-Safavid Baba Zünnun revolt near Yozgat in Anatolia in 1526 and the 1527 Kalenderoğlu revolt that erupted near Karaman because of problems related to fief-holdings, or *tımars*. In Egypt, he had to quell the Canberdi Gazali (1521) and Ahmed Pasha (1524) revolts, both of which broke out of efforts to reestablish the Mamluk state. It was only then that Süleyman I ventured further into new conquests.

During the reign of Süleyman the Magnificent, Charles V (1500–1558) was the Habsburg Holy Roman emperor, with familial connections to Hungary and Austria. The growth of Charles V's empire in Central Europe and the Mediterranean caused the sultan to mark Europe as the

Miniature of the servants of the Royal Apartments

Miniature of Sultan Süleyman the Magnificent in the War of Mohács by the court painter Nakkaş Osman in his *Hünername*, 1548

direction of his future campaigns. For this reason, the Ottoman army operated in the West during the reign of Süleyman the Magnificent while it had fought wars in the East and South during the reign of Sultan Selim I.

After visiting the tombs of his ancestors and of Abu Ayyub al-Ansari (also known as Eyüp Sultan) in Istanbul on May 19, 1521, Sultan Süleyman the Magnificent set up his military quarters in Halkalıpınar. Soon after, his army marked out its course, through Edirne—the main military base for all the sixteenth century campaigns of conquest westward into Europe—up to the north by way of Plovdiv, Sofia, and Niš. The army finally reached Belgrade, its final destination, and besieged the city for twenty-eight days. The siege ended with the conquest of Belgrade in 1521, the first conquest to Süleyman's credit. The sultan performed the Friday prayer in the first mosque in Belgrade and then returned to Istanbul as "the Conqueror of Belgrade," which his grandfather Sultan Mehmed the Conqueror would have been quite proud of. The conquest of Belgrade exacerbated the relations between the Ottomans and Hungarians as it paved the way wide open for the Ottomans toward Hungary and supplied them with a strategically vital military base for the ensuing conquests in Europe.

Süleyman the Magnificent entered his first naval warfare the following year; as a result, he captured Rhodes Island, another area that his grandfather Mehmed the Conqueror contended for in order to take the control of the Ottoman seas. Located eleven miles to the west of the Anatolian shores, Rhodes Island had turned notoriously into an island of pirates. The knights of St. John on Rhodes had been pirating in the Ottoman seas, obstructing the Ottoman commerce in the Mediterranean, and threatening the security of the Anatolian west coast. The conquest of the island on January 21, 1522 further consolidated the security of the sea route that followed from Egypt through Syria up to Anatolia.

Francis I of France was taken prisoner in Pavia by Charles V in the war that broke out between France and the Holy Roman Empire. As a last resort, the French decided to ask the Ottomans for help, and Francis' mother, Louise de Savoie requested that Süleyman the Magnificent save his son. Francis I thought that Charles V would release him if the Ottomans marched on Hungary.

On August 29, 1526, the Ottoman army commanded by Sultan Süleyman the Magnificent crushed the Hungarian army in Mohács on the right bank of the Danube in one of the shortest pitched battles in history. The French king was set free. The statement of Francis I of France to the Venetian ambassador Giorgio Gritti that he regarded the Ottoman Empire as the only power to protect the European countries against the belligerent expansion of Charles V is illustrative of how the Europeans perceived Sultan Süleyman the Magnificent.

After the great victory on the field of Mohács, Hungary came under the Ottoman suzerainty. The sultan knew that it would prove too difficult to directly incorporate the Hungarian territory into the Ottoman lands as they lay very far away from the Ottoman center beyond the Danube River;[23] therefore, he decided to keep Hungary under the Ottoman suzerainty with limited self-rule and appointed the Hungarian aristocrat Janos Zápolya as the new king of Hungary.

Ferdinand, the brother of Charles V and the Habsburg Archduke of Austria, claimed the Hungarian throne for himself, and thus he did not recognize Janos Zápolya as the new king in Hungary. He then moved to capture the Hungarian capital of Buda,[24] exiled Janos, and proclaimed himself as the new Hungarian king. These acts led Süleyman the Magnificent to another campaign into Hungary. The sultan recaptured Buda and proclaimed Janos as the king of Hungary once again on September 8, 1529. Janos agreed to pay annual tributes to the Ottomans; in return, the sultan reserved a Janissary garrison in the Fort of Hungary.

Although the campaign season ended, Sultan Süleyman continued to lead his army all the way to Vienna and placed the Austrian capital under siege in 1529 in an effort to intimidate the Habsburg Archduke Ferdinand. Since the main objective was not a long-lasting siege of Vienna to conquer it, the military preparations were short. Ferdinand must have been relieved at the onset of winter when the Ottomans lifted the siege that lasted for three weeks.

Ferdinand of Austria sent his envoy to Sultan Süleyman the Magnificent and asked him to recognize and support him instead of supporting Janos. Meanwhile, he attacked Buda, an Ottoman territory. This time, Süleyman the Magnificent prepared a military campaign against the Habsburgs. A successful end of the campaign would mean the end of the Habsburg emperor Charles V's support of Ferdinand. The sultan moved toward inner Austria and central Europe; despite his continuous invitations to come to the battlefield, neither Ferdinand nor Charles V braved the challenge. The campaign not only secured Sultan Süleyman's rule of Hungary but also forced Ferdinand to ask for a truce. The sultan, who also had to contend with the growing threat from Safavid Persia to the East, accepted Ferdinand's offer of peace in 1533. Thus, Ferdinand of Austria acknowledged the superiority of Süleyman the Magnificent, recognized Janos as the king, renounced his claims to Hungary, and promised to pay thirty thousand gold duchies per year to the Ottomans.

When Andrea Doria, the imperial admiral of Charles V's naval forces, captured Koroni on the southwest of the Morea from the Ottomans, Süleyman the Magnificent realized that rivalry for the Mediterranean had commenced. Therefore, he assigned Barbaros Hayreddin Pasha, the famous Turkish mariner and the conqueror of Algeria, as the imperial commander general of the Ottoman navy. The increasing insistence of the French, who had sought an official alliance with the Ottoman Empire as early as 1531, with the aim to bring itself under security culminated in the alliance signed in 1536.

Shah Tahmasp succeeded Shah Ismail for the Safavid throne. The Safavids had suffered a certain defeat at the Battle of Çaldıran during the reign of Sultan Selim I and when the new shah tried to establish alliances with the Austrian Kingdom and Holy Roman Empire,

Miniature from the illustrated manuscript of *Süleymanname* (The History of Süleyman the Magnificent) depicting
Sultan Süleyman the Magnificent attending the circumcision ceremony of his sons Şehzade Bayezid and
Şehzade Cihangir in the Fountain Hall of the Topkapı Palace

Painting of the Ottoman fleet's arrival, painter unknown

Süleyman the Magnificent marched against the Safavids.

Shah Tahmasp also had provoked several *beys* in Anatolia against the Ottoman authority and had threatened the Ottoman domination in eastern and southeastern Anatolia, another reason for Süleyman the Magnificent to begin the offensive against Safavid Persia. A few months after the death of his mother came the first expedition of the sultan to Safavid Persia. Grand Vizier İbrahim Pasha entered the capital of Tabriz with his army. Sultan Süleyman directed his campaign up to Hamadan soon after he captured Azerbaijan. Shah Tahmasp, who could not risk challenging the Ottoman Empire, fled to the inner Persia. The sultan moved down to the south and conquered Baghdad in 1534.

The conquest of Baghdad as a result of this campaign meant that the six holy cities of Islam—Mecca, Medina, Damascus, Istanbul, Jerusalem, and Baghdad—came under Ottoman domination. In addition, the campaign allowed Süleyman the Magnificent to bring under Ottoman control a larger portion of the Silk Road. On the Mediterranean theater, Charles V had captured Tunis in 1535. Ottoman naval forces under the leadership of Barbaros Hayreddin Pasha (also known as Hayreddin Barbarossa in the West) later plagued the Europeans when they captured several Venetian fortresses in the Aegean and conducted a score of round-ups along the shores of Italy. As a result, the three states (Venice, Genoa, and Malta) unified their forces in the Corfu Island off the coast of Albania to end the Ottoman domination in the Mediterranean. At this time, a remarkable crusader fleet was set up and submitted to the command of Andrea Doria.

Barbaros Hayreddin Pasha heard the news about the crusader fleet and sailed his fleet near Preveza located at the mouth of the Gulf of Arta on the Ionian Sea. The Ottoman naval forces, which were led by other distinguished Turkish admirals such as Salih Reis, Seydi Ali Reis, and Turgut Reis, succeeded in disbanding the crusader army, which initially seemed far stronger in size and manpower. On September 28, 1538, the Ottomans won one of the most prestigious naval victories in Ottoman history. Andrea Doria himself fled and barely saved his own life.

The Victory of Preveza sealed the Ottoman sovereignty in the Mediterranean. September 28, the anniversary of the victory, is still celebrated in Turkey as "The Day of Turkish Maritime Forces." In addition, this victory forced the Venetians to recognize the Ottoman control over the fortresses in the Morea and the Dalmatian shores, and of the regions that Barbaros Hayreddin Pasha had conquered.

Süleyman the Magnificent responded to the envoys of Charles V that he would sign no peace agreement until the French lands were returned to the French. France indeed reaped the benefits of the alliance with the Ottoman Empire, the superpower of the period.

When the Hungarian King Janos died in 1541 and was replaced by his infant son Sigismund, Ferdinand of Austria announced that he would not acknowledge Sigismund as the new king and invaded Hungary once again. Sigismund's mother Isabella asked Süleyman the Magnificent for help this time. The sultan replied with another march on Hungary, and adopted Hungary as a direct Ottoman province under the administration of a governor general, or *beylerbeyi*.

The French King Francis I called on Süleyman the Magnificent when he had failed in his challenges against Charles V. The sultan dispatched to France the Ottoman fleet commanded by Barbaros Hayreddin Pasha. Barbaros anchored in Marseilles in 1543; he captured the Fort of Niš and gave it to the French. The same year, the sultan made an expedition to Esztergom on the right bank of the Danube River about thirty miles northwest of the Hungarian capital, for the European states had intervened in the internal affairs of

Miniature of Sultan Süleyman the Magnificent by Nigari, Topkapı Palace, 1560

Hungary. He conquered Esztergom and Stolni Belgrade (now Fehérvár), but the well-deserved joy of his victory was interrupted by the sad news of his son, Şehzade Mehmed's death. He asked that the dead body of his son, who was the governor of Manisa, to be brought to Istanbul, and he performed the funeral prayer with the public in the Bayezid Mosque, which is located in the Bayezid Square. The sultan ordered Mimar Koca Sinan (the Great Architect Sinan) to construct the Şehzade Mosque (including a *külliye*) in memory of his son.

The Safavids had initiated a counter-attack against the Ottomans by the time Süleyman the Magnificent was fighting in Central Europe; thus the sultan declared a second campaign over Safavid Persia in 1548. The battles that lasted for seven years with intermissions came to an end with the signing of an agreement in Amasya in 1555. The Treaty of Amasya, signed by Süleyman the Magnificent and Shah Tahmasp, is the first Ottoman-Persian agreement in history. It stipulated that the Ottomans retain possession of eastern Anatolia, Azerbaijan, Tabriz, and Mesopotamia, including Baghdad, giving the Ottomans access to the Persian Gulf.

Charles V took a large number of the knights of St. John in Rhodes and placed them in Tripoli, which was assigned to the knights as a base for naval operation in the Mediterranean. Süleyman the Magnificent then authorized the Ottoman admiral Turgut Reis (known as Dragut in the West) to strike Tripoli. Turgut Reis attacked Tripoli and conquered this strategic port city, incorporating it into the Ottoman domain in August, 1551.

The crusaders aimed to get rid of the Ottomans in Africa and obstructed Turgut Reis' advances in the Mediterranean; thus, Turgut Reis lay a siege to Djerba, the largest island off North Africa in the Gulf of Gabes, which belonged to the Spanish. When Andrea Doria, Genovese condottieri and admiral, heard about the siege, he sailed with his fleet near Djerba, forcing Turgut Reis to call for reinforcements. The Ottoman fleet under the Admiral-General Piyale Pasha confronted the crusader fleet and crushingly defeated the crusaders a second time. Djerba was conquered by the Ottomans in 1560; in addition, Europe acknowledged Ottoman dominance over the western Mediterranean as well as the Ottoman presence in North Africa, which lasted four centuries.

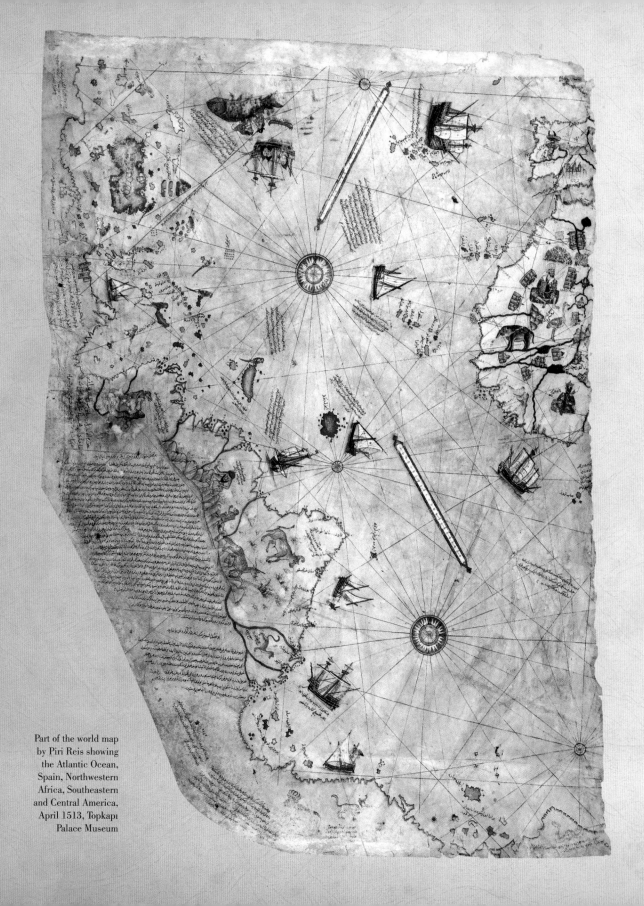

Part of the world map
by Piri Reis showing
the Atlantic Ocean,
Spain, Northwestern
Africa, Southeastern
and Central America,
April 1513, Topkapı
Palace Museum

112

فوتوغرافيا السيد العفاطي تكبير

It was Sultan Süleyman the Magnificent who had conducted the most extensive reparations in the Haramayn.
The photo illustrates the Grand Mosque (Masjid al-Haram) in the 1890s.

Sultan Süleyman the Magnificent ordered the siege of Malta in 1565. Turgut Reis had been assigned to the conquest of Malta, but the ongoing siege of Malta was halted after he died a martyr during the siege. The Ottomans did not attempt to take Malta again. The next year, the Chios Island in the Aegean Sea waved the Ottoman flag.

The Ottoman fleet gained enough strength to compete with European states during the reign of Mehmed the Conqueror, and it underwent a golden age during the reign of Süleyman the Magnificent, who won great victories against the formidable enemies of the Ottoman Empire.

The conquests of Istanbul and Egypt assured the Ottoman control of the vital commercial routes, so the Europeans began to look for new networks to facilitate their commercial activities. The Portuguese sailed to the Indian Ocean, established colonies in India, and took the Indian commercial sea-routes under their control. Furthermore, they exerted pressure

Night view of the Süleymaniye Mosque, which is situated at the top of a hill, dominating the landscape of the historic peninsula of Istanbul

on the Muslim states in India and plundered the ships of the Muslim merchants. In response to all of this and to the call for Süleyman the Magnificent from the Gujarat state in India, the Ottoman Empire made four successive expeditions to India.

The first expedition under the command of Hadım Süleyman Pasha in 1538 added Yemen, Aden, Sudan, and some tracts of Ethiopia to the Ottoman domains. The second naval expedition in 1551 under the command of Piri Reis brought about the conquest of Muscat in the southeast of the Arabian Peninsula. The third and fourth expeditions by Murad Reis in 1552 and Seydi Ali Reis in 1553 did not yield any tangible results. Overall, the naval expeditions to India resulted in fulfilling the Ottoman responsibility of holding the Caliphate.

Sultan Süleyman the Magnificent, who had not waged any major campaigns for many years, led his army for the last time in the year 1566 against Ferdinand of Austria, who broke the peace agreement with the Ottomans by attacking the principality of Transylvania under Ottoman suzerainty. Despite his illness and age of seventy-two years, Grand Vizier Sokullu Mehmed Pasha convinced him to command the Ottoman army in person on this campaign. The sultan was too sick to mount his horse; worse his illness became more critical after he passed Edirne. The Ottoman army besieged the Fort of Szigetvár, and after about a month of following the siege from his sickbed, Süleyman the Magnificent passed away on September 7, 1566. The death of the sultan was kept secret in an effort not to distract the Ottoman army. The fort was conquered following a thirty-four day siege, and the march to Szigetvár turned out to be the last successful campaign of Süleyman the Magnificent.

The conquests, cultural activities, and a civilizational flourishing marked the forty-six-year reign of Süleyman the Magnificent. His achievements—one of which is his incredible record of riding his horse for ca. 30,000 miles—earned him the deserved title "the Magnificent," which was attributed to him in the West. A major shift of emphasis occurred in his political orientation toward Europe and the Mediterranean countries after the European economy was boosted by the age of discoveries in the 16th century.

Sultan Süleyman the Magnificent had neither a benign character like his grandfather nor was he nervous and fierce like his father. He was foresighted and acted diligently. His father left him not only a treasury full to its capacity and a powerful army but also a legacy on which he built his future leadership and commandership skills. He led his army in many battles in the East and West, and he died on the battlefield, not in the palace.

Süleyman the Magnificent was not only a brilliant strategist and statesmen but also an acclaimed legislator. He led a systematically functioning state administration and a modern, powerful, and quite mobile army. During his period of reign, there was no army or fleet stronger than his; he had an absolute authority over his military forces. Along with his great victories in the East and West, the sultan became famous for his administrative and legal reforms, which earned him the name *Kanuni*, or Lawgiver and ensured the survival of the state long after his death. Thanks to his unerring decisions regarding the division of labor and his impressive talent in assigning duties to the right person as well as in training his staff, the state affairs were handled very successfully during his reign.

The forty-six year long reign of Süleyman the Magnificent also witnessed the zenith of the Ottoman arts and culture. Various imperial artistic societies, called the Community of the Talented,[25] were administered under his patronage. According to the registers of the Ottoman arts industry and its organization (still preserved in the archives of the Topkapı Palace), Süleyman the Magnificent personally inspected the works of the artists and rewarded them for their outstanding achievements.

During this period, developments occurred in both fine arts and decorative arts, especially in calligraphy, miniature painting, manuscript painting, gravures, *ebru* (water marbling), wood and stone carving, ceramics, tiles, and textiles. Among the most outstanding architec-

tural achievements of this golden age were the *selatin* (plural of sultan) mosques which were built by the sultan and the members of the imperial family and designed as part of a *külliye*, the complex of buildings for various benevolent services for the public good, comprising colleges, medical schools, hospitals, soup kitchens, inns and public baths. The sultan appointed Mimar Koca Sinan, who is considered as one of the greatest architects of the world history as the chief royal architect. His legacy amounts to more than three hundred structures in different parts of the empire from the Balkans to the Hijaz, including 57 colleges, 46 inns, 35 palaces and mansions, 42 public baths, 22 tombs, 17 almshouses, 3 hospitals, 7 aqueducts, 8 bridges, 8 granaries, and 135 mosques—the two mosques built in Süleyman the Magnificent's name in Istanbul and Damascus are considered the most notable monuments of both cities. His daughter Mihrimah Sultan also had the celebrated Ottoman architect Sinan build two mosques in her name in Istanbul, one in Üsküdar on the Asian shore of the city and the other located on the European side at the Edirne gate of the old city walls. This latter mosque is reminiscent of the foundress with its elegant style and graceful decoration.

The greatest projects, however, were undertaken in the Holy Lands during Sultan Süleyman's administration. First, shelters were erected to accommodate the pilgrims that would stay the night in Mecca around the premises of the Grand Mosque (Masjid al-Haram), and then a large Turkish bath was constructed for bathing and cleaning, preventing the huge crowd of pilgrims from soiling the Grand Mosque in 1566. It was also in this period that the wooden roofs of the portico around the Ka'ba were replaced with stone domes, which still stand today. In Mecca, the oldest *medrese* known to this day was also established in 1565 during the reign of Sultan Süleyman. The construction plan of the *medrese* was engineered by the great architect Sinan, and his operating budget was 30,000 gold coins. The *medrese* was built with specifications to accommodate the needs of the four main schools of Islamic law. The pilgrims had been threatened in Medina occasionally by the attacks of Bedouin raiders during the pilgrimage season, and the existing walls around the city could not deter the attacks. For this reason, the people of Medina submitted a request to Sultan Süleyman the Magnificent. The ensuing order of the sultan brought about the fortification

and elevating of the walls based on the Ottoman military's building experience. After seven years of hard work, the new strong, high walls emerged around the city of Medina in 1533. The watchtowers were added to the walls that included the Jannat al-Baqi cemetery. Furthermore, an inner fortress was constructed inside the walls, and ninety Ottoman soldiers were positioned in this fortress; thereby, the city of the Prophet was taken under protection. In Ottoman history, the tradition of the construction in the Mosque of the Prophet (Masjid an-Nabawi) began with Süleyman the Magnificent when he sent engineers and craftsmen from Istanbul. Those experts made reparations and renovations in the Mosque of the Prophet starting from the western walls of the Tomb of the Prophet (Hujra as-Saada) in 1540. Again in Medina, the scholars who taught in the Mosque of the Prophet were given permanent positions while an annual budget was allocated to pay others serving in the mosque. Sultan Süleyman the Magnificent further renovated the tomb of Aisha, the wife of the Prophet, located in the Jannat al-Baqi cemetery, and pursued in the Masjid al-Qiblatayn in Medina the most comprehensive construction plan since the time of the Abbasid Caliph Umar ibn Abdul Aziz (ruled 717–720). The sultan also commissioned the city walls encircling Jerusalem as well as fountains and large gateways in Jerusalem.

Mihrimah Sultan, the daughter of Süleyman the Magnificent, spent a fortune to bring from Ara-

The interior of the Süleymaniye Mosque is covered by a massive dome rising to a height of 174 feet (53 meters).

fat to Mecca the water reservoir of Ayn al-Zubayda, which had been constructed by Zubayda, the wife of the Abbasid Caliph Harun al-Rashid (ruled 786–809). From the reign of Süleyman the Magnificent onward, the Ka'ba's outer cloth was prepared in Egypt and its inner cloth in Istanbul.

The sultan did not limit his services to the Holy Lands; he also built a series of fortresses with water reservoirs on the caravan route for the pilgrims during their long, difficult journey across the desert from Damascus to Mecca. For this he constructed a fortress and dug new water wells in Ma'an, Jordan en route to Mecca, offering them a safe stopping place during their lonely desert travel which was fraught with the risks of exhaustion, scant food and water, and attack. Likewise, he constructed another wealth of wells and erected an Ottoman fortress in Dhat al-Hajj in the Tabuk region of Arabia. In praising the fortress that the sultan constructed in Uhud near Medina, the Persian pilgrims once said that "the building material of this fortress is not found even in Istanbul."

Ottoman tombac ewer-basin set

Sultan Selim II

Reign: 1566–1574

Honorifics and Aliases: *Sarı*, *Mest*, and *Selimi*
Father's Name: Sultan Süleyman the Magnificent
Mother's Name: Hürrem Sultan
Place and Date of Birth: Istanbul, May 30, 1524
Age at Accession to the Throne: 42
Cause and Date of Death: Cerebral hemorrhage, December 15, 1574
Place of Death and Burial Site: Istanbul – his tomb is located near Ayasofya
Male Heirs: Murad III, Mehmed, Abdullah, Cihangir, Mustafa, Osman, and Süleyman
Female Heir: Fatma Sultan, Şah Sultan, Gevherhan Sultan, and Esmahan Sultan

Ironically enough, Selim II was the first sultan to be born and die in the Ottoman capital of Istanbul. After long years of education in the Topkapı Palace, he acted as the governor of Konya (twice), Manisa, and finally of Kütahya. During his *şehzade* years, he prevented his brother Şehzade Bayezid's attempt to acquire the throne. When Grand Vizier Sokullu secretly informed him of his

Miniature of Sultan Selim II by Levni in his *Kebir Musavver Silsilenâme* (The Great Envisaged Portraiture Geneology)

father's death in Szigetvár, Hungary, he came from Kütahya to Istanbul. He proclaimed that he was the new sultan and travelled all the way up to Belgrade to claim his father's dead body. Meanwhile, the Janissaries created a serious unrest on the matter of receiving the gratuities of the sultan's accession, called *cülüs*. The new sultan secured peace by accepting the Janissaries' demands, which was an unusual policy that neither Sultan Selim I, his senior namesake, nor Sultan Süleyman the Magnificent, pursued. In fact, it was regarded as a sign that he would not masterfully command over the army the way his father and grandfather had done before him.

The competence of Grand Vizier Sokullu Mehmed Pasha, who received his training and gained experience during his father's reign, provided the state affairs with efficiency and discipline, so Sultan Selim II left him in charge of the administrative affairs.

The first notable event during the reign of Selim II occurred when Imam Mutahhar rebelled in Yemen. Sinan Pasha and Özdemiroğlu Osman Pasha, the governor general of Abyssinia (now Ethiopia), were sent to Yemen, and together they quelled the rebellion, affirming that the Ottoman authority would prevail in Yemen.

The capturing in 1557 of the Astrakhan region by Ivan IV Vasilyevich of Russia blocked the pilgrimage route of Muslims from that region, preventing them from reaching Mecca through Crimea. Upon their call to the Caliph of all the Muslims, the Ottoman sultan Selim II ordered a campaign to facilitate their pilgrimage; however, the campaign did not bear any results in the absence of support from the Crimean Khan.

The Sultanate of Aceh, the Muslim state in the Sumatra Island located in western Indonesia, had first called Sultan Süleyman the Magnificent for help to end the Portuguese oppression, and the sultan had responded to the call by dispatching an Ottoman garrison to the region. During the reign of Sultan Selim II, Aceh requested Ottoman help once again. In 1569, Selim II sent a naval fleet of twenty-two ships commanded by Kurdoğlu Hızır Reis, the Captain of Suez.

Sultan Selim II had the Selimiye (Selim's) Mosque built near the Tomb of Rumi while he was still a governor şehzade in Konya.

A number of Turkish soldiers sent to the region did not return but stayed in Sumatra, and their descendants have identified themselves with their Turkish origins to this day. The flag of Aceh looks quite similar to the Ottoman and Turkish flags; moreover, the peoples of Aceh are still attached to Turkey with a string of love.

The Venetians on the Island of Cyprus had long since threatened the security of the shores of Anatolia and Egypt and continued their acts of piracy on Muslim merchant ships and pilgrim boats. In fact, the island eventually turned into a nest of pirates. Therefore, the Ottoman envoys approached Venice to carry the following message: "Either cease piracy in Cyprus, or the Ottomans will capture it." The second round of correspondance followed when the Venetians rejected the Ottoman warning ordering the Venetians to surrender the island. In the advisory council to the sultan on the matter, Grand Vizier Sokullu Mehmed Pasha opposed the idea of the conquest of Cyprus, for he thought it would invite a new series of crusades; however, the sultan and the majority of others sitting in the council affirmed the campaign. The Ottoman fleet commanded by the Vizier Lala Mustafa Pasha went on to besiege the island; finally, it captured Cyprus in 1571 after a year-long siege. The sultan populated the island with an influx of Turcomans from Karaman.

During the conquest of Cyprus, the Ottoman fleet decided to return when Mağusa (Famagusta) on the east side of Cyprus came under siege. The navy switched its area of activity to the shores of the Adriatic when it seemed likely that a crusade fleet would hit Cyprus. After spending the winter in Istanbul, the fleet set sail in

early spring to the Mediterranean again; however, it unexpectedly confronted no crusade fleet. When the Ottoman fleet anchored at the Lepanto (İnebahtı) seaport, the Venetians and Spanish, who had combined their forces under the leadership of the Pope, prefered to ambush rather than fight the Ottomans and burned the Ottoman fleet at Lepanto in September 1571. Only Uluç Ali Pasha, the governor general of Algiers was able to move twenty ships through the enemy ambush and safely reach Istanbul.

The news of the naval disaster severely disappointed Sultan Selim II; he promoted Uluç Ali Pasha, who lived through Lepanto, to admiral general (*Kaptan-ı Derya*) and conferred on him the title *Kılıç* (Sword). The chronicles narrate that Grand Vizier Sokullu Mehmed Pasha, seeing the anxiousness of the new admiral general in reconstructing the Ottoman fleet, suggested the following: "Dear Pasha, the might and force of this [Ottoman] Empire is such that it deserves a fleet comprised of ships whose anchors are of silver, whose hawsers are of silk threads, and whose sail cloths are of satin weaves. Come get from me whenever you run short of stuff for your ships."

After a short four months of hard and continuous work, a new Ottoman fleet was built, comprising more than two hundred battleships. The size of eight newly constructed ships was more enormous than anyone previously had seen and caused a huge wave of panic in Europe.

Grand Vizier Sokullu Mehmed Pasha responded to the Venetian envoy, who came to understand the impact that the defeat at Lepanto had on the Ottomans, in the following metaphorical way: "Whereas we had chopped your arms by conquering Cyprus, you shaved our beard by burning down our fleet. There is no way you can get chopped arms back; however, the beard you have shaved will grow thicker for sure." This statement of Sokullu pointed to the undisputable power of the Ottoman Empire in the 16th century; in effect, Admiral General Kılıç Ali Pasha would support his speech by conquering Tunis from the Spanish in 1574 in a matter of three years.

Sultan Selim II planned to open a waterway running through the Isthmus of Suez and linking the Mediterranean Sea with the Red Sea. Although his grandfather Sultan Selim I before him had also wished to undertake this plan, neither his grandfather nor he was able to succeed in fulfilling it.

The main objective of the Ottomans in connecting the Mediterranean and Suez through a water canal was to protect the trade and pilgrimage route as well as the Holy Lands and

Night view of the Selimiye (Selim's) Mosque in Edirne which has imprinted its image on the city with its four graceful slender minarets with three balconies and the great single-domed silhouette.

The Selimiye Mosque in Edirne was considered by the great Ottoman architect Sinan to be his "master work."

other Muslim territories from the Portuguese attacks. The opening of the canal also would revive the Spice Route ending in the Mediterranean; furthermore, the canal would provide a significant shortcut to the Indian sea route that Europeans used to sail through the Cape of Good Hope. Finally, the commercial activities with Asia would operate through the Ottoman lands and would thus strengthen the Ottoman Empire in economic terms. Despite the fact that the governor of Egypt was assigned to research the project, no solid result emerged. The canal would be erected by British, only in 1869.

During the reign of Sultan Selim II, the opening of another waterway was discussed. A projected canal would open between the Volga and Don rivers and connect the Black Sea to the Caspian Sea. If realized, this project would have facilitated the Ottoman military engagement against Persia, helped the Ottomans establish their authority in the Caucasus, and blockaded the expansion of Russia in the Turkish Islamic states of Central Asia. It could have further led to the establishment of direct relations with the Turks in Central Asia. Although one-third of the waterway was spaded, the project remained unfinished in part because the Crimean Khan did not contribute enough to it and partly because the Russians encumbered

Splendid inner dome of the Selimiye Mosque, which is 142 feet (43 meters) high and 102 feet (31 meters) in diameter, rests on an octagonal arrangement of eight pillars, and the arches extending from the pillars open out onto smaller domes illuminated by windows.

the ongoing project in 1569. The canal between the Volga and Don rivers was finished and opened by the Russians, only four centuries later.

Sultan Selim II died of a sudden cerebral hemorrhage when he accidentally fell and hit his head on the marble floor in Hünkar Hamamı, the Bath of Sultans, located in the Topkapı Palace at the time. Selim II was the first Sultan to pass away in the Topkapı Palace in Istanbul. The period of his short reign lasted seven years like his grandfather's. But unlike his namesake, he did not invest his period of reign in a series of consecutive campaigns; instead he ruled the Empire from his palace. To his advantage, Sokullu proved to be an excellent grand vizier; moreover, Sokullu's efficiency and organizational skills averted any major administrative shortcomings.

Sultan Selim II wrote poetry under the pseudonym Selimi. He was also a very good archer. He was the first blonde sultan with blue eyes and was often called *Sarı* (Blonde) Selim. During the period of his reign, Selim II patronized and sponsored scholars and gave priority to construction works. For instance, he charged the great architect Sinan with renovating and extending various sections of the Topkapı Palace, especially the kitchens located on the right side of the Second Courtyard after they were destroyed by fire in 1574. The Topkapı Palace kitchens, which are larger than those of their European counterparts, are now used to display one of the richest porcelain collections in the world.

Ottoman architecture, the preeminent form of Ottoman art, reached its apex with the mosque Sultan Selim II built in his name in Edirne. The Selimiye Mosque is not only the masterpiece of the greatest Ottoman architect Sinan, but also that of world architecture. The sultan loved Edirne more than Istanbul, and for this reason he had the splendid Selimiye Mosque built in his beloved city of Edirne instead of the glorious capital of Istanbul. His reign was less impressive than those of his father and grandfather; nevertheless, the consolidation of the administrative system and the emergence of competent statesmen like Sokullu during his reign maintained the momentum of Ottoman expansion.

In addition, Sultan Selim II led a series of construction works for the safety of the blessed city of Mecca and for the welfare of the pilgrims.

16th century ewer, encrusted with rubies and emeralds

Ottoman bath clogs

Elegant marble fountain and
basin of the sultan's bath

The sultan's bath in the harem
section of the Topkapı Palace was
built by the celebrated architect
Sinan. Contrary to popular belief,
Sultan Selim II passed away not
in this bath but in the one next to
the Treasury Office which has not
survived as it was worn and torn
due to humidity in time.

129

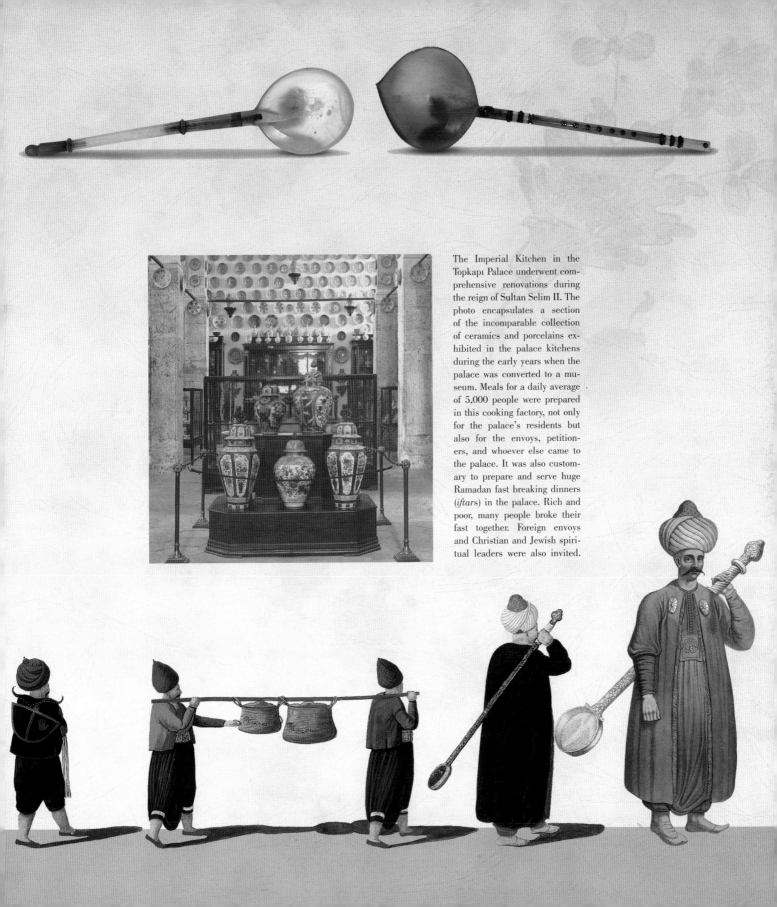

The Imperial Kitchen in the Topkapı Palace underwent comprehensive renovations during the reign of Sultan Selim II. The photo encapsulates a section of the incomparable collection of ceramics and porcelains exhibited in the palace kitchens during the early years when the palace was converted to a museum. Meals for a daily average of 5,000 people were prepared in this cooking factory, not only for the palace's residents but also for the envoys, petitioners, and whoever else came to the palace. It was also customary to prepare and serve huge Ramadan fast breaking dinners (*iftar*s) in the palace. Rich and poor, many people broke their fast together. Foreign envoys and Christian and Jewish spiritual leaders were also invited.

The Twelfth Ottoman Sultan
Sultan Murad III
Reign: 1574–1595

Honorifics and Aliases: *Muradi*
Father's Name: Selim II
Mother's Name: Nurbanu Sultan
Place and Date of Birth: Bozdağ, Manisa; July 4, 1546
Age at Accession to the Throne: 28
Cause and Date of Death: January 16, 1595
Place of Death and Burial Site: Istanbul— his tomb is located near Ayasofya
Male Heirs: Mehmed III, Selim, Bayezid, Mustafa, Osman, Cihangir, Abdurrahman, Abdullah, Hasan, Ahmed, Yakub, Alemşah, Yusuf, Hüseyin, Korkud, Ali, İshak, Ömer, Alaeddin, and Davud
Female Heir: Ayşe Sultan, Fatma Sultan, Mihrimah Sultan, and Fahriye Sultan

Following the sudden death of Sultan Selim II, Sokullu Mehmed Pasha once again assumed responsibility of informing a *şehzade* of the bad news, and invited Murad III to the throne; thus, the Ottoman throne hosted another Murad after 123 years as the twelfth Ottoman sultan. Oddly enough, the sequential order, which follows the reigns of sultans as the third, sixth, and twelfth, is a set of interrelated numbers and all point to the sultans named Murad.

Miniature of Sultan Murad III by Levni in his *Kebir Musavver Silsilenâme* (The Great Envisaged Portraiture Geneology)

The *tughra* (calligraphic imperial signature) of Sultan Murad III

Sultan Murad III was the governor of Akşehir and Saruhan prior to his accession to the throne. Upon succession, it was custom for the sultans to gird their sword of office in the Eyüp Sultan Mosque, where Abu Ayyub al-Ansari, standard bearer to the Prophet, died and was buried. Murad III went to the Eyüp Sultan Mosque on the twenty-second day of the month of Ramadan. He wore his imperial sword in line with the Ottoman imperial tradition and paid visits to the tombs of preceding sultans, his ancestors.

Murad III extended the tenure of Grand Vizier Sokullu Mehmed Pasha, who had previously worked in the same capacity under his father and grandfather; therefore, Sokullu Mehmed Pasha became the first and only statesman in Ottoman history whose administrative functions as the grand vizier spanned the reign of three different sultans. Sokullu indeed had such a profound role in the administration that this time period would later be called the Era of Sokullu. In particular, he cast a long shadow on the reign of Sultan Murad III until his later assassination.

Murad III's first political involvement in Europe was to replace the late Polish king with Bathory, the Prince of Transylvania. This decision would terminate the Russian and Habsburg influence in the region, and the Kingdom of Poland eventually went under the Ottoman protectorate in 1575. Hence, the Ottoman dominance spread as far as the Baltic Sea.

The Ottoman borders stretched even further to the Atlantic Ocean by way of southwestern Africa. Sultan Murad III commissioned Governor General Ramazan Pasha of Algeria to

Splendid decorations of the high ceiling of the entryway of the Privy Chamber of Murad III, the Topkapı Palace

conquer Morocco. Morocco fell under Ottoman control when Ramazan Pasha honored Abdul Malik ibn Muhammad as the sultan of Morocco in 1576. Reinforced by the Moroccan military forces, the Ottoman army faced the crusade army, which the Portuguese had formed with the support of the Papacy, French, and Spanish and gave it a crushing defeat in Qasr al-Kabir near Tangier on the Strait of Gibraltar in 1578. King Sebastian of Portugal died at war, and the entire North Africa passed into the Ottoman hands.

In Safavid Persia, Shah Ismail had triumphed in the contest for the throne following the death of Shah Tahmasp. As the new king, he nullified the Treaty of Amasya in 1555 and transgressed the Ottoman borders. Thus Murad III sent the Ottoman army under Lala Mustafa Pasha to the Safavids and led the campaign in person. The Ottomans defeated the Safavids in the Valley of Çıldır in the southeast of the Black Sea region in 1578. Then they plunged into Georgia and conquered Tbilisi, the largest city in the Caucasus. The following year saw another battle in which the Ottoman army defeated the Safavid army once more.

Miniature depicting the funeral of Sultan Murad III's mother Valide Nurbanu Sultan.
The coffin of the Valide (Mother) Sultan is carried on the shoulders for burial out of the Funeral Gate of the palace

In 1583, in a battle against the Safavids called "the War of Torches,"[26] the Ottoman army led by Özdemiroğlu Osman Pasha won a great victory despite its initial disorientation. Osman Pasha then moved to Kaffa and posted İslam Giray as the new Crimean Khan. When the Pasha returned to Istanbul, he gave Murad III a three-hour briefing about his experience. While listening to him, the sultan was pleasantly surprised and occasionally excited, and offered him gracious gifts and his prayers. Furthermore, Murad III promoted Özdemiroğlu Osman Pasha to the grand vizierate. Özdemiroğlu Osman Pasha, the new grand vizier, was dispatched to the conquest of Tabriz. Tabriz recognized the Ottoman authority shortly after in 1585; nonetheless, it proved a daunting challenge to run the city. Özdemiroğlu Osman Pasha unexpectedly fell sick and died. The news of his death drowned the city of Istanbul in a sea of sorrow. But the Ottoman army did not stop; instead it marched forward under the new leadership of Ferhad Pasha. The advance of the Ottoman troops coupled with the disturbances in the Safavid reign yielded the signing of a treaty between the Ottomans and Safavids which stipulated that the newly conquered lands would merge into the Ottoman territories. Indeed, the intermittent wars with Safavid Persia continued from 1578 to 1590 until Safavid Persia asked for an agreement. The Treaty of Ferhad Pasha, also known as the Treaty of Istanbul, was signed in 1590 and sealed the Ottoman frontiers in the East to the furthest limits it could attain.

The financial difficulties that the Persian wars caused triggered a host of other problems, however. For instance, a subsequent Janissary revolt severely threatened the sultan's future and was barely quashed. During the ongoing battles with Persia, Istanbul lamented the news of another death: Sinan, the masterful architect of monumental works like the Süleymaniye and Selimiye mosques, had met his destiny in 1588.

During his reign, Sultan Murad III pursued a policy of "the enemy of my enemy is my friend." Particularly speaking, Murad III gave priority to maintaining closer relations with Britain while competing and warring with Spain and Portugal; furthermore, he allowed the British merchants to pursue free-trade on the Ottoman sea routes in 1580. He established relations with the Uzbek Khanate in Central Asia. In fact, the extension of the Russian threat into the Caucasus and Siberia ushered in closer ties between the two countries. Although the Uzbek envoys informed the sultan that a greater danger would emanate from the Russian settlement in Astrakhan, opening the entire Central Asia to Russian venture, and offered a collaborative effort to thwart such a danger, the sultan declined the offer due to the ongoing events in the West.

The Treaty of Istanbul, signed by the Ottoman Empire and Austria in 1533, was renewed in 1568. In violation of the treaty, however, Austria refused to pay the agreed-upon tribute to the Ottomans. Moreover, Austrian forces began attacking the Ottoman frontier lands and agitated the princes of Wallachia, Transylvania, and Moldavia against the Ottoman Empire. All of these acts brought the two countries to the verge of war. Then the assassination of Telli Hasan Pasha, the governor-general of Bosnia, was the straw that broke the camel's back. The Ottoman army under Grand Vizier Koca Sinan Pasha had continuously won victories in the early theaters of war; however, the Ottoman army was crippled later by the revolts of the princes of Wallachia, Transylvania, and Moldavia. Amidst the deteriorating circumstances came the news of Sultan Murad III's death in 1595. The sources do not have a consensus on the cause of his death. Among the causes cited are various illnesses such as cold, gastric bleeding, epilepsy, and bowel inflammation.

The sources narrate that Murad III was devoted to literature, calligraphy, and arts and was interested in the world history. In addition, he was very kind and generous to the members of his family. He was brown-haired and middle-sized and had a vivacious and benign nature. He refrained from shedding blood and rarely said "no." He liked to wear splendid costumes with plumed ornaments and precious gems on his turban. He was a talented equestrian and marksman. He has been criticized for involving irrelevant and incompetent people, and especially women of the palace, in state affairs and for failing to march on campaigns in person. Although a warrior type, Murad III was surrounded by those who defended the idea that he should rule the state from his palace; therefore, it seems that it was not him but the people around that influenced him not to campaign.

During his reign, the Ottoman Empire had engaged in long-lasting and expensive wars against Persia and Austria, causing a spiraling series of unfavorable developments: the fief (*tımar*) system dete-

The Suyuf-u Mübareke (Sacred Sword of the Prophet)—the hilt, cross guard and the scabbard were studded with pieces of turquoise and rubies at later periods.

137

The elaborate mantelpiece and canopied sofa in the Privy Chamber of Murad III demonstrate the Ottomans' elegant taste in the art of decoration

riorated, a significant number of villages were abandoned, migration to Istanbul was boosted, the number of the members of the regular army, the *Kapıkulu*, increased and more incapable soldiers began to be recruited, and soldier salaries were not able to be paid on time. The Black Death endemic and a powerful earthquake in Istanbul also aggravated the situation.

Sultan Murad III was a man of charities. During his reign, Murad III renovated the Ka'ba and the Grand Mosque (Masjid al-Haram) in Mecca. He also restored the Mosque of the Prophet (Masjid an-Nabawi) in Medina and all the waterways on the pilgrimage route, and constructed one *medrese*, alms house, school, and a *zawiya* (Sufi lodge) in both of the holy cities of Mecca and Medina. Furthermore, he erected in Manisa, the city where he spent his *şehzade* years, the Muradiye Mosque, whose plan was drawn by the great architect Sinan. It was a magnificent complex comprising a mosque and *medrese*, a decent inn, and a caravanserai. He also constructed mosques in the Morea and Navarino (now Pylos); the latter still survives today. In Istanbul, Murad III erected the Throne Room (*Has Oda*) in the Topkapı Palace. He also adorned the Ayasofya Mosque with the two northside minarets, the elegant pulpit, and the *mahfil* (the sultan's gallery) made of fine latticework. The construction project in Mecca that commenced during his father's reign continued, and close attention was given to the safety of the pilgrims and the protection of the Prophet's sacred relics in Mecca. The *Suyuf al-Mubaraka*, or the "Blessed Sword" that the Prophet Muhammad used at the Battle of Uhud and later gave to Umar as a gift, was passed on successively to the Umayyads, Abbasids, and Mamluks. It was finally brought to Istanbul and submitted to Sultan Murad III. This sword is still exhibited in the Pavilion of the Sacred Relics in the Topkapı Palace.

The sultan's gallery, Ayasofya

The Thirteenth Ottoman Sultan
Sultan Mehmed III
Reign: 1595–1603

Honorifics and Aliases: *Gazi* [Warrior for the Faith], *Eğri Fatihi* [the Conqueror of Eger] and *Adli* [as his pseudonym]
Father's Name: Murad III
Mother's Name: Safiye Sultan
Place and Date of Birth: Manisa, May 26, 1566
Age at Accession to the Throne: 29
Cause and Date of Death: Heart attack, December 20, 1603
Place of Death and Burial Site: Istanbul– his tomb is located near Ayasofya
Male Heirs: Ahmed I, Mustafa I, Selim, Mahmud, and Cihangir

The chronicles mention that Mehmed III was born during the Szigetvár Campaign led by his great grandfather Sultan Süleyman the Magnificent, and it was Süleyman the Magnificent who named him after his grandfather Sultan Mehmed the Conqueror. Mehmed III, then the governor of Manisa, ascended to the throne in 1595 following the death of his father Murad III. Mehmed III is the last of the Ottoman sultans to rise to the throne after serving as governor during his *şehzade* years.

Miniature of Sultan Mehmed III by Levni in his *Kebir Musavver Silsilenâme* (The Great Envisaged Portraiture Geneology)

The Ottoman-Austrian war was underway by the time Mehmed III became the sultan. As a result of the poor management of the Wallachian, Transylvanian, and Moldavian principalities by Grand Vizier Sinan Pasha, these principalities turned against the Ottomans and allied with Austria. Meanwhile, the Austrian army besieged and finally captured the forts of Esztergom and Visegrád. The Ottomans burst into sorrow when they heard the news, especially the fall of Esztergom. The famous Turkish folksong that goes, *Estergon Kalesi su başı durak/ Kemirir içimi bir sinsi firak* (The Fort of Esztergom, a station at a water top; My heart broods over the pain of separation) serves as testimony of the yearning for Esztergom.

The statesmen and the Janissaries requested that the sultan march a campaign against Austria in the face of the score of defeats. His mother Safiye Sultan had kept him vigilantly under surveillance during his *şehzade* years, which had caused him to be an introvert and easily manipulated by her. But despite her filibustering, Sultan Mehmed III did march, and thus he injected a shot of morale into both the soldiers and public, who had not seen a sultan engaged in a war since the times of Süleyman the Magnificent. The army marched from Istanbul to Belgrade in 1595. During the campaign, the news of the death of Cihangir, the sultan's three-month old son, reached him. Soon after, Eger Vár, one of the strongest fortresses in northern Hungary not yet under Ottoman control was conquered. Following the conquest, Mehmed III came to be called the Conqueror of Eger.

Austria reacted to the conquest of the fort by organizing a crusader army to confront the Ottomans. The two armies met in Mezőkeresztes (also known as Haçova) near Eger and fought a fierce battle. Sultan Mehmed III set up his imperial tent on a spot suitable to efficiently command his army. The Ottoman army was suffering heavy casualties, so the soldiers began to scatter and desert the battlefield. When the crusaders neared Mehmed III's tent, the Ottomans felt the danger their sultan was in. Some even suggested that he change his clothes and escape in disguise. However, the sultan, who had taken the holy mantle and sword of the Prophet on the campaign, decided to stay on the battlefield and led his soldiers to victory. He was especially inspired by the advice of Hoca Sadeddin, the *Sheikhu'l-Islam*, or highest official of religious law, at the time: "My Sultan! As an Ottoman Sultan who is Caliph on the path of the Prophet, it would be appropriate for you to put on the holy mantle and pray to God." This was an example of the rare but invaluable political determination of the sultan, taking command at such a critical moment.

Having seen that their sultan was determined to stay and fight, the army pulled itself together for a last stand: not only the soldiers but also the supply services including cooks, palace servants, stablemen, camel-riders, and muleteers got directly involved in the war. Such a powerful resistance took the crusaders by surprise. At the end of the day, the rejuvenated army turned the tide from a possible defeat into a certain victory. Following the victory, the new grand vizier, Cigalazade Sinan Pasha took attendance and announced the names of the fugitive soldiers. Soon after, imperial edicts were sent to the provinces with orders to seize the fugitives' properties. Such a massive confiscation program caused the Celali revolts to sweep across Anatolia. It was these revolts that disturbed the order and security in Anatolia and caused the Ottoman state much hardship during Sultan Mehmed III's reign.

Austrian forces captured Esztergom and Gyor in northwest Hungary in 1598, the following year. The sultan, disappointed by the news of consecutive defeats, also lost Selim, his fourteen-year old son. In 1600, the Ottoman army fought back to reclaim the lands lost to Austria and conquered the Fort of Kanizsa in Hungary, one of the most significant strongholds of Europe. The army then returned to Istanbul, leaving Tiryaki Hasan Pasha as the guardian of the fort. A new crusade army under the leadership of Austria besieged Kanizsa to get it back. As a result of the heroic defense of the commander Tiryaki Hasan Pasha and his clever tactics, the crusaders could not hold long and retreated in 1601.

Abbas I of the Safavids exploited the circumstances: the Ottoman army was fighting the Austrians, and the Celali revolts were causing havoc in Anatolia. At such an opportune moment, Abbas I moved to recapture the lands that the Safavids had lost under the Treaty of Ferhad Pasha. He further sought alliances for support with the Papacy and European countries. In the absence of Ali Pasha, the governor general of Tabriz, Abbas I conquered the Tabriz and Nakhchivan regions. Amidst ongoing struggles with Austria in the West and Safavid Persia in the East, Sultan Mehmed III's health deteriorated. When entering the palace on September 27, 1603, a saint-like dervish had warned Mehmed III that he should not be caught unaware and unprepared as something important would happen in fifty-six days. On December 18,

In the miniature, dating from the early 17th century painted by Talikzade Suphi Çelebi, Sultan Mehmed III is shown on horseback leading the army during the Eger Campaign. Among a group of figures there is a man on horseback carrying the holy mantle (wrapped in a cover) on his head.

his illness became insufferable, and the sultan died two days later on December 20, 1603, as the dervish had foretold.

During the chaotic reign of Sultan Mehmed III, the central and provincial security had been often and severely breached, mainly because of the Janissary mutinies in Istanbul and the Celali revolts in Anatolia. The Ottoman Empire indeed went through dire straits: economic distress mounted, inflation boomed, the pashas struggled for power, and Istanbul was first consumed by a big fire in 1598 and then plagued by the Black Death. Furthermore, more problems arose because the sultan had been advertently manipulated by his mother Safiye Sultan and the Valide (mother) Sultan had directly intervened in state affairs and interfered with administrative appointments. Consequentially, Sultan Mehmed III failed to reflect during his reign all the administrative experience and skills he obtained from his prior position as the *sancak* governor. In fact, he was the last of the Ottoman *şehzade*s sent out into the provinces to gain military and administrative experience.

Sultan Mehmed III had a character of tranquility; he was indecisive, moody, easily manipulated, and a true introvert. Along with these character traits, the sultan was an observant Muslim and quite tolerant to believers in a diversity of religions. The chronicles refer to how seriously he took his daily prayers and to his reverence to the Prophet.[27] He abandoned some of his father's practices. He was the first sultan for many years to march on a campaign in person, and he made many efforts to connect with his subject peoples. His reign spanned over a relatively short period of time; nevertheless, it heralded a host of turmoil impending.

Gravure of the inauguration of the annual Surre (Imperial Gifts Caravan) procession in the presence of the sultan in front of the Pavilion of Sultan Mehmed III. In Tableau Généra de L'Empire Othoman (General Picture of the Ottoman Empire) by Mouradgea d'Ohsson, Paris 1790. In the place of the pavilion now stands Istanbul Archeology Museum.

The fourteenth Ottoman Sultan

Sultan Ahmed I

Reign: 1603–1617

Honorifics and Aliases: *Gazi* and *Bahti*
Father's Name: Mehmed III
Mother's Name: Handan Sultan
Place and Date of Birth: Manisa, April 28, 1590
Age at Accession to the Throne: 14
Cause and Date of Death: Typhus and gastric bleeding; November 22, 1617
Place of Death and Burial Site: Istanbul – his tomb is located near the Sultan Ahmed Mosque, Istanbul
Male Heirs: Osman II, Murad IV, İbrahim, Bayezid, Süleyman, Kasım, Mehmed, Hasan, Selim, Hanzade, and Ubeyde
Female Heir: Gevherhan Sultan, Ayşe Sultan, Fatma Sultan, and Atike Sultan

Subsequent to his father Mehmed III's death, Ahmed I rose to the throne at an early age as the first sultan without prior governorship experience, which would have been too risky in the face of the rising Celali revolts in the Anatolian provinces.

By the time Ahmed I received the throne, the Ottoman Empire was in a state of war against Austria in the West and the Safavids in the East. The Ottoman army un-

Miniature of Sultan Ahmed I by Levni in his *Kebir Musavver Silsilenâme* (The Great Envisaged Portraiture Geneology)

der the commandership of Cigalazade Sinan Pasha spent that winter in Van in the southeast of Anatolia without waging a campaign. Sinan Pasha moved the army to Erzurum no sooner than the Safavids attacked; however, his undertaking raised discomfort among the soldiers and led the army to spare a campaign season in vain. Finally, the army marched with the purpose of conquering Tabriz in 1605. The Ottoman army defeated the Safavids, but Commander General Sinan Pasha was put in a difficult position when Köse Sefer Pasha, the governor general of Erzurum, detached his troops from the Ottoman army to chase the enemy and was captured and held prisoner of war. Shah Abbas of the Safavids organized an ambush at a critical moment and vanquished the troops of Köse Sefer Pasha. The remaining Ottoman forces retreated first to Van and then to Diyarbakır located on the banks of the Tigris River. After the sudden death of Sinan Pasha in Diyarbakır, Shah Abbas easily captured Şirvan, Şamakhi, and Ganja in the south Caucasus. The Ottoman Empire did not assign its entire forces to fight against the Safavids, for it was simultaneously fighting Austria, and the internal strife in Anatolia was getting worse. Therefore, the war against the Safavids ended with the signing of a truce named after Grand Vizier Nasuh Pasha.

The daunting challenge during the reign of Sultan Ahmed I came with the revolts that broke in Anatolia. The rise of the revolts occupied much of his attention and extended to a broader sphere of influence. The hardly-thwarted revolts would lead to others in the years to come. In addition, the discontent that stemmed from the intermittent Ottoman-Austrian wars increased when more taxes burdened the Ottoman subjects. Also, the fief-holder timariot cavalry units—who were bound to assemble with the army during wartime and to take care of and control the land entrusted to them in times of peace—showed signs of weaknesses and turned out lesser cavalrymen for the campaigns. The care and control of the provincial lands entrusted to the timariots also declined. This gave momentum to the migration from rural areas to cities, caused the villages and farms to be abandoned, and reduced the government's tax income for agricultural production on timariot land.

By the time Ahmed I rose to the throne, the Ottomans had been waging fierce battles against Austria just as they were during the reign of his father. The reconquest of the forts of Visegrád and Esztergom in 1605 contributed to the consolidation of the Ottoman authority in Wallachia, Moldavia, and Transylvania, and the retained status quo was also recognized by the Wallachian, Moldavian and Transylvanian princes who were agitated by Austria against the Ottoman Empire. At that point, Austria had no other choice but ask for peace. The following Treaty of Zsitvatorok, signed at the former mouth of the Zsitva flowing into the Danube in 1606, stipulated that the Ottomans would keep the forts of Egri, Esztergom, and Kanizsa. Although the treaty seemed to favor the Ottoman Empire, it was nonetheless indicative of the future Ottoman stagnation in Europe. By concluding the treaty with the *Nemçe Çasarı* (Austrian Kaiser), the Ottoman sultan recognized the Austrian ruler for the first time as his diplomatic equal. This was the first occasion of diplomatic equality between an Ottoman sultan and the neighboring European monarchs, whom the Ottomans had previously assigned a subordinate status equal to the grand vizier of the sultan. Hence, this marked the end of absolute Ottoman superiority in international diplomacy that had prevailed since the times of Sultan Süleyman the Magnificent. The renewal of the treaty in the following years was largely due to the unceasing Celali revolts that caused severe problems for the Ottomans. Sultan Ahmed I also renewed the free-commerce privileges of Britain, France, and Venice that the preceding sultans had granted; he also granted the same privileges to Holland.

The massive structure of the Sultan Ahmed Mosque, which is also known as the Blue Mosque due to its exquisite interior blue İznik tiles, is studded with its great domes and six slender minarets rising high above the vast Sultan Ahmed Square.

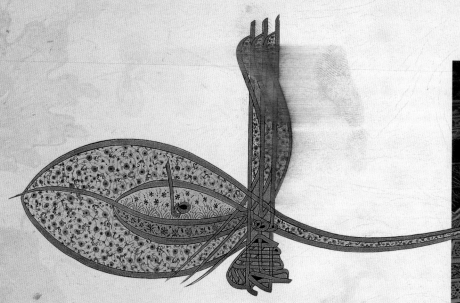

The *tughra* (calligraphic imperial signature) of Sultan Ahmed I

The chronicles state that Ahmed I, who became the fourteenth Ottoman Sultan in his fourteenth year and reigned for fourteen years, met his destiny owing to gastric bleeding at an early age on December 22, 1617. Like many other sultans, Sultan Ahmed I wrote numerous poems under his pseudonym "Bahti." Sultan Ahmed I, a man of religion and charities, was appreciated and respected by his subject people in part because he abstained from pleasures and amusements. In state matters, he was unrelenting in his execution of punishments for those who showed dereliction or treachery in their posts. As a matter of fact, the rise of revolts and his failure to suppress them during his reign seems to have compelled him to govern in a harsh manner in order to restore his authority.

During his reign, the most significant change in state apparatus occurred with reforming of the rules of accession to the throne; particularly, he abolished the execution of fratricide—which had emerged when the *şehzade*s contested for succession during the civil strife after Sultan Bayezid I's loss at the

Splendid ceiling decorations of the massive domes of the Sultan Ahmed Mosque. Many Ottoman mosques built by the members of the Ottoman dynasty are far more majestic and richer than the Ottoman seats of government. Indeed, Ottoman sultans preferred to lead modest lives in their small living quarters in the palace. Neither the Topkapı nor the Dolmabahçe Palaces in Istanbul were the grandest or most expensive palaces of their time although they are stunning in regard to their humility and beauty.

Ankara Battle in 1402—and issued new laws of succession based on *ekberiyet* (seniority) and *erşediyet* (personal and political maturity). In line with the new laws, Mustafa I, Sultan Ahmed I's brother, became *de jure* heir to the throne. In addition, the practice of sending out *şehzade*s to the provinces as governors to gain military and administrative experience was discarded; instead they came to be reserved in the Twin Pavilions in the Topkapı Palace.

The new succession system of seniority and maturity led the Ottoman sultans to come to rule at far older ages; furthermore, the abolishment of the tradition of *şehzade*s serving as *sancak* governors diminished the opportunity for *şehzade*s to gain administrative training and experience. From Sultan Ahmed I onward, the throne began to pass rarely from the sultan to his own son but usually to his brother, the elder member of the dynasty. Today, the head of the family in the Ottoman dynasty is still determined by the rule of seniority. Contrary to expectations, the principles of seniority and maturity did not halt the contests for the succession among brothers. A conventional consensus among the historians, however, is that the newly enthroned sultan's fratriciding heirs to the throne had been applied particularly during the reigns of Murad III and Mehmed III in order to quell any ambitions of potential rivals to the throne. Other unfortunate incidents seem to have occurred when they could not be avoided: it was inescapable that the dynasty members who waged bloody contests for the throne through fire and water would lose their lives in case of failures.

Sultan Ahmed I constructed the Sultan Ahmed Mosque, the *magnum opus* of the Ottoman architecture, across from the Ayasofya mosque. The sultan attended the breaking of the ground with a golden pickaxe to begin the construction of the mosque complex. Sultan Ahmed I became delightedly involved in the eleventh comprehensive renovations of the Ka'ba, which had just been damaged by flooding. He sent craftsmen from Istanbul, and the golden rain gutter that kept rain from collecting on the roof of the Ka'ba was successfully renewed. It

Rosewater flask, the Topkapı Palace

The Privy Chamber of Ahmed I is impressive with a rich variety of İznik tiles covering the walls up to the dome

was again during the era of Sultan Ahmed I that an iron web was placed inside the Well of Zamzam in Mecca. The placement of this web about three feet below the water level was a response to lunatics who jumped into the well, imagining a promise of a heroic death.

In Medina, a new pulpit made of white marble and shipped from Istanbul arrived in the Mosque of the Prophet and substituted the old, worn-out pulpit. It is also known that Sultan Ahmed I erected two more mosques in Üsküdar on the Asian side of Istanbul; however, neither of them have survived. The sultan had a crest carved with the footprint of Prophet Muhammad, peace and blessings be upon him, and illustrated one of the most significant examples of affection to the Prophet in the Ottoman history. Engraved inside the crest was a quatrain he composed: "If only could I bear over my head like my turban forever thee…"

155

Sultan Mustafa I

Reign: 1617–1618 (first term)
1622–1623 (Second term)

Miniature of Sultan Mustafa I by Levni in his *Kebir Musavver Silsilenâme* (The Great Envisaged Portraiture Geneology)

Father's Name: Mehmed III
Mother's Name: Handan Sultan
Place and Date of Birth: Manisa, 1592
Age at Accession to the Throne: 30
Date of Death: January 20, 1639
Place of Death and Burial Site: Istanbul, his tomb is located near the Ayasofya Mosque.

Mustafa I was the first Ottoman sultan to follow his late brother to the throne. The stresses and strains of his paternal uncles' executions during his father Mehmed III's reign and his life under vigilant surveillance in the palace during the reign of his two-year elder bother Ahmed I impacted the young *şehzade* psychologically for many years.

Though his neurotic strains were apparent, it was hoped that the *şehzade* would recover once he assumed the reign. Nevertheless, after the first three months of reign, the statesmen unanimously

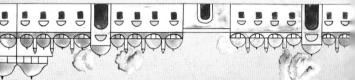

agreed that he "was not able to rule," and dethroned him. Sultan Mustafa I was taken once again into custody, and Osman II, the son of Sultan Ahmed I, was announced as the new sultan on February 26, 1618. The newly enthroned young sultan ruled out that his paternal uncle's being in custody would suffice and spared the life of Mustafa I when he could get rid of him for the sake of averting potential risks. However, the Janissaries and the Sipahi cavalry corps raided the palace suddenly, and executed the young sultan Osman II in order to bring Mustafa I back to the throne so that they could manipulate him in his fragile mental state. Mustafa I returned to the throne once more, but his mental state grew much worse.

In the course of Sultan Mustafa I's second term of reign, the tragic murder of Sultan Osman II by the Janissaries brought about a widespread public abhorrence to the Janissary and cavalry corps, and a series of revolts erupted across the land. Sultan Mustafa I was in great agony; in the eyes of the common people, however, he was held as responsible as the military corps.

The sources on Sultan Mustafa I narrate that he withdrew into solitude during the month of Ramadan and mourned; however, he did not unburden himself to anyone, and in one of his dreams saw his brother Osman elevated up on holy levels. The chronicles further refer to the fact that the religious public coming to pray in the mosques were asked to pray also for the improvement of the sultan's health. Other sources record this brief anecdote that followed the death of Osman: Sultan Mustafa I went hither and yon in the Topkapı Palace in search of the late "Osman," screeching and screaming Osman's name, and begging Osman to relieve him from the insufferable pain of sovereignty.

After a year and a half of internal turmoil, the statesmen decided that the leadership of Sultan Mustafa I was no longer legitimate, so they dethroned Mustafa I for the second time and hailed Murad IV as their new sovereign. Exposed to tremendous pressure of many kinds, confined to his room in the palace, then suddenly announced as sultan (twice!), Mustafa I had sorrowfully observed the vanishing of Osman II. All these challenges incapacitated his already deteriorated mental health. Fifteen years after being held in the palace, Mustafa I met his destiny on January 20, 1639, and was buried in the gardens of the Ayasofya Mosque.

158   Gravure of the Mevlit Alayı (Holy Birth Procession) celebrated in the Sultan Ahmed Mosque after the pilgrims return from the Hajj

European ambassadors lunching with the grand vizier at the Imperial Council Chamber (Kubbealtı) by Jean Baptist Hilaire

159

Sultan Osman II

Reign: 1618–1622

The Young

Honorifics and Aliases: *Genç* [the Young], *Şehid* [the Martyr] and *Farisi* [as his pseudonym]
Father's Name: Ahmed I
Mother's Name: Mahfiruz Sultan
Place and Date of Birth: Istanbul, November 3, 1604
Age at Accession to the Throne: 14
Cause and Date of Death: Martyr, May 20, 1622
Place of Death and Burial Site: Istanbul – his tomb is next to his father Sultan Ahmed I at the Tomb of Ahmed I near the Sultan Ahmed Mosque
Male Heirs: Ömer and Mustafa
Female Heir: Zeyneb Sultan

Sultan Osman II, the eldest son of Sultan Ahmed I, was named by his father after Osman Gazi, the first Ottoman sultan. In accordance with the fundamental change in the procedures of accession to the throne, Osman II was recognized and proclaimed in his fourteenth year as the new sultan by the will of the statesmen due to the inability of his paternal uncle Mustafa I to rule.

Miniature of Sultan Osman II by Levni in his *Kebir Musavver Silsilenâme* (The Great Envisaged Portraiture Geneology)

Sultan Osman II received an excellent education; he acted wisely and supported innovations in the state apparatus in a more mature way than expected from his very young age. Soon after ascending to the throne, Osman II asserted himself, dismissing from positions of authority not only Mustafa I's followers but also the statesmen and his spiritual guide and advisor that led him to the throne. The Ottoman Empire fought against the Safavid Persia and the Polish Kingdom during his reign.

By the time of his ceremony of accession to the throne, Grand Vizier Halil Pasha of Kayseri was marching a campaign against the Safavid Persia. The Safavid army had defeated the forces of the Crimean Khan in the plains of Serav. The Khan had merged his troops with the Ottoman army on September 10, 1618, and Halil Pasha marched toward the city of Ardabil where Shah Abbas of the Safavids was at the time. The Treaty of Serav, a response to the offer made by Shah Abbas in 1618, stipulated that the amount of silk the Safavids had to pay to the Ottoman Empire as annual tribute, which had been determined by the Treaty of Nasuh Pasha, would be reduced by half. The young sultan affirmed the treaty; nevertheless, he replaced Halil Pasha with Damad Kara Mehmed Pasha as the grand vizier, mainly in reaction to the former's inefficacy against the Safavids.

There had been friendly relations between the Ottomans and the Polish Kingdom. However, the Kingdom of Poland that had come under the protectorate of the Ottoman Empire by Grand Vizier Sokullu Mehmed Pasha (d.1579) now interfered in the internal affairs of the neighboring Moldavia, an Ottoman land that Poland has its sights set on. Furthermore, Poland vigorously encouraged and supported the Cossacks, who were assaulting the Ottoman lands in the northern region of the Black Sea. Therefore, Ottoman-Polish relations escalated to belligerence followed by the call to war against the Kingdom of Poland by the new grand vizier, Güzelce Ali Pasha in 1621. During the period in which the Thirty Years' War occupied a significant part of the Christian Europe, Sultan Osman II commanded the Ottoman army himself

Miniature of Sultan Osman II's accession ceremony

with the objective to revive the Ottoman Empire in a way comparable to its golden age.

The sultan took the name of every Janissary prior to the campaign, which caused enormous discontent in the army. The Ottoman army made a failed attempt to capture the Khotyn Fortress on the shores of the Dniester on the northern border of Moldavia. In the face of the strong reinforcements that fed the Polish and Cossack armies, many incursions led by Osman II would be to no avail. The sultan had seen the Janissaries fighting reluctantly and the winter approaching fast; therefore, he responded favorably to the offer of peace in favor of the Ottomans made by the Kingdom of Poland, and the two countries signed the Treaty of Khotyn in 1621. This treaty gave the Khotyn Fortress to the Voivode of Moldavia, an allegiant of the Ottoman Empire.

The sultan called in his wife Ayşe Sultan and son Ömer while in Edirne. Unfortunately, the sultan's son Şehzade Ömer died when a bullet ricocheted and hit him during the celebrations of the Khotyn Victory, which the sultan had ordered at the request of his wife Ayşe Sultan.

Miniature of Sultan Osman II seated on throne

Sultan Osman II was a sultan who tried to carry out a wide array of reforms to stop the decline of the Ottoman Empire. In his view, the reason for the empire's stagnation was the statesmen of the *devşirme*[28] who tolerated bribery and nepotism and ignored visible administrative malfunctions. In order to heal the empire's wounds, the sultan considered replacing the *devşirme* court officials and the Janissary corps with a new army recruited from the Anatolian population as well as transferring the imperial capital from Istanbul to Anatolia.

The rumors about the sultan's intent to abolish the Janissary corps as a result of its unruliness manifested during the Khotyn Campaign and to recruit a new army reached their ears rather swiftly. The announcement of the sultan that he would set out for Syria to thwart a widespread rebellion in Lebanon and then pay a pilgrim's visit to Mecca had even greater repercussions. The Janissaries were in outraged disbelief, believing the rumors that the sultan was preparing to move against them. In fact, the rumors spread that the sultan would pick up soldiers from Anatolia, Syria, and Egypt, and attack the rebellious Janissaries. According to the sources, the sultan's choice of the Sultan Selim Mosque for the Friday Prayer before that great Janissary mutiny was a sign that the sultan would soon be on the move toward Syria and Egypt, just as Sultan Selim I had moved down the Upper Euphrates into Syria and Egypt. The rising host of gossip prompted the Janissaries to rebel shortly thereafter; the *ulema* (Islamic scholars) supported the Janissaries as they too had become estranged from the sultan.

Sultan Osman II strongly opposed the Janissaries' demand that he hand over several statesmen, and at this point he decided to resist to the Janissary Corps. When the rebels

Equestrian miniature of Osman II

plunged into the Topkapı Palace and proclaimed Mustafa I as the new sultan, it became obvious that the tremendous efforts of the Skeikhu'l-Islam (the Grand-Judge) Esad Efendi, the father-in-law of Osman the Young, to end the mutiny and avert the ex-sultan Mustafa I's accession back to the throne had been unsuccessful. Even the fact that Osman II finally submitted and delivered the wanted statesmen to the rebels did not recover the situation. Osman II took refuge with Janissary Commander in Chief Ali Pasha and asked him to please the Janissaries; the Janissaries responded to Ali Pasha by killing him brutally. Captured and insulted by the rebels, Sultan Osman was presented to Mustafa I in 1622. They then imprisoned and executed him in the Yedikule Zindanları (the Dungeons of the Seven Towers). Osman the Young was recorded in the annals of history as the first Ottoman sultan assassinated by his own soldiers.

The striking deficiencies of Osman II were derived from his inexperience as a juvenile sultan, his rough nature, and his undeveloped temperament in handling difficult issues. As a result of his extensively visible exposure to the public in casual clothes and his sudden surprise raids of the *meyhane*s (taverns), Osman II lost his reputation in the eye's of the soldiers, men of books, and the broader public. He strived to enact a wealth of fundamental reforms to revive the empire along the lines of the glorious eras of Sultan Selim I and Sultan Süleyman the Magnificent. Sultan Osman II aimed to bring about military order; he secretly inspected the soldiers in disguise and did not hesitate to severely punish those whom he caught were guilty.

A remarkable poet, Sultan Osman wrote splendid poems under the pseudonym of "Farisi." Keen on sports, the sultan was a marvelous equestrian and marksman.

General view of the Historic Peninsula of Istanbul during the Ottoman times

Sultan Murad IV

Reign: 1623—1640

Honorifics and Aliases: *Bağdad Fatihi* [Conqueror of Baghdad], *Gazi* [Warrior for the Faith], *Sahibkıran* [the Always-Successful Ruler], *Şah Murad* [Murad the Sovereign], and *Muradi* [as his pseudonym]
Father's Name: Ahmed I
Mother's Name: Mahpeyker (Kösem) Sultan
Place and Date of Birth: Istanbul, July 27, 1612
Age at Accession to the Throne: 11
Cause and Date of Death: Gout, February 9, 1640
Place of Death and Burial Site: Istanbul – he was buried next to Sultan Ahmed I in the Tomb of Ahmed I near the Sultan Ahmed Mosque
Male Heirs: Süleyman, Mehmed, Alaeddin, Ahmed, and Mahmud
Female Heir: Kaya İsmihan Sultan, Rukiye Sultan, and Hafize Sultan

The Janissaries dethroned Sultan Osman II and brought Mustafa I back to the throne in 1622. Nevertheless, the grand vizier and notable statesmen forced Mustafa I to relinquish his throne once more in part because of his own mental deficiencies and in part because he failed to effectively settle the administrative havoc that emerged in the course of his one and a half year reign. Murad IV, an eleven year old heir to the throne, was proclaimed to be the new sultan in 1632.

Miniature of Sultan Murad IV by Levni in his *Kebir Musavver Silsilenâme* (The Great Envisaged Portraiture Geneology)

Ceremonial knobbed mace with metal shaft

The accessional address was held at the Tomb of Eyüp Sultan, and it was his spiritual mentor Aziz Mahmud Hüdayi who girded Murad IV his sultanic sword. The Valide (mother) Sultan Maypeyker Kösem and Grand Vizier Kemankeş Ali Pasha undertook running the central administration as the new sultan was still too young. He was also too young to respond to the outbreak of violence in Istanbul by the military as a punishment for the statesmen who espoused the Janissary mutinies for their own benefit. Nor was he able to quell the revolts that had erupted in particular provinces. Murad IV disguised himself and roamed the streets of Istanbul in search of answers for why the events went wrong; in addition, he carried out preparations to change his nominal sovereignty into a *de facto* one.

Murad IV spent his first nine years of reign gaining experience in Ottoman state administration. In May, 1632 he made a courageous attempt to thwart the rebels. As a capable sultan, he counter blasted the women of the palace and the *ağa*s (the chief court officers) of the palace and eventually deprived them of their manipulative force that had influenced the state affairs to no small degree.

Abaza Mehmed Pasha, the governor general of Erzurum, led a counterinsurgency to avenge the murder of Sultan Osman II; in 1624 he captured Erzurum and its vicinity in Eastern Anatolia and slayed the Janissaries located in the region. Murad IV's forces defeated Abaza Mehmed Pasha near Kayseri in central Anatolia and the pasha retreated to Erzurum only to rise in rebellion at a later date. Grand Vizier Hüsrev Pasha captured and brought him to Istanbul. After Abaza Mehmed Pasha came to the presence of and was forgiven by the sultan, he was reassigned as the governor general of Bosnia.

The most striking revolt in Istanbul erupted on February 7, 1632. Hüsrev Pasha, who replaced Hafız Ahmed Pasha as the new grand vizier, had oppressed people in Anatolia during his campaigns to Hamedan and Baghdad and failed in the siege. Therefore, Hafız Ahmed Pasha was called back to replace Hüsrev Pasha as grand vizier once again. Topal Recep Pasha, willing to be promoted to a provincial governorship, provoked the pro-Hüsrev Pasha soldiers, and a major revolt ensued.

The soldiers gathered in the Sultan Ahmed Square; they marched to the palace for three consecutive days and requested the execution of the grand vizier Hafız Ahmed Pasha, the grand judge Zekerriyyazade Yahya Efendi, the chief of the Janissary Corps Hasan Halife as well as seventeen others, the men most loyal to the sultan. When Sultan Murad IV strongly opposed their request, the head of the rebels breached the Babu's-Selam (Gate of Salutation), the second gate to the palace, rushed into the courtyard of the Council Hall (*Divan Meydanı*), and requested the presence of the sultan. Following a two-round drop-in meeting (Ayak Divanı) with the mob, Sultan Murad IV felt compelled to take seriously the advice of Topal Recep Pasha, who warned him of the danger of becoming dethroned and yielded to the demands of the rebels.

Aware of his destiny, Hafız Ahmed Pasha, a manifest loyal Grand Vizier, revealed himself to the sultan saying, "My Sultan! Always has Hezar Hafız, the humble subject of yours [addressing himself], been ready to sacrifice himself for your sake; however not to die by your respected orders but to be killed by the mob is my wish because only so would I fall martyr." He then moved on to attack the rebels; he was able to eliminate one of the ferocious members of the mob but he was eventually martyred. The sultan, having seen the dramatic series of events unfolding, receded back to his chamber, grumbling and pledging vengeance. From then on, his tone changed into a far more aggressive one against the rebels. Later, the rebels gathered again in the Sultan Ahmed Square for a meeting with the sultan during which they demanded to see the *şehzade*s. The sultan, very aware of the collusion underway behind his back, could do nothing but sacrifice Şehzade Bayezid and Şehzade Süleyman, his sons, on the way back from the Yerevan campaign.

A successive score of rebels had become the norm in Istanbul, thanks to the agitation of Grand Vizier Recep Pasha. In an effort to quash the rebellions and establish his sovereignty, the sultan first disposed of the statesmen who had turned corrupt. For instance, he executed Recep Pasha, who played a profound role in several major rebellions in Istanbul and Anatolia. The execution of the pasha appalled the unruly members of the Sipahi cavalry units and their proponents, but eventually order was restored in Istanbul and Anatolia.

The Safavids recaptured Baghdad during this period. Hüsrev Pasha embarked on a campaign series in Hamedan and Baghdad; nonetheless, the victories of his forces, which had been reinforced by the soldiers present in the region from the time of Abaza Mehmed Pasha, were insufficient for a reconquest of Baghdad after its siege quite some time before.

Sultan Murad IV marched two campaigns against Persia. During the first campaign on March 28, 1635, he moved his army through the route that followed İzmit, Eskişehir, Konya, Kayseri, and Sivas; eventually the enormous Ottoman army that consisted of more than 200,000 soldiers passed through the Erzurum-Kars region and reached the gates of Revan (present-day Yerevan). The army besieged and conquered the Fortress of Yerevan. The sultan sent Emirgûneoğlu, the last commander-in-charge of the fortress, to Aleppo as the new governor general of that region. Emirgûneoğlu would later become a Sunni and change his name to Yusuf; however, people persistently addressed Yusuf Pasha as Emirgûneoğlu for the rest of his life even when he was summoned to Istanbul to be promoted to the grand vizierate. In fact, the marvelous orchard that was given to him on the Bosphorus is one of today's favorite excursion spots in Istanbul and is named Emirgan after him. In memory of the Yerevan Victory, a pavilion was constructed in the Fourth Courtyard of the Topkapı Palace, and it was called the Revan Pavilion.

The Safavids recaptured Yerevan after Sultan Murad IV returned from Yerevan and dispatched an emissary to call for truce. Sultan Murad did not allow him to enter his presence; instead, he sent a message to the Safavid emissary that "he would answer the message [request for peace] back in Baghdad," and the emissary left.

The Ottoman army commanded by Murad IV himself marched a campaign to Baghdad; meanwhile, his son Şehzade Kasım too was executed as a result of the disturbing rumors that spread prior to the campaign. The sultan led a magnificent Ottoman army, reminiscent of the armies of the early period. With the sultan as a soldier, the Ottoman forces laid a siege to the Baghdad Fortress, which culminated in the reconquest of Baghdad and the incorporation of the city back into the Ottoman domain in 1638.

Following the conquest of Baghdad, Sultan Murad IV travelled around the Baghdad Fortress and paid a visit to the Tomb of Imam al-A'zam Abu Hanifa—founder of the Hanafi school of Islam. Then he ordered the renovation of the tombs of Abu Hanifa and Abdu'l-Qadir al-Jilani, two prominent figures in the history of Islam. The sultan could have advanced much further into Persia, but he did not, and returned to Istanbul primarily because of

The Baghdad Pavilion viewed from the marble-paved terrace. Built by Sultan Murad IV, the pavilion has a beautiful view of the Bosphorus.

his deteriorating health. A long and difficult journey back to Istanbul also gave him sore feet. It came down to the grand vizier to lead the peace talks; consequently, the Treaty of Qasr-e-Shirin (also known as the Treaty of Zohab)was signed on May 17, 1639 near the city of Qasr-e-Shirin, symbolizing the official end of the ongoing wars between the Ottoman Empire and Safavid Persia. The treaty brought about peace to the region for long years to come; in fact, it also laid the groundwork for future references in the diplomatic relations between the two countries.

During the wars with Persia, the Kingdom of Poland had neglected to pay the annual tributes found in the agreements, and moreover, Poland had agitated the Russian Cossacks to attack the Ottoman lands. Hence, Sultan Murad IV ordered a campaign against the Kingdom of Poland. Shortly after, the Kingdom of Poland asked for peace and promised to pay annual tributes to both the Ottoman Empire and the Crimean Khanate.

During an expedition, Ali Piçinoğlu, the admiral of the Ottoman fleet in Algeria and Tunis, had docked his fleet of ships at the Port of Vlora, which is the closest in proximity to the Italian port of Bari. The Venetians exploited this to their advantage and sent a huge fleet to blockade Vlora. Finally, they confiscated and carried the Ottoman ships away in 1638. Frustrated by the news, Sultan Murad IV ordered the termination of commercial relations with Venice, and the closure of the customs station located at the port city of Split on the eastern shores of the Ad-

Interior of the Revan Pavilion, Topkapı Palace

Interior of the Baghdad Pavilion decorated with beautiful ornamentations with minute details

riatic Sea. Considering the detrimental consequences, Venetians rushed to call for peace. A new treaty that would resume the commercial terms and compel Venetians to pay reparations was signed on July 16, 1639.

Sultan Murad IV stubbornly struggled to cast the Ottoman Empire back to its glory; he eliminated corruption from the administrative structure to a certain extent and undertook drastic measures to quell the Celali revolts. In accordance with the recommendations of the historian Koçi Bey, who, at the request of the sultan, presented a concise briefing concerning the present situation of the Sublime Ottoman State, Sultan Murad IV prepared for a wide range of reforms.

Sultan Murad IV's health severely deteriorated on the journey back from his military expedition to Baghdad; the sultan critically relapsed two days after celebrating the coming of the holy month of Ramadan, and met his destiny following the night-time prayer on Thursday, February 8, 1640. He was buried, before a big gathering, in the Tomb of Sultan Ahmed I, his father, near the Sultan Ahmed Mosque. The famous contemporary chronicler Naima recorded in his annals the following anecdote: The Baghdad Pavilion was raised in the Topkapı Palace in remembrance of the re-conquest of Baghdad, and when the walls of the pavilion were being tiled with the calligrams in the *cel'i divani* script,[29] the calligrapher came to a point where he had to write the Qur'anic verse in Arabic that reads "And when İbrahim [Abraham] raised the foundations of the house..." (Baqara 2:127). The death of Sultan Murad IV coincided with the time he began to write the name of İbrahim, and the sultan's younger brother İbrahim succeeded him to the throne.

Sultan Murad IV was tremendously heavily-built and famous for his physical strength with incredible stamina to travail. A fan of sports, the sultan constructed in the gardens of the Topkapı Palace "the Stone Throne," a solid marble throne on which he later sat and watched the competitions of the students from the free-boarding Enderun School within the Topkapı Palace. He also participated in the sports on this spot once in a while. The epigraph behind the marble throne records the fact that Sultan Murad IV successfully threw an oak club approximately 263 feet (80 meters) while riding his horse at full speed in the month of Ramadan in the year of 1636, illustrative of his outstanding physical strength. Other instances of his strength included the heavy-lifting of a 565-pound (256-kilo) mace and wrestling famous contemporary professional wrestlers. Quite interestingly, it is also recorded that he once lifted from his belt a certain fat Silahtar Musa Pasha (a man of distinction and the principle of the Enderun School) and carried him around in the Imperial Chamber of the palace several times.

Sultan Murad IV was a remarkable equestrian and was a talented marksman who mastered many types of guns. Quite devoted to his horses, the sultan took particular care of the *Has Ahur*, the imperial stables. The thoroughbred horses with the names Dağlar Delisi (the Mountain-Crazed), Ağa Alacası (the Lord-Speckled), and Tayyar (the Flying)[30] were raised in these stables. In line with ancient Turkish customs, these select horses of the deceased sultan trotted from the Topkapı Palace to the Sultan Ahmed Mosque with their saddles belted upside down.

Sultan Murad IV's marble throne in the palace garden. A fan of sports, he watched the sporting contests from here.

The Baghdad Pavilion viewed from the Tulip Garden

The sources further report that Sultan Murad IV, prior to his death, had shot an arrow and pierced one of the iron-made gates of the Topkapı Palace. He also punctured a shield, which was made from the rhino leather and sent by Shah Jahan, the ruler of the Mughal India, to the sultan during his stay in Mosul on the banks of the Tigris before campaigning to Baghdad. It was said to be arrow- and bullet-proof; nonetheless, the sources record that the sultan, right before the eyes of the Mughal emissary, punctured two clear-cut holes in that shield with both a spear and an arrow. Consistent with this anecdote, it is said that the sultan's arrows would range far greater distance than decently shot rifle bullets and that "there was no match against his javelin throw." In fact, he was a proven talent in both archery and piking; for instance, he could launch spears from the Eski Saray, or Old Palace, (in whose place now stands the rectorate building of Istanbul University) to the bottom of a Bayezid Mosque minaret in the Bayezid Square and again from the Fortress of Aleppo to near the saddlers' workshop area of Saraçhane in Aleppo.

Sultan Murad IV was an extraordinary sultan with an unorthodox character. In an era of stagnation, the sultan diligently dealt with state affairs, tried to inquire into and understand the events outside of his palace by his local visits in disguise. He succeeded to a certain extent in recovering the empire from an impending chaos. The Western sources also mention that he established a domestic intelligence bureau.

Murad IV knew Arabic and Persian as well as Turkish; he penned poems under the name "Muradi" and composed the military marching songs for the Ottoman military band called the *Mehter*—the oldest variety of military marching band in the world. Among the Islamic chants that he wrote is the famed hymn that goes, *Uyan ey gözlerim gafletten uyan* ("Awake eyes of mine, awake to the negligence"). He penned splendid Ottoman calligraphic works in the *talik* script, which has short verticals with no serifs and long horizontal strokes. The sultan was a devout Muslim and respected the scholars and religious notables. During his reign emerged numerous renowned Ottoman scholars, historians, poets, calligraphers, and musicians. They included Evliya Çelebi, Katip Çelebi, Nef'i, Sheikhu'l-Islam Yahya, Veysi, Koçi Bey, and Azmizade.

Extensive rainfall had poured on the city of Mecca in April of 1639, flooding the Masjid al-Haram. The flood swelled two fathoms high and severely damaged the mosque. No sooner than the news of the flood reached the sultan did he meet up with the Sheikhu'l-Islam and received a *fatwa* (an authoritative religious decree) on how to proceed with the reparations. The sultan then appointed for the reparations the Ottoman *qadi* (judge) Mehmed Efendi and the renowned architect Rıdvan Ağa. Finally, a team of crafty workers under their supervision handled the damage that the flood inflicted on the Ka'ba, and undertook the reparations so completely that they even inspected the infrastructure and fortified the foundations of the Kab'a. In addition, a unique approach was applied in the reparations: the pieces and stones of the Ka'ba, which fell off or simply became dysfunctional, were replaced only with those collected where the originals had come from.

Despite the fact that Sultan Murad IV's reign spanned over sixteen years, his *de facto* sovereignty lasted merely eight years for it was his mother that led during the early years of the reign of the young and inexperienced sultan. Sultan Murad IV's character resembled that of one of his forebears, Sultan Selim I, but his administrative fate was the opposite. First, the sultan rose to the throne at the age of eleven; second, he was deprived of exceptionally talented statesmen. Otherwise, it seems highly likely that he would have changed the course of the Ottoman Empire in quite a different way. The sultan marched no single campaign to Europe; nevertheless, his sheer presence was frightening enough to the Europeans. The European monarchs burst into joy and happiness simply when they heard he was gone. His brother İbrahim would succeed him to the throne.

Miniature of the Mehter band in their official Ottoman costumes. The Mehter band was the oldest military marching band in the world.

Galicia
Austria
Vienna
Uyvar
Zsitvatorok
Eger
Vasvár
Mezokövesd
Esztergom
Kanizsa
Transylvania
Szeged
Szigetvar
Mohács
(1566)
(1526)
Karlowitz
Wa
Belgrade
Bosnia
(1521)
Herzegovina
Niko
Niš
Serbia
Ragusa
Montenegro
Sofia
Albania
Serres
Salonica

ATLANTIC
OCEAN

France

Venice

Genoa

Italy

Dalmatia

Spain

Corsica

Rome

Sardinia

Otranto

Naupactus
Preveza
Athe
Sicily
Morea

Algiers
Tunis

Malta
MEDITERRAN

Cr

A l g e r i a
Tunisia

(1533)

Tripoli

Benghazi

B e r k

T r i p o l i

(1551)

N
W   E
S

Ottoman Empire

	Territory annexed by Sultan Mehmed the Conqueror (1451–1481)
	Territory annexed by Sultan Bayezid II (1481–1512)
	Territory annexed by Sultan Selim I (1512–1520)
	Territory annexed by Sultan Süleyman the Magnificent (1520–1566)
	Territorial expansion from Sultan Murad III to Sultan Mehmed IV (1566–1683)

Boundaries of the Ottoman Empire (1451–1683)

Ukraine

Donets

Russia

Dnieper

Don

Volga

Bender

Yedisan

Astrakhan

ARAL
SEA

Arabia

Crimean
Khanate

Kuban

ilia

Akkerman

Sevastopol

Caucasia

Dagestan

CASPIAN SEA

Varna

BLACK SEA

Sinop

Georgia

Istanbul

Samsun

Kars

Shirvan

İznik

Ankara

Trabzon

Erzurum

Yerevan

Azerbaijan

Bursa

Otlukbeli

Serav

Manisa

Erzincan

Van

Tabriz

zmir

Konya

Adana

Diyarbakır

Tehran

Rhodes

Antakya

Marj Dabik

Mosul

Hamedan

Aleppo

Tigris

Qasr-e-Shirin

Latakia

Syria

Safavid
Persia

Cyprus
(1570)

Beirut

Euphrates

Baghdad

SEA

Damascus

Isfahan

Dumyat

Jaffa

Arabia

Alexandria

Ridanieh

Jerusalem

Basra

Cairo

Shiraz

Suez

Sinai

Aqaba

Hijaz

PERSIAN GULF

Egypt

RED SEA

Al-Qatif

(1517)

Medina

SCALE

Mecca

0   125   250   375   500 miles

The Eighteenth Ottoman Sultan

Sultan İbrahim

Reign: 1640—1648

Father's Name: Sultan Ahmed I
Mother's Name: Mahpeyker (Kösem) Sultan
Place and Date of Birth: Istanbul, November 4, 1615
Age at Accession to the Throne: 25
Date of Death: August 18, 1648
Place of Death and Burial Site: Istanbul,
he was buried in the Tomb of Mustafa I near the Ayasofya Mosque
Male Heirs: Mehmed IV, Süleyman II, Ahmed II, Murad, Orhan,
Bayezid, Cihangir, Selim, and Murad
Female Heir: Ümmü Gülsüm Sultan, Peykan Sultan, Atike Sultan, Rukiye Sultan,
Kaya İsmihan Sultan, Hafize Sultan, Ayşe Sultan, and Gerverhan Sultan

Sultan İbrahim was Sultan Ahmed I's third son to rise to the throne. His *şehzade* years passed in the Topkapı Palace, during which the state had been undergoing a period of internal turmoil. Sultan İbrahim lost his father Sultan Ahmed I when two years old and closely observed Sultan Mustafa I's mental anguish and the series of events related to his poor mental state. Furthermore, the dethronement of his older brother Sultan Osman II and his murder at a very

Miniature of Sultan Ibrahim by Levni in his *Kebir Musavver Silsilenâme* (The Great Envisaged Portraiture Geneology)

young age by his very own soldiers had a very profound influence on Sultan İbrahim. The events to follow led him to think he would meet his destiny soon: his younger brother Sultan Murad IV could not assume his *de facto* sovereignty in the first nine years of his reign; Murad IV had been forced to submit to the insulting impromptu meetings with rebellious mobs who had breached the gates of the Topkapı Palace forcing Murad IV to adopt an excessively brutal and bloody approach; and finally, his older brothers Bayezid, Süleyman, and Kazım were murdered. Waiting for the day he too would die profoundly influenced the psychology of Şehzade İbrahim, who had a sensitive nature in the first place.

Since his older brother Murad IV's sons all died when Murad IV was still alive, Şehzade İbrahim ended up remaining as the only heir to the throne. İbrahim did not want to leave his private room after he received the news of Sultan Murad IV's death mainly because he had regarded the news as part of a setup against himself. It was only after his mother Kösem Sultan convinced him by showing him the dead body of his older brother that he believed he would be the next sultan.

The first four years of Sultan İbrahim's reign elapsed in peace and order, thanks to the great contributions of Kemankeş Kara Mustafa Pasha—Sultan İbrahim's candid, respected, and experienced grand vizier. Compared to Sultan Murad IV's power-oriented administration, Sultan İbrahim took on a less aggressive, more tolerant approach, which finally brought about a period of tranquility. The instructions that the young Sultan İbrahim sent to his grand vizier suggest that he was very interested in and very concerned with the state and the public welfare. Sultan İbrahim took short walks around the city in disguise, and notified the grand vizier about the social ills that called for urgent remedies to be conducted by a better functioning government.

Four years later, the execution of Kemankeş Mustafa Pasha under Sultan İbrahim's order would cripple the order of state. Koçi Bey, the contemporary chronicler, submitted a brief, or *risale*, to Sultan İbrahim in a similar vein to the one previously addressed to Sultan Murad IV; in particular, his brief lamented the irresponsibility of the imperial institutions, the complaints, and the status quo.

The Ottoman army marched to the Fortress of Azov on the Sea of Azov, which had been captured by the Cossacks living along the Lower Don River. Upon hearing that the Ottomans were

The Circumcision Chamber in the Topkapı Palace with its rare İznik tiles is one of Sultan İbrahim's contributions.

Built-in marble fountains at the windows of the Circumcision Chamber
constructed to sound-proof the chamber

en route, the Cossacks destroyed and fled the city. The Ottomans reconquered Azov and put it under tremendous construction-works.

On another front, Emirgûneoğlu, the old ruler of Yerevan, began to sow the seeds of discord soon after the death of Sultan Murad IV. He had readily surrendered the fortress to the Ottomans during the siege of Yerevan and had gained the acclaim of the sultan's older brother, Sultan Murad IV. However, Emirgûneoğlu now became impudent and insisted on returning to Persia. The sultan had advised him on many occasions, but this last time, Emirgûneoğlu would have to face the sultan's wrath. Shortly after, he was executed.

The *iftariye* (fast-breaking dinner) bower is one of Sultan İbrahim's contributions in the Topkapı Palace.

On their pilgrimage journey to Mecca, Sümbül Ağa, one of the chief officers of the palace, and his extended company were ambushed and looted and many were slaughtered by the pirates of Malta near Crete Island. Fed up with the pirates, the sultan gave orders, right away, for a campaign to Malta. Reflective of his diplomatic talents at the time, the sultan imposed secrecy on the coming campaign to Crete, one of the most strategically important islands in the Mediterranean; at the same time his fingers were pointing directly to Malta. Moreover, he successfully kept his secret from the foreign ambassadors residing in Istanbul. This diplomatic maneuver would deny any united mobilizations against the Ottomans by the enemy.

The Ottoman administration chose to hit the Venetian colony of Crete specifically because of its strategic significance in the Mediterranean Sea. First, the Ottoman forces laid a siege to Hania on the north coast of the island. When Hania surrendered in 1645 within a couple of months of the siege, Sultan İbrahim ordered a grand jubilation that lasted three days and nights. Hüseyin Pasha, now assigned as the new guardian of Hania, continued the operations. He captured the Fortezza, the Castle of Rethymno to the east of Hania. The complete conquest of Crete would prove too expensive and difficult, and so it took long years to integrate all of Crete into the Ottoman domain.

Candia (now Heraklion), the largest city of Crete, went under siege as well, but the Venetians imposed a naval blockade on the strait of the Dardanelles, which was more than the Ottomans could contend with at the time. Besides the war, the Ottomans also had to grapple with new revolts erupting in Istanbul and Anatolia; worse, Grand Vizier Kemankeş Kara Mustafa Pasha was executed in 1645 and his execution triggered a polarized struggle within the palace. Indeed, there was a power struggle within the palace between Grand Vizier Kemankeş Kara Mustafa Pasha and Yusuf Pasha; furthermore, Kösem Sultan was involved in the struggle, albeit behind the scene. Eventually, Sultan İbrahim was dethroned in the aftermath of a highly organized coup on August 8, 1648.

The execution of Kara Mustafa Pasha brought about major changes in the Ottoman administration. Generally speaking, a period of chaos followed the previous era of relative peace and order. Even if Sultan İbrahim had desired to take on a *de facto* leadership, like his older brother Murad IV, all of the stress and the resulting depression prevented him from doing so. Moreover, during

Miniature of Sultan İbrahim in front of the *iftariye* bower

185

the successive grand vizierates of Sultanzade Mehmed Pasha, Salih Pasha, and especially of Hezarpare Ahmed Pasha, irresponsible and iniquitous statesmen disturbed law and order. These statesmen did all they could to keep the sultan away from the administration, encouraging him to amuse himself and deliberately causing him to act inconsistently and imbalanced so that they could exploit the state. Particularly, Sultan İbrahim's unusual manners multiplied when Ahmed Pasha was the grand vizier. For instance, fomenting the sultan's interest in furs, Ahmed Pasha levied taxes on sable furs. All in all, he aimed to amuse the sultan and distracted him from the state affairs in order to secure his own position.

The people in the major cities and provinces had become even more discontent since Sultan İbrahim remain removed from the state affairs. His mother Kösem Sultan attempted to caution Sultan İbrahim, but she was forced to leave the Topkapı Palace and to live in the İskender Bahçesi—a coastal grove in Istanbul—for a certain period. What's more, the frequent shift of experienced governors and governor generals served as a harbinger to new tragedies. It was during this period that Varvar Ali Pasha, the governor general of Sivas, revolted and was restrained with difficulty. The fact that Grand Vizier Ahmed Pasha had been concerned only with his own interests incited a number of destructive rumors; eventually, a large-scale revolt broke out in reaction to the grand vizier's uncompromising approach.

The revolt had emerged only against Ahmed Pasha, but it resulted in the dethronement of Sultan İbrahim and his replacement by Mehmed IV, İbrahim's young son. The rebels involved in the revolt caught and executed Ahmed Pasha, and cut his body into bits in the Sultan Ahmed Square. From then on, he was called *Hezarpare*, or "smashed to bits." Meanwhile, Sultan İbrahim was confined to the Twin Pavilions in the harem section of the Topkapı Palace. And after his seven-year-old son Mehmed IV's accession ceremony, Sultan İbrahim's pitiful cries could be heard throughout the harem, which profoundly touched and appalled the people there. Those who replaced Sultan İbrahim with Mehmed IV executed İbrahim right where he had been confined in the palace mainly because they suspected that he would be placed back on the throne. The ex-Sultan İbrahim's final discussion with the statesmen who visited him in his chamber prior to his execution is recorded in several contemporary sources: İbrahim had defended himself against the accusations with solidly convincing evidence, but it was to no avail. The body of the deceased Sultan was buried in the Tomb of Mustafa I near the Ayasofya Mosque on August 18, 1648.

The Ottoman dynasty continued through the late Sultan İbrahim's progeny. İbrahim's three sons—Mehmed IV, Süleyman II, and Ahmed II—all became sultans while others passed away at early ages. Indeed, it was much later towards the end of the Ottoman state that some historians of the Second Constitutional Monarchy (1908–1922) had unjustly labeled him *deli* (mad) and began calling him Sultan İbrahim the Mad. Though he went through a period of mental distress, especially during his childhood, Sultan İbrahim's mental state was not incapacitated like his paternal uncle. The sultan sometimes expressed the mental anguish he had been experiencing in his writings to his vizier; his calligrams mentioned his mental distresses and terrible headaches. Despite all, Sultan İbrahim tried hard to manage state affairs, joined in the imperial council meetings, and scrutinized the decisions. He wanted more knowledge about the ongoing events in the Ottoman borderlands. Sultan İbrahim's sensibility, manifest in the early years of his reign, faded away later for interrelated reasons: his health steadily deteriorated, his state responsibilities became far more complicated, the statesmen consulted and acted in their own interests, and the women of the palace, especially the *Valide* Sultan, intervened in the state affairs.

Reputedly, during one of his incognito visits, Sultan İbrahim witnessed a very long line in front of a bakery. Upon returning to the palace, the sultan penned a *hat* (an imperial mandate) to his grand vizier, strongly rebuking what he'd seen and ordering him to urgently take measures so that his subject people would not have to wait to obtain essential commodities.

The Ottoman economy did fairly well particularly during the early years of the reign of Sultan İbrahim, who was a generous sultan. In fact, the Ottomans experienced an era of economic welfare. Clearly, had İbrahim been sent out into the provinces to gain administrative experience as a governor instead of experiencing the dramatic events in the palace during his childhood, he would have most likely turned out to be a different sultan, far more capable of changing the course of Ottoman history the way he wanted it to be.

Sultan Mehmed IV

Reign: 1648–1687

Honorifics and Aliases: *Avcı* [the Hunter]
Father's Name: Sultan İbrahim
Mother's Name: Hadice Turhan Sultan
Place and Date of Birth: Istanbul, January 2, 1642
Age at Accession to the Throne: 7
Cause of Death: Gout, Mental Anguish, or Poison
Place of Death and Burial Site: Edirne – he was buried in the tomb of his mother Hadice Turhan Sultan near the Yeni (New) Mosque in Istanbul
Male Heirs: Ahmed III, Mustafa II, Bayezid, İbrahim, and Süleyman
Female Heir: Hadice Sultan, Fatma Sultan, and Ümmi Sultan

Mehmed IV became the new sultan in his seventh year, an exceptionally early age to assume the throne, thanks to the support of his grandmother Kösem Sultan, the statesmen, and the Janissaries, after his father Sultan İbrahim was dethroned on August 8, 1648. As the youngest sultan in the Ottoman history, Mehmed IV was certainly not capable of ruling the Empire; those who had brought him to the throne would inevitably exerci-

Miniature of Sultan Mehmed IV by Levni in his *Kebir Musavver Silsilenâme* (The Great Envisaged Portraiture Geneology)

se their authority to the utmost extent. Thus the first eight years of his reign brought with it the power struggles of his grandmother, mother, and their supporters.

Initially, the Empire was in complete flux: his father was executed, his grandmother Kösem Sultan entered into a bitter battle against Grand Vizier Sofu Mehmed Pasha, the salaries of the cavalry units were not paid in due time, and the Janissaries became politicized, gaining far more influence. Consequently, "The Incident of the Sultan Ahmed Mosque" erupted as the first revolt during Mehmed IV's reign on October 25, 1648. The chiefs of the Janissaries successfully quelled the revolt; however, their role in dealing with the revolt caused them to gain greater influence in state matters.

When the revolts mushroomed in Istanbul and Anatolia, the Venetian blockade of the strait of the Dardanelles continued, and the discontent in association with the unruly Janissaries spread in the imperial capital. Furthermore, inflation rose when the Janissary chiefs kept for themselves the true-value *akçe*s (the Ottoman monetary unit of silver-coins) and paid the soldiers their salaries with lower-scale silver *akçe*s. The child sultan was kept out of state affairs. To amuse and distract him from administration, Sultan Mehmed IV had frequently been taken on hunting parties in Kağıthane, which is located along a stream that runs into the Golden Horn and the Gülhane Park near the palace. Hunting soon turned into his favorite hobby and would be his addiction later on, earning him the nickname "the Hunter."

The *Büyük Valide* (Grand Mother) Kösem Sultan had assigned her followers to key administrative positions. Such arbitrary staffing paved the way for odd complications; eventually, the Ottoman palace became the stage of an ongoing struggle between a daughter-in-law and a mother-in-law. The *Küçük Valide* (Minor-Mother) Turhan Sultan eliminated her mother-in-law Kösem Sultan with the help of the palace chiefs. Thus Kösem Sultan failed to carry out her plan to replace Sultan Mehmed IV with Süleyman II mainly because she thought that she could better manipulate Süleyman's mother, who was apparently more naïve than Mehmed IV's mother Turhan

Sultan. Hadice Turhan Sultan played a profound role in state administration for five successive years. During this period, Tarhuncu Ahmed Pasha was promoted to Grand Vizier on 1652 with his condition that no one could oppose his authority in financial matters. Tarhuncu Ahmed Pasha attempted to balance income and expenditures with strict regulations; however, he fell into contempt and was soon discharged shortly after he levied taxes on government officials and proposed a list of spending-cuts for the palace.

In addition to the continuous replacement of grand viziers, a revolt emerged in reaction to the fact that the Janissary salaries were paid with lower-scale silver *akçe*s funded by the administration's borrowings. The rebels crowded in the Sultan Ahmed Square, invited the sultan out to the First Courtyard of the Topkapı Palace to hold a *fait accompli* emergency, impromptu meeting with him. In the meeting, they requested that Sultan Mehmed IV deliver thirty palace chiefs to them. The young sultan initially rejected this request; however, the unremitting pressures compelled him to yield, so he ordered the execution of the chiefs whom the rebels had requested on March 4, 1656.

A change of grand viziers in 1656 soon proved to be a marvelous occasion to Sultan Mehmed IV's credit. This change translated into fundamental innovations in government affairs. The new grand vizier Köprülü Mehmed, whose preconditions to assume his new post had been accepted by Valide Turhan Sultan, inaugurated what comes to be known as the Köprülü Era, the period of grand viziers from the Köprülü family. Köprülü Mehmed Pasha completed what was missing in Mehmed IV because of his very young age: competence and experience in administration. Köprülü Mehmed Pasha first thwarted a collective effort for a rebellion; in general, he directed his full force toward the rejuvenation of the empire.

Köprülü Mehmed Pasha quelled several revolts and effectively forced the Venetians to remove their blockade on the Dardanelles. His son Fazıl Ahmed Pasha succeeded him in accordance with Mehmed Pasha's deathbed recommendation. With this, the grand vizierate pursued a lineal succession for the first time in Ottoman history. During the grand vizierate of Köprülüzade Fazıl Ahmed Pasha, the Ottoman Empire accomplished many achievements and victories, reminiscent of glorious preceding centuries historians conventionally call the Rise of the Ottoman Empire. Particularly speaking, the Ottomans defeated Venice and France on the sea, and their army crushed Austrian and Polish forces at war. They conquered the Fortress of Uyvar (now Nové Zámky) on the Nitra River in 1664. Furthermore, the Tre-

The Yeni (New) Mosque on the shore of Eminönü has a beautiful view of the Golden Horn and the Bosphorus.

The golden chest for
the Mantle of the Prophet

aty of Vasvár was signed with Austria, who was obliged not only to pay war reparations but also to recognize the Ottoman suzerainty of Transylvania. The treaty also stipulated that the fortresses of Uyvar and Nógrád belonged to the Ottoman Empire. Köprülüzade Fazıl Ahmed Pasha also successfully ended the siege of Crete by capturing Candia in 1669.

While the sultan's young vizier Fazıl Ahmed Pasha was on the campaign to Candia, Sultan Mehmed IV remained in the Morea and marched a campaign to Kamianets, Podolia against the Kingdom of Poland in the presence of a magnificent cortege in 1672. During the siege, which proved too difficult due to drenching rains, the sultan did something quite extraordinary in terms of Ottoman imperial customs. He dressed *incognito* in a regular soldier uniform and participated in the assault. As a result of the conquest, which the young sultan and the young grand vizier collaboratively achieved, the Treaty of Buchach was signed and the lands of Buchach and Podolia were incorporated into the Ottoman territory.

Three years later, the Polish Monarch John Sobieski (John III) declared war on the Ottoman Empire; in response, Sultan Mehmed IV mobilized his army but suspended the march before confronting the enemy in face of the coming winter. The following year, the Ottoman forces marched back, defeated the Poles, and renewed the Treaty of Buchach. Fazıl Ahmed Pasha had discontinued the march, along with the sultan, on account of his worsening illness. Finally, he met his destiny, leaving the sultan in grief. The sultan replaced late Fazıl Ahmed Pasha with Merzifonlu Kara Mustafa Pasha, another member of the Köprülü family.

The first of the Ottoman-Russian wars was fought around this time as well mainly because of the Dnieper Cossacks. Following two campaigns, the Ottoman Empire concluded a treaty with the Russians that would last for twenty years. Sultan Mehmed IV, in fact, was complying to an extent with the aggressive foreign policies of Merzifonlu Kara Mustafa Pasha.

Merzifonlu Kara Mustafa Pasha countered France on the issues concerning the province of Trablusgarp (modern day Libya). He overreacted to the French bombardment of the Chios Island in the Aegean Sea off the west coast of Anatolia and pressured the French to pay war reparations.

Inner domes of the Yeni (New) Mosque in Eminönü, Istanbul

Catholic Austria, meanwhile, had begun to exert political and religious pressure on the Protestant Hungarians, who had allegiance to the Ottoman sovereignty. Although Köprülüzade Fazıl Ahmed Pasha previously denied the Transylvanian prince's request for assistance on account of the Treaty of Vasvár with Austria, Merzifonlu Kara Mustafa Pasha now accepted the Hungarian's appeal for help. A number of statesmen opposed the idea; nevertheless, Merzifonlu Kara Mustafa Pasha persuaded the sultan and marched a campaign on Austria. In 1682, Sultan Mehmed IV attended the campaign too and went as far as Belgrade. Merzifonlu Kara Mustafa Pasha besieged Vienna a second time after Süleyman the Magnificent in 1683.

Reinforced by the troops of Transylvania, Wallachia, Moldavia, and Crimea, the Ottoman army fought exceptionally well. The Austrian Emperor then called the crusaders for support. Encouraged by the Pope, the Habsburgs, French, and Poles came to rescue Vienna. During the two-month siege, Murad Giray Khan of Crimea did not stop the Polish army led by John Sobieski on its way to Vienna through the Danube, exactly when the fall of Vienna was only a matter of time. Now that the Ottoman army was surrounded by the Polish forces, the army stood between two fires. Amidst this unexpected turn of events, Mustafa Pasha withdrew his forces back to Belgrade successfully enough to avoid major casualties and devised the strategy of another attack. Back home, several statesmen became jealous of Merzifonlu Kara Mustafa Pasha's growing reputation. They coveted his position as grand vizier and thus successfully provoked and brainwashed Sultan Mehmed IV with delusive advice to get rid of the grand vizier. Eventually, Merzifonlu Kara Mustafa Pasha's death warrant was sent to him. Despite being hundreds of miles away from the capital and the commander-in-chief of a powerful Ottoman army, Merzifonlu Kara Mustafa Pasha submitted, performed his last two *rak'at*s (cycles) of prayer, and requested the executive order carried out in a surprisingly faithful way. The failure at the second siege of Vienna became a turning point in Ottoman history; indeed, it precipitated a streak of successive defeats, which suggests that the course of ensuing events could have transpired entirely differently if Merzifonlu had been given another chance.

The Ottoman failure at Vienna also had broader ramifications: it inspired and energized the crusaders with the idea that they could drive the Ottomans out of Central Europe. Encouraged and led by the Pope, Austria, Poland, Russia, Venice, and Malta set up a "holy alliance." Although the Ottoman army initially defeated the Polish, the Austrian army advanced along the Danube and attacked Transylvania and Hungary. Esztergom and Belgrade fell;

The Ka'ba standing in the courtyard of the Grand Mosque and its vicinity in around 1910

Interior of the Tomb of Valide Hadice Turhan Sultan by Ouannin, in Turquie Paris, 1853. What makes this tomb special is that it is the only place where as many as five sultan tombs are found together. The sarcophaguses of Sultan Mehmed IV, his mother Valide Hadice Turhan Sultan, his sons Sultan Mustafa II and Sultan Ahmed III as well as his grandsons Sultan Mahmud I and Sultan Osman III are all in this tomb in the garden of the Yeni (New) Mosque, Istanbul.

195

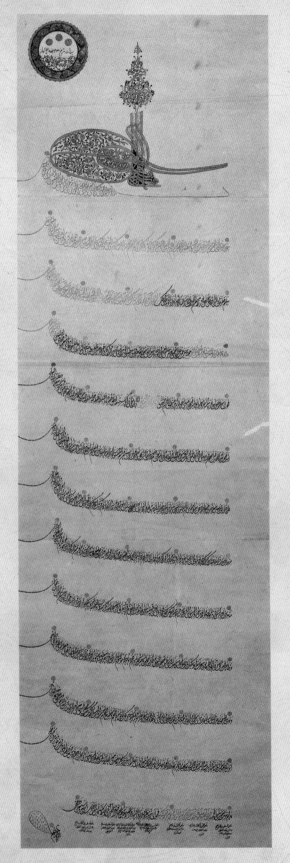

unfortunately, the Muslim residents of Buda were massacred extensively after the city had been lost. In other theaters of war, the Polish forces captured Podolia and infiltrated Moldavia, and the Venetians attacked the shores of the Morea and Dalmatia with Spanish and Maltese support. Eventually, the Morea split off, and then Athens passed into Venetian hands.

A losing series brought about a wave of indignation in the Ottoman society. Rumors spread that "the sultan occupied himself with hunting parties rather than taking care of the state." The Ottoman army, which suffered a crushing defeat in Mohács, revolted up to the grand vizier and began to move toward Istanbul, using unpaid salaries as an excuse to revolt. Their primary intent was to dethrone Sultan Mehmed IV. While the Ottoman army was marching toward Istanbul, its very own capital, the Austrians captured, with relative ease, the lands that the Ottomans had conquered under hardships and diligence. Still nothing changed even when Sultan Mehmed IV proved to the soldiers, who reached Istanbul, that the grand vizier had already been replaced and that he swore not to go hunting again. They secured an executive *fatwa* that authorized the soldiers to dethrone Mehmed IV for overly amusing himself with hunting parties and impeding state affairs. Süleyman II succeeded him in 1687. Mehmed IV, now the ex-sultan, was confined in *Şimşirlik*, or the Boxwood section of the Topkapı Palace, until he was carried away to Edirne, his favorite city. By this time, Sultan Süleyman II had set out on a campaign to Hungary. Mehmed IV, who would also live through the reign of Ahmed II, his other brother, passed away in Edirne as the first sultan after Süleyman the Magnificent to die outside of Istanbul.

Sultan Mehmed IV's edict on the land grants in some of the villages under the jurisdiction of the district of Negropont that have been deeded to the mosque erected by the Mother Sultan in Bahçekapı, Istanbul.

Sultan Mehmed IV had become a sultan at a very young age, and so he was unable to receive a thorough education as a young *şehzade*. In fact, it seems that his tutors raised him as a hunter, not as a sultan. Those who had been struggling for power in the palace kept him strictly within the confines of the palace. The appointments of competent grand viziers from the Köprülü family contributed to reviving the empire in many ways. It was after the death of his mother Turhan Sultan and the dissociation of the Köprülüs from administration that the sultan showed his ineptitudes in governing. Although his sons had inalienable rights to the throne, he spared his brothers; in this way, he paved the way for their rise to the throne after he had been dethroned.

Mehmed IV was very kindhearted and generous. He led quite a regular life of simplicity though he had all the means to lead a lavish lifestyle as the sultan of a superpower. Sultan Mehmed IV was very enthusiastic about history and patronized the arts. It was during his long reign that the celebrated Evliya Çelebi (1611–1682) penned his renowned *Seyahatname* (Travelogue) in ten volumes, describing his travels that started in his native city of Istanbul and covered Anatolia, Caucasia, Middle East, Egypt in North Africa, Rumelia, Central, Eastern, and Northern Europe up to the Baltic Sea. It was again during his reign that the renowned Turkish classical music composer Buhurizade Mustafa Itri (d.1712) composed many masterpieces of religious musical compositions in various *makam*s,[31] including the *takbiru't-tashriq*,[32] which is still popular in Turkey to this day. As sultan, Mehmed IV undertook substantial renovations in Mecca and its environs, especially the water system of the Arafat valley[33] in an effort to comfort the pilgrims.

Protective case for the Qur'an, early 17th century

197

The Twentieth Ottoman Sultan

Sultan Süleyman II

Reign: 1687–1691

Father's Name: Sultan İbrahim
Mother's Name: Saliha Dilaşub Sultan
Place and Date of Birth: Istanbul, April 15, 1642
Age at Accession to the Throne: 45
Cause and Date of Death: Edema, June 22, 1691
Place of Death and Burial Site: Edirne – he was buried in the Tomb of Sultan Süleyman the Magnificent in Istanbul

Süleyman II ascended to the throne when the Janissaries revolted in 1687 and dethroned Sultan Mehmed IV, his two-years-older brother. Several revolts broke out during the first few days of his reign in the Aksaray and Sultan Ahmed squares of the Ot-

Miniature of Sultan Süleyman II by Levni in his *Kebir Musavver Silsilenâme* (The Great Envisaged Portraiture Geneology)

toman capital. The newly enthroned sultan even had to melt down silver objects found in the palace in order to raise sufficient funds to pay the Janissaries the *cülüs* (accession) gratuities. Janissary mutinies became the norm in Istanbul during his time.

Sultan Süleyman II continued the wars with the Polish Kingdom, Venice, and Austria; furthermore, the Ottomans went to war with Russia. Believing that leading his army in person as commander would make a difference in view of soldiers and the public, Sultan Süleyman II attended the campaign to Hungary. However, he could not go any further than Sofia, for he had been terribly sick. When the news of defeat reached him, he returned to Edirne.

Following the failure at the siege of Vienna during his brother's reign, Austrians had captured the forts of Esztergom, Buda, and Belgrade. Sultan Süleyman II replaced Grand Vizier Bekir Mustafa Pasha, whose negligence added to the failures in 1689, with Fazıl Mustafa Pasha of the Köprülü family.

In conformity with the legacy of his father and older brother, Fazıl Mustafa Pasha restored order in administrative affairs, improved the economy, and fortified the imperial army. Sultan Süleyman II then dispatched his thriving grand vizier Fazıl Mustafa Pasha to a campaign on Austria in 1690. Fazıl Mustafa Pasha first reclaimed the Fort of Niš, and then he subsequently reconquered the fortresses of Vidin, Smederevo, and Belgrade from the Austrians. On the way back, Sultan Süleyman II greeted him with tears of joy in Davutpaşa Sahrası, an important station in Istanbul from which the Ottoman army set out on their campaigns to Europe. He took off his cloak and gave it and his personal dagger to Fazıl Mustafa Pasha.

The following year, Sultan Süleyman II, in an ever-worsening state of health, sent Grand Vizier Köprülü Fazıl Mustafa Pasha from Edirne on another campaign. The sultan had suffered from edema for a long time, and his body was exposed to extensive swelling. The sultan eventually passed away on June 22, 1691.

Topkapı Palace, by Loos, 1710

Ceiling decorations of the School of Şehzades, the Topkapı Palace Museum

Sultan Süleyman II was gentle, calm, and a devout Muslim. He had a weak constitution mainly because he was held in confinement in the Şimşirlik section of the palace for long years during his *şehzade* years. The sultan was masterful in the art of calligraphy; it was during his reign that the Turkish master calligrapher Hafız Osman Efendi (1642–1698), considered the greatest 17th century calligrapher of the Ottoman style, penned splendid Qur'an manuscripts, especially in the *nesih* script—the highly legible script of choice for the Qur'an.

Like his namesake Süleyman the Magnificent, Süleyman II took special care of the holy cities of Mecca and Medina; in particular, he increased the portion of the imperial budget allocated to these cities from 0.12 percent to a high of 2 percent, which along with other such acts showed the great value he attributed to them.

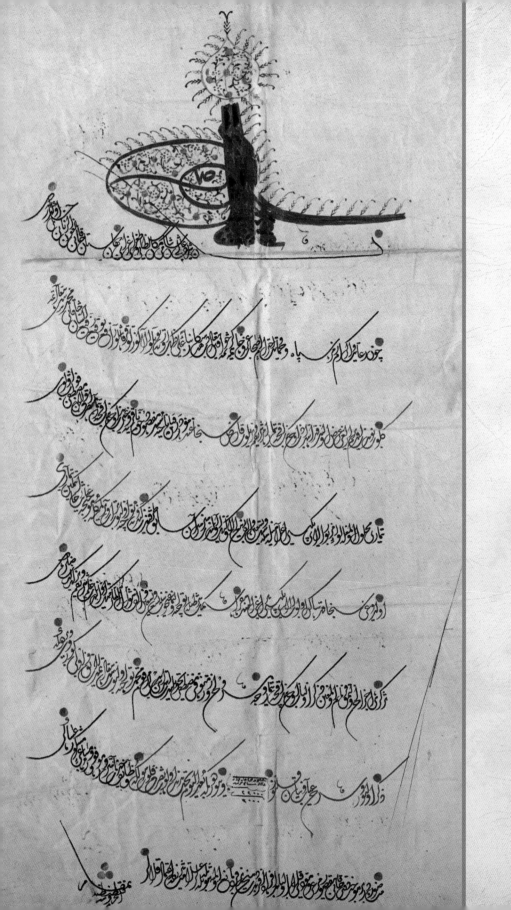

Sultan Süleyman II's edict on the
distribution of fiefs (*tımar*) dated 1688,
from the Prime Ministry Ottoman Archives'
Imperial Edicts

Sultan Ahmed II

Reign: 1691—1695

Father's Name: Sultan İbrahim
Mother's Name: Muazzez Valide Sultan
Place and Date of Birth: Istanbul, February 25, 1643
Age at Accession to the Throne: 49
Cause and Date of Death: Edema, February 6, 1695
Place of Death and Burial Site: Edirne – he was buried in the Tomb of Sultan Süleyman the Magnificent in Istanbul
Male Heirs: İbrahim and Selim
Female Heir: Atike Sultan, Hadice Sultan, and Asiye Sultan

By the time Ahmed II succeeded his older brother to the throne, Grand Vizier Köprülü Fazıl Mustafa Pasha had been commanding the Ottoman army in a campaign against Austria. The new sultan kept the grand vizier at his post; however, Köprülü Fazıl Mustafa Pasha died a martyr in Slankamen when the Austrian army was on the verge of being defeated. The grand vizier's death caused his army to disband and suffer a crushing defeat in 1691.

Miniature of Sultan Ahmed II by Levni in his *Kebir Musavver Silsilenâme* (The Great Envisaged Portraiture Geneology)

After the Ottoman defeat in Slankamen, Austria captured all the Ottoman lands in Hungary except Timişoara in 1693. Meanwhile, Venice captured the Morea and besieged the city of Hania in the Crete Island; nevertheless the Ottoman forces there effectively defended the city.

Recruitment needs had increased in the Ottoman army because of the campaigns to Austria and Poland. The number of guardians had dwindled in the islands except for Crete. Venice, which recently failed in Hania, leagued with the Papacy and Malta and invaded the Aegean island of Chios in 1694. Distressed by the bad news from the field, Sultan Ahmed II ordered his army to do whatever it would take to capture the island. Poland captured the Castle of Varad in Oradea; however, the Poles were pushed back by the Ottoman army shortly after they stormed in Kamianets, Podolia. On February 6, 1695, Sultan Ahmed II died in Edirne on account of edema; like his older brother Sultan Süleyman II, he was fifty-two years old when edema took his life. The body of the deceased Sultan was brought to Istanbul and buried in the Tomb of Sultan Süleyman the Magnificent, his namesake and great grandfather.

Sultan Ahmed II was emotional and tough in nature. Ahmed II was also interested in calligraphy and poetry as well as music. His orders were reflective of the fact that he always gave priority to the rights of his subject people. The number of meetings for the *Divan*, or the Imperial Council, increased from two to four per week, like during the reign of Sultan Süleyman the Magnificent. Moreover, Sultan Ahmed II made himself accustomed to observing the council's discussions directly. Ahmed II did not give up attending the meetings even when his health deteriorated. He particularly aimed to protect his subjects' rights and avoid revenue losses.

Sultan Ahmed II undertook a number of reparations in Mecca and Medina, and provided maintenance for the waterways and pools for storing drinking water on the plain of Arafat.

The Imperial Hall, Topkapı Palace. This spacious hall was used for miscellaneous purposes such as ceremonies for exchanging greetings on religious festive days, spiritual lessons, weddings, and accepting guests. The canopied sofa is in the middle and the *sedir*s (fixed window seats) are along the windows.

The Twenty-second Ottoman Sultan

Sultan Mustafa II

Reign: 1695—1703

Honorifics and Aliases: *Gazi*, *İkbali*, and *Meftuni*
Father's Name: Sultan Mehmed IV
Mother's Name: Rabia Gülnuş Emetullah Valide Sultan
Place and Date of Birth: Edirne, June 2, 1664
Age at Accession to the Throne: 31
Cause and Date of Death: Edema, December 29, 1703
Place of Death and Burial Site: Istanbul – he was buried in the
Tomb of Hadice Turhan Valide Sultan near the Yeni (New) Mosque, Istanbul
Male Heirs: Mahmud I, Osman III, Mahmud Mehmed, Selim, Murad, Hasan,
Hüseyin, Süleyman, and Ahmed
Female Heirs: Ayşe Sultan, Emine Sultan, Safiye Sultan, and Emetullah Sultan

Sultan Mustafa II ascended to the throne, succeeding his paternal uncle Sultan Ahmed II. Meanwhile, the crusaders had been massively attacking the Ottomans on several fronts since the failed siege of Vienna. Mustafa II tried to assume *de facto* control of the state in the face of the continuous power struggle waged by many different factions within the government. The sultan replaced the high-ranking officials with the new ones he trusted most, reflec-

Miniature of Sultan Mustafa II by Levni in his *Kebir Musavver Silsilenâme* (The Great Envisaged Portraiture Geneology)

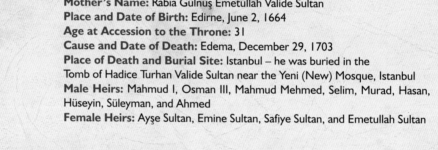

 tive of his vision of a strong and coordinated central state, and of his desire to fulfill the objectives he set during his *şehzade* years.

The Ottoman navy defeated Venice, supported by the Papacy and the Morea, and eventually recaptured the Chios Island, which had been invaded by Venetians during the reign of his uncle Ahmed II. This early victory was interpreted as a sign of future successes; jubilations were held and accession gratuities bestowed. In addition, the victorious incursions into the Polish lands of the Shahbaz Giray, the Khan of the Crimean Tatars who fought in the name of the Ottomans, inspired and motivated the sultan.

Sultan Mustafa II wanted to lead the campaigns in person like many other preceding sultans. He further declared, "God Almighty has bestowed upon me the caliphate, for this reason, I am obliged to refrain from any sort of comfort and amusement." In his opinion, it was the sultans' indulgence in joy and amusement and their negligence in state affairs that had caused successive defeats. Mustafa II intended to occupy himself with *gaza*s; with the help of God, the Ottomans would reclaim Muslim lands that had been captured by the European powers and reconquer the lands lost to them.

An admirer of Sultan Süleyman the Magnificent, Sultan Mustafa II revealed to the statesmen his intention to directly command the army. The statesmen, including the grand vizier, opposed the idea and recommended that the sultan stay in Edirne, for his involvement in a campaign would dearly cost the imperial treasury. Sultan Mustafa II replied that he would spend like a regular soldier, eat and drink like them, and no extra funding had to be allocated for him. Finally, he put his armor on, girded his sword, mounted on his horse, and marched on Austria on June 30, 1695. The Ottoman troops banded together in Timişoara and Belgrade and conquered Lippa first. The sultan took command of the army when they confronted the Austrian forces in the forest region of Buldur. Reinforced by the Crimean forces and inspi-

View of the Bosphorus from the Justice Tower of the Topkapı Palace

red by the sultan, the Ottoman army crushed the Austrian forces; however the deaths of the governor generals of Anatolia and Rumelia, Şahin Mehmed and Mahmud pashas, during the war dejected the sultan, who reputedly expressed his sorrow: "That I have seen the victory in Buldur, but at the enormous cost of losing my beloved Şahin and Mahmud."

A score of fierce battles were fought between the Ottomans and Russians as a result of the Russian participation in the "Holy League" and subsequent surrounding of the Fort of Azov, part of their ultimate objective of reaching into the Black Sea region. Tsar Peter I of Russia besieged Azov both in the land and on the river, and the Ottomans could no longer defend the fort. The city fell on August 6, 1696. The fall of Azov caused tremendous sorrow among the public and the palace circles; in response, the sultan ordered a set of instructions to reclaim it. Meanwhile, the victories of the chief commander of the Ottoman navy, *Kaptan-ı Derya* (Captain of the Sea) Mezemorta Hüseyin Pasha in the Morea and the Aegean Sea against the Venetians boosted the morale, albeit partially.

No sooner than returning from Edirne to Istanbul did Sultan Mustafa II launch preparations for a second campaign; oddly enough, the sultan requested the statesmen of means to recruit soldiers and pay their expenditures. For the first time in Ottoman history, even the *Bostancı*s that were responsible for the security of the Ottoman capital and the palace were drafted into service. Before proceeding from Belgrade for his second campaign towards Austria in the month of Ramadan, 1696, the sultan opened the golden chest that held the Mantle of the Prophet before his imperial war council and ardently implored God to bestow upon them a victory comparable to the Victory of Mohács during the reign of Sultan Süleyman the Magnificent. The course of the Ottoman campaign changed following the siege of Timişoara by the Austrians. On August 27, 1696, the Ottomans won a remarkable victory at a pitched battle, an answer to the sultan's prayers. The same year the Ottomans won their battles against the Venetians.

Austria remained between two fires, for it had to fight against both the Ottomans and French; thus, they offered peace to the Ottomans. Sultan Mustafa II had won two consecutive victories against the Austrians and expected more coming. For this reason, he postponed their offer, waiting for a more profitable one. The next year, the sultan marched his third and last campaign. Once more, he assembled his war council in Belgrade and discussed the plans and details of the attack. Two notable proposals emerged in the council meeting concerning the campaign route: whereas Amcazade Hüseyin Pasha recommended marching to the northwest towards Petrovaradin, many other statesmen suggested Timişoara as the ideal target. As a result, the sultan sanctioned the rule of majority and ordered his army to head to the northeast toward Timişoara.

The choice of Timişoara indeed led the Ottomans to a lot of problems: instead of Petrovaradin, which is near Belgrade, the army headed from Belgrade toward the further Timişoara on whose route there were many rivers and marsh lands, requiring plank ways to be erected in order to cross. The Ottoman army tried to ford the river Tisza when they arrived in Zenta, but the Austrian army, informed of the Ottoman battle-plans, attacked the Ottoman army in an unexpected and swift way. When the troops that had already crossed the bridge could not offer any help, the remainder of the army panicked and routed, and Grand Vizier Elmas Mehmed Pasha died a martyr. Extremely upset with this debacle, Sultan Mustafa II took the army to Timişoara. In the aftermath of their victory at the Battle of Zenta, the Austrian forces advanced as far as Sarajevo; they

Short-sleeved royal caftan,
Topkapı Palace

burned and inflicted extensive damage on the cities they passed through.

The defeat at Zenta had a profound influence on Sultan Mustafa II. He was well aware of the fact that it was he who had to offer peace to the enemy; however, he thought that it would be too insulting for an Ottoman sultan to do so. The sultan then decided to continue the battle; however, statesmen including Grand Vizier Amcazade Hüseyin Pasha advocated for an end to the series of simultaneously-fought, time- and resource-consuming battles.

The wars against Austria, Poland, Venice, and Russia took a downturn during the reign of Sultan Mustafa II. To end all wars, the British and Dutch ambassadors stepped in. In 1699 the Treaty of Karlowitz was signed in Karlowitz near Belgrade and concluded the Ottoman war series that had lasted for sixteen years. This treaty marked the beginning of the steady loss of the Ottoman territories. In particular, all Hungarian lands but Timişoara were given to Austria, the Morea and part of Dalmatia to Venice, and Podolia to Poland. Russia took the Fort of Azov with the Treaty of Istanbul a year after in 1700.

The ongoing, multi-front battles undermined the economic and social structures of the Ottoman Empire to a large extent. In particular, new taxes were levied and old ones increased in association with enormous war expenditures paid directly from the imperial treasury. In the spirit of finding financial resources for wars, Sultan Mustafa II further confiscated the properties of the wealthy and introduced the collection of state revenues earlier than they were due. Since the systems of imperial military recruitments, both for the regular and cavalry corps, had degenerated, Mustafa II inducted a number of soldiers among his subject peoples; however, these temporarily enlisted troops, similar to mercenary units, would later cause severe security crises once they left the army and returned home.

In reaction to the growing bandit movements in Anatolia and Rumelia, Sultan Mustafa II appointed new local governors and abolished the Sarıca and Sekban troops, which were irregular troops of musketeers in the provinces. The sultan either sent military forces against or made concessions with the rebels who revolted in provinces away from the center.

Calligraphy exhibition held at the Imperial Stables of the palace during the early years the Topkapı Palace Museum

Buda •   Debrecen

Vasvár •

Hungary

Zagreb •

Brașov •

Karlowitz •   Timișoara •

P o d o

Sarajevo •   Belgrade •

Bucharesi

Bosnia
Herzegovina •

Passarowitz •

Dalmatia

R U M E L I A

Niš •

Nikopol •

Sil

Mostar •

O

Sofia •

Tarnovo •

Ragusa

Plovdiv •

Bu

Shkodra •

T

Skopje •

O

M

E

Kavala •

A

Ohrid •

Salonica •

Enez

Vlorë •

Ioannina •

Otranto

Trikala •

AEGEAN
SEA

Naupactus •

Kefalonia

Morea

Athens •

Kalamata •

Territories lost after the treaties of
Karlowitz (1699) and Istanbul (1700)

Territory ceded to Austria

Territory ceded to Kingdom of Poland

Territory ceded to Venice

Territory ceded to Russia

MEDITERRANEAN SEA

Crete

Territorial losses by the treaties of
Karlowitz (1699) and Istanbul (1700)

Dniester

Özü

Bender

Akkerman

Kilia

Azov

SEA OF AZOV

Crimea

Bakhchisaray

Kerch

Kaffa

Anapa

Kuban

rna

BLACK SEA

Sukhumi

Sinop

Amasra

Kastamonu

İstanbul

İzmit

Bolu

E M P I R E

Giresun

Trabzon

Bursa

sir

Sivas

Kütahya

Ankara

R E

ANATOLIA

Alaşehir

Bitlis

Konya

Muğla

Antalya

İskenderun

N

W   E

S

SCALE

0   150   300 miles

Pieces from the Prophet's standard (which has disintegrated to small pieces over time) as well as Qur'anic verses along with the names of the ten Companions of the Prophet who are promised Paradise are embroidered on this green satin standard, called Sancak-ı Şerif. Sultan Mahmud II was the last Ottoman sultan to take the Sancak-ı Şerif on military campaign.

Although the sultan exerted a good deal of pressure on state officials to reform the military, administration, and finance, as well as reinvigorating in particular the Janissaries and the Sipahi corps, all attempts to fulfill his objectives would come to no avail.

The first golden coins stamped with the *tughra* (calligraphic seal or signature) of an Ottoman sultan were also minted during Mustafa II's reign, providing a yardstick for distinguishing the real-valued coins from lower-scaled ones, especially after the merchants had collected large amounts of real-valued golden coins from the Istanbul market and put them on the market in the provinces, particularly in Egypt.

The period of peace following the Treaty of Karlowitz seems to stabilize and improve the Ottoman imperial budget; furthermore, a wide array of changes was introduced. For instance, emergency taxes were removed and imperial edicts were posted to the local administrations not to impose new taxes on the subjects. Sultan Mustafa II retired to himself though; he disassociated himself from state affairs and chose to live in Edirne. His self-isolation invited numerous criticisms from scholars, soldiers, and the public, and rumors spread that he was now following in the footsteps of his father, channeling his interest to hunting. The ensuing period of peace notwithstanding, the criticisms, coupled now with reactions to the lost wars and lands, gave rise to a revolt, which came to be called the Edirne Incident. The revolt first targeted Grand Judge Seyyid Feyzullah Efendi, the sultan's tutor and advisor; however, it grew in a short time into a revolt against the sultan himself. The rebels took over Istanbul, and then marched to Edirne to replace the sultan. A *fatwa* was issued in their favor, and they led Şehzade Ahmed to the throne. It was the efforts of Ahmed Pasha and Second Vizier Hasan Pasha that avoided a head-on clash between the troops in Edirne and those in Istanbul.

Sultan Mustafa II lost his forces when his army in Edirne joined the troops that arrived from Istanbul. Mustafa II went to meet his brother Ahmed III and said, "My brother, our sub-

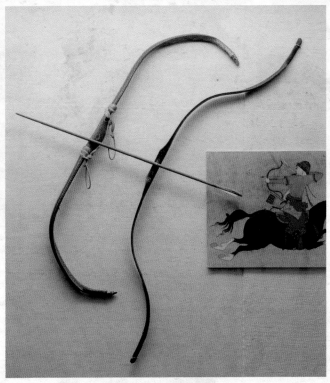

Ottoman bows and arrows displayed in the weapons exhibition at the Former Treasury Office, Topkapı Palace

Rabia Gülnuş Valide Sultan
(1647–1715)

216

ject people want to see you as the sultan." Mustafa gave up the throne willingly and strongly recommended Ahmed to certainly punish the rebels for they would attempt to dethrone him as well, sooner or later. Four years after relinquishing the throne, Mustafa II died of edema on December 29, 1703.

Sultan Mustafa II was the last sultan to command the Ottoman army on the battlefield. On the third day of reign, Mustafa II said, "I am obliged to refrain from any comfort and amusement." Until the defeat at Zenta in 1697, the sultan was enthusiastic about engaging *gaza*s; however, this crushing defeat destroyed his philosophy and compelled him to isolate himself and take to hunting as his father used to do quite often. Indeed, he spent greater number of his days in Edirne, for the campaigns to Europe began there.

Under the pseudonyms *İkbali* and *Meftuni*, Sultan Mustafa II wrote many poems and religious hymns, some of which would later be composed. Mustafa II was an accomplished calligrapher, tutored by Hafız Osman and Hocazade Mehmed Enveri—the celebrated calligraphers of his reign. Along with his finesse with arrow-shooting and javelin-throwing, the chronicles reported that the sultan was stronger, more mature and balanced than his predecessors.

Sultan Mustafa II took good care of the holy cities even during the years-long battles against Austria and continued to send regularly both financial and military help to the region. He began a comprehensive renovation in the two Holy Sanctuaries in Mecca and Medina. For instance, the columns that supported the ceiling of the Ka'ba as well as the worn-out gold frame around the blessed *Hajaru'l-aswad* in the southeast corner of the Ka'ba were meticulously renewed. Mustafa II also constructed a dome on four massive pillars right at the *Mabraku'n-naqa*—the famous spot in Quba on the outskirts of Medina where the Prophet built the first mosque in Islam—and donated a 400-carat emerald for the support of the *Rawda* area of the Prophet's Mosque between the Prophet's grave and pulpit. During the reign of Mustafa II, the Ottoman engineers and craftsmen worked to fix the wells, dykes, and waterways on the route from Damascus to Medina, drilled many more wells, and renovated the water works of Mecca, all of which were primarily undertaken for the good of the pilgrims.

Sultan Mustafa II ordered Fındıklılı Silahdar Mehmed Ağa to write a book on the political and military events of his time and even suggested the table of contents. Eventually Mehmed Ağa published his great work titled *Nusretname*. Most of sultan's sons passed away when he was alive, but Mahmud I and Osman III, two of his surviving sons, rose later to the throne.

Following pages: Tableau of the Imperial Gifts Caravan to the Haramayn by Stefano Ussi, the Dolmabahçe Palace, Istanbul

The Twenty-third Ottoman Sultan

Sultan Ahmed III

Reign: 1703–1730

Honorifics and Aliases: *Necib* [Sublime, of gentle birth]
Father's Name: Sultan Mehmed IV
Mother's Name: Rabia Gülnuş Emetullah Valide Sultan
Place and Date of Birth: Hacıoğlupazarı, Dobrudja; December 31, 1673
Age at Accession to the Throne: 30
Cause and Date of Death: June 24, 1736
Place of Death and Burial Site: Istanbul – he was buried in the Tomb of Hadice Turhan Valide Sultan near the Yeni (New) Mosque, Istanbul
Male Heirs: Abdülhamid I, Mustafa III, Süleyman, Bayezid, Mehmed, İbrahim, Numan, Selim, Ali, İsa, Murad, Seyfeddin, Abdülmecid, and Abdülmelik
Female Heir: Emine, Rabia, Habibe, Zeyneb, Zübeyde, Esma, Hadice, Rukiye, Saliha, Atike, Reyhan, Esime, Ferdane, Nazife, Naile, Ayşe, Fatma, Emetullah, Ümmüselma, Emine, Rukiye, Zeyneb, and Sabiha

Şehzade Ahmed was first confined to the Topkapı Palace and then transferred to Edirne during the reign of his paternal uncle Sultan Süleyman II. When the Edirne Incident transpired, he succeeded Mustafa II to the throne on August 17, 1703. Although he initially paid lip service to those who took him to the throne and appointed them to temporary positions, he eventually followed his brother's advice and dodged their sway by removing them from office one after another.

Sultan Ahmed III stayed neutral to the Russo-Swedish wars, which resulted from the matters con-

Detail from the miniature of Sultan Ahmed III seated on throne by Levni in his *Kebir Musavver Silsilenâme* (The Great Envisaged Portraiture Geneology)

cerning the status of the Polish Kingdom in Europe. However, Ottoman-Russian relations severed after when Charles XII of Sweden, also known as Charles the Habitué, took refuge with the Ottomans after his defeat by Tsar Peter I of Russia. Grand Vizier Çorlulu Ali Pasha had not informed the sultan of Charles' admission. In an act that breached the Treaty of Istanbul that had ended the Russo-Ottoman War in 1700, Peter I of Russia attacked the Ottoman lands in 1710; consequently, Sultan Ahmed III declared war against Russia. The Ottoman army commanded by Grand Vizier Baltacı Mehmed Pasha crushingly defeated the Russian army led by the Tsar Peter I near the Prut River. Huddled in the quagmires of Prut, the Russians offered a truce. Baltacı Mehmed Pasha could not rely on his Janissary corps to keep fighting, so he accepted Russia's offer and signed the Treaty of Prut in 1711. As a matter of fact, it was very likely that Mehmed Pasha would have signed a treaty with far better terms and conditions if he had not accepted truce right away and instead continued fighting.

The Victory of Prut energized the Ottomans, who had been distressed and continuously disheartened by the losing streak of their army at war. Because the Russians reneged on the treaty, Baltacı Mehmed Pasha was dismissed. Ahmed III further mobilized his army to Edirne for another campaign against Russia. It was only the intermediation of the British and Dutch ambassadors that prevented the army from fighting the Russians once again. The Treaty of Prut gave back to the Ottomans the Azov region, which the Russians had acquired in the Treaty of Istanbul.

The spirit of hope that the achievements in Prut gave to the Ottomans prompted the idea that the lands lost by the Treaty of Karlowitz were also recoverable. This idea survived up until the fall of the Ottoman Empire. The Ottomans drifted into a series of successive battles to reclaim lost territories, but these would finally result in more and more territorial losses.

Galvanized by the conclusions of the Prut Treaty, the Ottomans sought to regain the Morea Peninsula, which Venice had acquired with the Treaty of Karlowitz in 1699. They began to look for the best occasion to declare war against Venice. The occasion came when Venice provoked the Montenegrins to revolt, and the

Venetians attacked the Ottoman fleet led by Enişte Hasan Pasha. As a result, Sultan Ahmed III assigned Grand Vizier Ali Pasha to a mission to conquer the Venetian islands in the Mediterranean and the Morea. Ahmed III accompanied the army up to Edirne and sent them off from there.

The Ottomans applauded the news that the Ottoman forces had conquered the Morea; on the other hand, the Ottoman conquest of the Morea outraged Austria, and so Austrian forces had joined the enemy ranks by the time the Ottomans surrounded the Corfu Island in the Ionian Sea. Grand Vizier Damad Ali Pasha had died a martyr at the battles in Petrovaradin, which had proven very difficult for the Ottoman army. The sultan ultimately ended the siege of the Corfu Island. The Ottoman army did not achieve a military victory against the Austrians; moreover, the internal strife in Hungary, which emerged when the Ottomans encouraged the Transylvanian king to turn against Austria, proved to be futile. The Ottoman forces could not give the good news of a longed-for victory to the sultan. When Austrian forces effectively marched down to Niš, Grand Vizier Nevşehirli Damad İbrahim Pasha was forced to

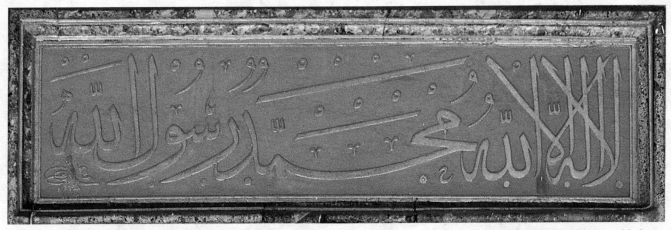

Calligraphy of the *Kalima at-Tawhid*: *La ilaha illallah Muhammadan rasulullah* (There is no deity other than God, and Muhammad is the Messenger of God) inscribed by Sultan Ahmed III at the entry of the Pavilion of Sacred Relics, the Topkapı Palace

sign the Treaty of Passarowitz in 1718. This treaty stipulated that the Austrians would take control of the west of Wallachia, including Belgrade with parts of northern Serbia, while the Ottomans reacquired the Morea. Thus, the Venetian threat in the Mediterranean lessened in favor of the Ottoman Empire. Although the Treaty of Passarowitz averted more territorial losses in Serbia and precipitated a long period of peace with Austria, it marked the end of Ottoman westward expansion. From then on, we see the change in Ottoman policy toward Europe as the Ottomans moved from a policy of conquest to a defensive policy with the aim of holding onto the lands in their possession.

The most significant events of the last years of Sultan Ahmed III's reign took place in the East. Afghans captured Asfahan from Persia, and Russia pushed through Persia to expand down to the Persian Gulf, thereby oppressing the Muslims of Shirvan and Daghestan. When the oppressed Muslims eventually called on Sultan Ahmed III, the Caliph of all Muslims,

Wall Fountain in front of the Library of Sultan Ahmed III

Sultan Ahmed III Library, which the sultan constructed in his name in the middle of the Third Courtyard of the Topkapı Palace

Calligraphic work , the Ulu (Great) Mosque in Bursa

Ahmed III put a far more intense focus on Persia. An internal crisis was well underway in Persia because of interdenominational strife that threatened to spread throughout the region, and the sultan was seeking ways to secure the eastern frontiers of his empire. Therefore, the Ottoman army penetrated into Persia from three different lines simultaneously. The army annexed the western cities of Persia while Russian forces captured Derbent and Baku. Eventually, the Ottoman army confronted the Russian troops in the eastern Caucasus. The French mediatorship efficiently avoided a pitched battle between the Ottomans and Russians, who instead signed the Treaty of Istanbul in 1724.

According to the treaty, the Ottomans and Russians split several Persian cities among themselves. Shah Tahmasp II, who was defeated by the Ottoman army, finally approved the articles of the Treaty of Istanbul. Later, Tahmasp II's successor Ashraf Khan rejected the terms the treaty had drawn. Persian-Afghan joint forces faced the Ottoman troops near Nihavend and crushingly defeated them. This defeat would mark a turning point for the sovereignty of Sultan Ahmed III: although the treaty included certain clauses in favor of the Ottomans, the Ottomans back home became extremely discontent with the defeat. The sultan's previously-positive public image had taken a downward twist.

The following years were filled with negative events: the Afghan leader Nadir Shah reclaimed the Persian cities under Ottoman control and killed the Ottoman soldiers living in the cities, new taxes were levied to pay military expenditures consumed mainly by the campaigns to Persia, a wave of in-migration flooded the city of Istanbul mostly because the rural regions of the provinces were plagued by explosively harmful revolts. In addition to this, various other economic and social problems amplified a common reaction to the government. This period also came to be called "the Tulip Era" (1718–1730) as a rich variety of tulips was planted in and garnished many gardens of Istanbul, and the sultan and statesmen amused themselves with a frenzy of parties. These parties coupled with the fact that the grand vizier and the grand judge designated their kinsmen to take over high administrative positions which caused the Ottoman administration to fall under heavy criticism of the notable state officials, scholars, and the general public. Following an idle period of silence during which the Ottoman government did literally nothing to reclaim the lands lost recently in Persia, a revolt instigated by the Albanian Patrona Halil erupted in 1730. Grand Vizier Nevşehirli İbrahim Pasha was executed, but his execution did not appease the rebels. Finally, the sultan was dethroned and replaced with his nephew Mahmud I.

Ahmed III and his *şehzade* sons were confined to the Şimşirlik section of the palace. While relinquishing his throne, Sultan Ahmed III recommended to Mahmud I, the next sultan, that he should run the empire himself and trust no one. He survived another six years and passed away where he was detained on June 24, 1736. His body was buried near the Yeni Mosque, in the Tomb of Valide Hadice Turhan Sultan, his paternal grandmother.

Historians conventionally suggest that the reign of Sultan Ahmed III was the first time in Ottoman history that a wealth

Water Fountain of Sultan Ahmed III in front of the main gate of the Topkapı Palace

of Western-oriented reforms went into effect. The reforms, which were initiated during his twenty-seven-year reign, significantly changed the mode of life in Istanbul. This was thanks in part to the report by Yirmisekiz Çelebi Mehmed Efendi, the Ottoman ambassador to Paris who had served in the twenty-eighth battalion of the Janissary corps and thus came to be known for his entire life by the nickname *Yirmisekiz* (twenty-eight). The establishment of numerous tulip gardens, elegant kiosks, and the Sadabad Palace on the banks of the Kağıthane River that runs into the Golden Horn also coincided with the Tulip Era. Named after the palace, the region came to be known as *Sadabad* (Prosperous Place).

A flower and garden enthusiast, Sultan Ahmed III helped floriculture to flourish and turned florists into decently-paid professionals. The tulips were elevated in the view of the Ottomans to a highly-respected status unknown in their countries of origin. The most remarkable cultural achievement was, however, the opening of a printing press to publish books in Ottoman Turkish for the first time in Ottoman history. Although non-Muslims had been running publishing houses all across the empire, particularly in Istanbul, İzmir, Salonica, and Aleppo, no single publishing house owned by Muslims existed. İbrahim Müteferrika partnered with Said Efendi, the son of Yirmisekiz Çelebi Mehmed Efendi, and with the permission of Sultan Ahmed III opened the first printing press to publish books and booklets in the Ottoman Turkish language in 1727. In addition, a paper factory opened in Yalova in the south of the Marmara Sea, a ceramics plant in the Tekfur Palace of Istanbul, and a drapery factory in Istanbul. The first quarantine methods were applied during this period; for instance, passengers on the sea were quarantined to prevent the spread of contagious diseases.

In addition, *Tulumbacı Ocağı*—a firefighter unit affiliated under the Janissary corps—was organized to facilitate extinguishing fires in Istanbul, which were commonplace in 1722.

Sultan Ahmed III was a talented calligrapher; he studied the art under the supervision of Hafız Osman, an eminent artist of calligraphy. Ahmed III scribed many calligraphic works that would garnish the marble panels on top of the water fountains in various locations in the capital as well as numerous panels in the Topkapı Palace. He was an excellent marksman; chroniclers note that he could hit with one precise shot a golden coin eighty-five footsteps away.

During his reign, Ahmed III patronized numerous poets, including the celebrated Nedim, whose work is often seen as representative of the spirit of Tulip Era. The sultan also wrote poems under the pseudonym "Necib." For the first time in Ottoman history, some French works were translated into Turkish and vice versa. The Ottomans found the cure to treat smallpox before the Europeans; in fact, the Ottoman doctors effectively cured the sultan who had caught the smallpox once.

Sultan Ahmed III opened several libraries to encourage learning, including the one in the Topkapı Palace under his name. He also erected monumental drinking fountains near the first gate to the Palace, called *Bab-ı Hümayun* (Imperial Gate), a second one in Üsküdar on the Asian shores of Istanbul, and a third near Çağlayan, Istanbul. In memory of his mother Rabia Emetullah Gülnuş Sultan, he constructed the Yeni Valide Camii and a splendid drinking fountain next to it as well as a public library next to the Tomb of Valide Turhan Hadice Sultan in Istanbul. He established two more mosques, one outside of the Galata Palace at the northern shore of the Golden Horn and one in Bebek on the European shores of the Bosphorus.

Since the reign of Süleyman the Magnificent, the outer cloth of the Ka'ba in Mecca had been made in Egypt and its inner cloth in Istanbul. From Sultan Ahmed III's reign onward, all the fabrics began to be woven in Istanbul. Like his brother Sultan Mustafa II before him, the sultan undertook reparations and renovation works in the Prophet's Mosque in Medina and regularly sent royal gifts to the holy cities.

Miniature of Sultan Ahmed III watching festivals by Levni in his *Surname-i Vehbi*, the Topkapı Palace Museum

Miniature of Sultan Ahmed III and his attendants, by Levni in his *Surname-i Vehbi*, the Topkapı Palace Museum

The Twenty-fourth Ottoman Sultan
Sultan Mahmud I
Reign: 1730—1754

Honorifics and Aliases: *Gazi*, *Kambur*, and *Sebkati*
Father's Name: Mustafa II
Mother's Name: Saliha Valide Sultan
Place and Date of Birth: Edirne, August 2, 1696
Age at Accession to the Throne: 34
Date of Death: December 13, 1754
Place of Death and Burial Site: Istanbul – he was buried in the Tomb of Valide Hadice Turhan Sultan, Istanbul

Mahmud I was brought from Edirne to Istanbul in the company of other *şehzade*s who were transferred to Edirne with their father Mustafa II when he was dethroned by the Edirne Incident in 1703. During his *şehzade* years, Mahmud was engaged in goldsmithing in Edirne. As a result of the Patrona Halil Revolt, he succeeded to the throne his paternal uncle Ahmed III, who had been forced to relinquish his sovereignty on October 2, 1730.

During his early years of rule, Mahmud I endeavored to meet the demands of the rebels. The

Portrait of Sultan Mahmud I seated on throne

kiosks and pavilions erected during the Tulip Era were demolished, newly instituted taxes were annulled, and the rebels' favorites were given administrative positions. Disturbed by the fact that Patrona Halil and his followers manipulated the state affairs at will, Sultan Mahmud I obtained the support of the influential army officers, who would later supply him with military support against the rebels and put an end to the rebellion by having Patrona Halil, the corrupt instigator of the uprising, and his circle of men executed. He would also drive his fellow countrymen and Janissaries away from Istanbul back to their lands of origin. The sultan also dealt in person with moral corruptions at large, inspected the merchants, and applied *narh*, or government initiative to fix market prices, for the protection of the consumer interests.

Once Sultan Mahmud I managed to suppress the revolt and successfully restore order, he turned his focus to foreign relations. He ordered a campaign to the Safavids in 1731; consequently, the Ottoman forces mobilized in Persia inflicted a serious defeat on Tahmasp II of Persia near Hamedan and reclaimed Tabriz and Hamedan. When Shah Tahmasp II called for truce, Ahmed Pasha, the governor of Baghdad who had been promoted to the ministry of Eastern defense, signed with him the treaty in 1732. According to the Ahmed Pasha Treaty, the Ottomans kept the regions of Ganja, Tbilisi, Yerevan, and Daghestan in the Caucasus whereas they had to give up the regions of Tabriz, Hamedan, Kermanshah, and Lorestan. Sultan Mahmud I had opposed delivering Tabriz to the Safavids; he substituted the high-ranking officials favoring peace with those that did not, and then declared war against the Safavids. Nadir Shah, the leader of the Turkoman Avşar tribe, deposed Shah Tahmasp, and appointed the eight-month old Abbas III as nominal ruler of the Safavid Persia. He then took over the administration as the chief deputy in 1732. Nadir Shah did not agree to the treaty and besieged Baghdad. But he lost, and the Ottomans reclaimed the city of Tabriz, giving Sultan Mahmud I the title of *Gazi*. Nevertheless, they could not hold Tabriz for long. After the Ottoman forces commanded by Abdullah Pasha were defeated in the Battle of the Arpaçay in the south Caucasus

Miniature depicting the Divan (Imperial Council) meeting held at the Council Hall. The sultan is following the council meeting from behind the window upstairs, and the preparations are being made outside in the Divan Square

in 1735 and the chance to fight the Russian forces became quite likely, Sultan Mahmud I signed a treaty in 1736 based on the Treaty of Qasr-e-Shirin concluded back in 1639. This treaty rejected the recognition of Ja'farism by the Ottomans as a fifth school (*madhab*) of Sunni Islam but acknowledged Nadir Shah as the new ruler of Persia and his official proclamation of Sunni Islam in Persia.

Russia, an ally of Austria, refused to let Crimean forces through the Kabardin region in Caucasus into Persia to reinforce the Ottoman army. Soon after, Russians attacked the Fort of Azov in Crimea in March 1736; in the face of the Russian attacks, the Ottoman imperial council reached a decision of war against Russia. Meanwhile, Austrians were determined to help their Russian ally and took the offensive against the Ottomans in 1737 in a three-sided assault. While Russia captured the forts of Azov, Kinburn, and Ochakiv, Austria seized Niš and Bucharest. Sultan Mahmud I felt tremendous sorrow upon hearing about the losses; nevertheless, he had to fight the Austrians and Russians in different theaters of war. He split his army into two main regiments to simultaneously fight the Russians and Austrians.

Sultan Mahmud I assigned Köprülü-zade Hafız Ahmed Pasha as the governor general of Rumelia and dispatched him with the mission to recapture Niš. In addition, preparations were made with the objective of reclaiming Belgrade. Niš was retaken and fierce battles took place between the Ottomans and Austrians, who attacked from the Timişoara region. The Ottoman army passed through the Danube River and made incursions into Timişoara. In 1738, the Ada Kaleh on the Danube fell to the Ottomans. The sultan's Grand Vizier Yeğen Mehmed Pasha arrived later in Niš and moved from there into Belgrade.

On the Russian front, the Ottoman army fought off the Russians who were trying pass through the Dniester River. The Russian fleet, on their way to the Black Sea through Azov, was scorched by the Ottoman fleet led by the Ottoman Admiral-General (*Kaptan-ı Derya*) Süleyman Pasha.

Sultan Mahmud I replaced his staff again; this time, İvaz Mehmed Pasha became the new grand vizier. The new target of the Ottoman army was Belgrade. Eventually, the Ottomans recaptured Belgrade following a series of fierce combats. Austria waved the white flag helplessly. The treaty that followed forced the Austrians to surrender all the lands (except the Banat) they had claimed with the Treaty of Passarowitz. Following the Treaty of Belgrade, Austria retreated up to the north of the Danube River on September 18, 1739.

In the meantime, Russia intended to attack from Bessarabia. In fact, the French fleet had sailed into the Baltic Sea after the alliance concluded between Sweden and France, after Prussian and Ottoman relations had observed manifest rapprochement, and after the Ottomans had signed a commercial treaty with Sweden. Consequently, the Russians were in panic of these victories as well as diplomatic and economic developments all to their disadvantage. It was when Austrians ended the fighting that they had to make peace with the Ottomans in 1739. The treaty stipulated the terms below: Russia could keep the Azov port with the condition that they would demolish the Azov Fort; there would be

The crest of an Ottoman flag-pole, molded in the shape of the Prophet's Sacred Sandal, the Topkapı Palace Museum

no Russian fleet in the Black Sea; and the Kabardin region was to be a neutral zone. In lieu of its pro-Ottoman mediatorship in the peace talks, the capitulations granted to France earlier were revised and extended in 1740. The same year, the Ottomans signed a defense treaty with Sweden and another of commerce with Spain. As a result of these treaties, the Ottomans off-set a diplomatic balance of power vis-à-vis Europe. The Treaty of Belgrade also led to thirty long years of peace on the Western front. Sultan Mahmud I's military reforms brought about tangible consequences. Eventually, the Treaty of Belgrade proved to be the most profitable of the treaties the Ottoman Empire had ever signed.

In the East, Nadir Shah laid a siege to Baghdad in 1743, demanding the city be surrendered to him. A new Ottoman-Persian war broke out shortly after the capture of Kirkuk and the siege of Baghdad by Nadir Shah. The combats near Kars did not yield any conclusive results. The martyrdom of Yeğen Mehmed Pasha, the commander of the Eastern front, bro-

This golden throne embellished with precious stones was presented by Nadir Shah of Persia to Sultan Mahmud I

View of the Göksu Palace from the Bosphorus

ught a tidal change to the course of the battle near Yerevan. The Ottoman army defeated the enemy, and Kars fell. Pressed by the ongoing Ottoman raids into Hamedan, Nadir Shah offered a truce to the Ottomans. Founded on the earlier Qasr-e-Shirin Treaty in 1639, the Treaty of Kerden (also called the Second Qasr-e-Shirin Treaty) followed in 1746. The treaty further acknowledged that the Persians would respect the Prophet's late Companions and secure the pilgrimage route through their country. As a symbol of friendship, Nadir Shah gifted Sultan Mahmud I with a golden throne, called *Taht-ı Tavus*, which still survives in the Topkapı Palace. Oddly enough, this splendid throne remained in Baghdad quite some time after Nadir Shah was assassinated. It only arrived in Istanbul after the death of Mahmud I. It was Sultan Mustafa III who would actually see it.

Faithful to his words and a lover peace, Sultan Mahmud I wanted neither to exploit the succession wars that shook Europe nor to march a campaign against Persia during the internal strife that emanated from Nadir Shah's assassination.

Sultan Mahmud I dealt with domestic affairs during his reign and strived to fortify and modernize the imperial army. Mahmud I did not attempt to eliminate the Janissary corps, but instead paid particular attention to paying the Janissaries on time and wanted to keep them under his control. The sultan further consulted İbrahim Müteferrika on the causes of military defeats and what to do about them. In response, Müteferrika wrote his advice down in his famous *Usulu'l Hikem fi Nizam'ul Umem* ("Essential Wisdom for Ruling Peoples"). In light of his suggestions, the sultan appointed Humbaracı (artillerist) Ahmed Pasha, the name assumed by the French Comte de Bonneval after his conversion to Islam, the duty of modernizing the *Humbara* (artillery) units. Soon after, the Imperial Technical College (also called *Humbarahane*, or house of bomb-making) opened at Üsküdar, Istanbul. It was this college that would provide the foundations for later engineering colleges.

During Sultan Mahmud I's reign, the *ayan*s, or the local notables, gained considerable power and exercised suppression and control over people in the provinces. The sultan issued an *adaletname* (edict of justice) to defend the public against their oppression. The sultan further sought to balance the imperial treasury income and expenditures; in conformance with this financial project, he paid the debts, basing the fiscal year on the Gregorian calendar instead of the Hijri calendar. It was during the reign of Sultan Mahmud I that the Ottoman Empire had its last period of greatest peace and prosperity in the 18th century. He pursued coherent diplomatic relations and eventually signed successful and conclusive treaties that would leave the succeeding sultans long years of peace on Eastern and Western fronts. Sultan Mahmud I died on his horse in the Topkapı Palace on his way from the Friday prayers on December 13, 1754.

The sultan was closely attentive to state matters; he regularly attended the *Divan* (Council) meetings of his viziers held at the *Kubbealtı* (Council Hall), and he discussed with the members of the Imperial Council[34] the affairs of the state as well as public affairs. Sultan Mahmud I was kind, just, intelligent, peace-loving, dignified in character, and a devout Muslim. Mahmud I wrote poems in Turkish and Arabic and set some to music. He enjoyed javelin-throwing and horse racing.

The sultan initiated construction projects in Istanbul; for instance, he established the enormous Nuruosmaniye (the Light of Osman) *külliye* next to the Grand Bazaar, which would be completed during the reign of his brother and successor sultan Osman III and so remembered with the latter's

The Topkapı dagger, 1741

237

name. Indeed, the complex was originally given the name *Osmaniye*, and later in time it came to be called *Nuruosmaniye*. The inscription of the Qur'anic verse, "God is the Light of the heavens and the earth," inside the dome of the mosque as well as the existence of interlacing pieces of colored and plain glass windows providing much light inside the mosque justified its name. Its complex consisted of a library containing rare manuscripts most of which were personal collections of Sultan Mahmud I and Osman III, a college, soup kitchen, water fountain, some shops and a tomb where Sultan Osman III's mother Şahsuvar Valide Sultan is buried.

Mahmud I erected the *Topkapı Sahil Sarayı* (Topkapı Seaside Palace) on the shores of the present-day Topkapı Palace. The name of this palace was given later to the bigger and well-known seat of government only after the *Topkapı Sahil Sarayı* was destroyed by fires.

The sultan undertook the reparations of numerous mosques, big and small, all across the land. Furthermore, he constructed the Hacı Kemaleddin Mosque in Rumelihisarı and the Arab port in Beşiktaş, both on the European side of the Bosphorus, as well as the mosques of Sultan Mahmud and Kandilli in Üsküdar on the Asian side. He converted the vault of Kurşunlu into a mosque (known today as the Yeraltı, or Underground Mosque) and redrew the boundaries of the mosque to include the nearby tombs of the Companions of the Prophet. The sultan also oversaw the urban water supply; in particular, the dams and aqueducts that he constructed channeled potable water to a network of fountains across the city. Sultan Mahmud I constructed a reservoir in the European part of the capital. The major tourist and shopping region in present-day Istanbul that came to be called *Taksim* (meaning "division" or "distribution") derived its name from this stone reservoir, where the main water lines from the north of Istanbul converged and then branched off to other parts of the city.

Reputedly, Sultan Mahmud I's mother Valide Saliha Sultan cracked her earthenware jug when she dropped it on the street as a young girl. A woman from the palace saw young Saliha Sultan bursting into tears, consoled her, and helped her to enter the palace. In the palace, Saliha Sultan received a remarkable education, was trained in elaborate Ottoman etiquette, and finally married Mustafa II. When she became the *Valide Sultan*, Saliha Sultan had the means to construct a magnificent fountain called the Saliha Sultan Fountain in the Azapkapı region of Istanbul, right where she had dropped and cracked her jug many years ago. Valide Saliha Sultan participated in the opening ceremonies of the fountains for the first time and gave the-go to filling them up with water.

During the reign of Sultan Mahmud I the *Darü'l Kütüb* (House of Books) opened. This library held rich collections of sources particularly on history for use at the imperial chambers of the Revan Pavilion at the Topkapı Palace. Over time, the library accumulated a rich collection of rare manuscripts submitted to the sultan. Furthermore, the sultan sponsored the construction of libraries in Belgrade and Vidin on the Danube, as well as the imperial mosques in Istanbul. He also supervised the transfer of rare manuscripts from the provinces to these libraries. He opened a seminar house near the Fatih Mosque for the purpose of studying *Sahih al-Bukhari*—the most trusted collection of sayings and traditions of the Prophet.

A man of charities, the sultan had the Prophet's sacred footprint, which had been in the Pavilion of the Sacred Relics in the Topkapı Palace, placed for public visits within a marble belt at the Tomb of Eyüp Sultan, a Companion of the Prophet, on the wall facing the direction of the Ka'ba. He gifted the Grand Mosque in Mecca with invaluable chandeliers and candelabrums and conducted extensive reparations on the walls of the city of Medina.

The Twenty-fifth Ottoman Sultan
Sultan Osman III
Reign: 1754–1757

Father's Name: Mustafa II
Mother's Name: Şehsuvar Valide Sultan
Place and Date of Birth: Edirne, January 2, 1699
Age at Accession to the Throne: 56
Cause and Date of Death: Cancer, October 30, 1757
Place of Death and Burial Site: Istanbul – he was buried in the Tomb of Hadice Turhan Valide Sultan near the Yeni (New) Mosque, Istanbul

Sultan Osman III was confined in the Şimşirlik section of the Topkapı Palace for long years and ascended to the throne in his fifty-sixth year as the oldest heir assuming the Ottoman throne up to that time. He enjoyed doing carpentry during his *şehzade* years. Long years of confinement in the palace made him short-tempered, and Osman III would usually make up his mind quite fast though he sometimes regretted what decision he had made.

Portrait of Sultan Osman III

As the new sultan, Osman III meticulously chose his statesmen and replaced his grand viziers quite often. The frequent rotations in grand vizierate indeed brought about instability and interrupted the proceedings in state matters. It is very likely that Osman III recurrently got rid of his grand viziers frequently because they had gained increased influence and power during his reign and came to dominate the administration.

Economically, the Ottoman imperial budget presented surpluses during Osman III's rule as had been the case during the last fifty years. During this period, the *Sikke-i Cedid* (new coin) was sealed as minted in *Islambol* (literally, "where Islam abounds"), another name for Istanbul.[35]

It was during his reign that the Ottoman capital was exposed to a flood disaster, two minor earthquakes, and a winter hard enough to surprisingly freeze the Golden Horn in the year 1755. The sultan visited in person the scenes where these disasters inflicted losses and severe damages. He had the officials evaluate the damage caused by the extensive fires that had plagued a significant part of Istanbul. The sultan took particular care in covering the losses and putting in effect scores of measures to avoid future fires.

The Ottoman Empire engaged in no wars during the reign of Sultan Osman III as the sultan devoted his time to internal issues. He took action against all the banditry in Anatolia and Rumelia during this period and ordered severe penalties for the brigands who attacked the pilgrims on their journey as well as those who corrupted their administrative positions by exploiting the endowment property devoted for religious or charitable purposes. The sultan further gave priority to handling the issues of the pilgrims in Mecca and Medina.

A momentous interdiction during Osman III's rule concerned the migration to Istanbul, which had become a huge, populous metropolis. In practice, the government granted admission of entry only for business purposes, and in that case, not to large companies but to individuals.

Inner dome of the Nuruosmaniye Mosque, whose construction was initiated by Sultan Mahmud I and completed during the reign of Sultan Osman III

Sultan Osman III often mingled with public, albeit incognito. He not only closely observed the problems his subject people had to go through but also found out what they thought of the administration. While Sultan Osman III banned the show and use of tobacco in public, no restrictions applied to those who smoked responsibly in private.

For the first time in Ottoman history, the Ottomans signed a treaty of amity and commerce with the Kingdom of Denmark.

Sultan Osman III became severely ill before he attended the *Cuma Selamlığı*—a public ceremony held after the Friday congregational prayer—and passed away two days after. Some sources suggest that he had cancer. He was the fifth and last Ottoman sultan buried in the Tomb of Valide Hadice Turhan Sultan next to the Yeni Mosque.

Sultan Osman III's mother Şehsuvar Valide Sultan, who met her destiny in the third year of the sultan's reign, was known for her devotion and piety. The sultan, who grew up in a devout Muslim family environment, was also an observant Muslim. He abhorred wastefulness, falsehood, and bribery. He sympathized with local people, paid his incognito visits among the general public, and tried to meet their needs.

Osman III was an accomplished calligrapher and man of the arts. Some of his calligraphic works have survived up to the present in the Topkapı Palace Museum. On top of the footprints

Night view of the Nuruosmaniye Mosque

View of the Nuruosmaniye and Sultan Ahmed Mosques from the Bayezid Fire Tower with Kadıköy on the other side of the Bosphorus(circa 1910)

View of the Pavilion of Osman III from the marble-paved terrace in the Topkapı Palace

243

of the Prophet that are preserved in the palace and several other tombs, Osman III commissioned talented artists to draw a tableau of the sacred footprints to be placed in the Tomb of Eyüp Sultan. Sultan Osman III constructed İhsaniye, a new quarter in the Üsküdar district of Istanbul and erected there the İhsaniye Mosque and many other smaller mosques which have endured up to today. In addition, he reconstructed the Yanık Minare (Burnt Minaret) Mosque. The Nuruosmaniye mosque-complex, whose foundations Mahmud I had laid, was also completed by Osman III.

After a large vessel ran aground on the Ahırkapı shores of Istanbul one night, Sultan Osman III began the construction of the first lighthouse in the region. In Topkapı Palace, the sultan also constructed the Pavilion of Osman III, which faces the Gülhane Park and consists of a main room and two rooms off to the sides. In addition, he put the *Şimşirlik Dairesi*, in which he had been confined for long years, under extensive reparations and added adjacent buildings.

Inner view of the pavilion constructed by and named after Sultan Osman III in the Topkapı Palace

Sultan Mustafa III

Reign: 1757–1774

Honorifics and Aliases: *Cihangir* ["World-conqueror", dominant over the world] and *Gazi* [Warrior for the Faith]
Father's Name: Ahmed III
Mother's Name: Mihrişah Emine Sultan
Place and Date of Birth: Edirne, January 28, 1717
Age at Accession to the Throne: 40
Cause and Date of Death: Edema; January 21, 1774
Place of Death and Burial Site: Istanbul – he was buried in the tomb under his name near the Laleli Mosque, Istanbul
Male Heirs: Selim III and Mehmed
Female Heirs: Şah Sultan, Fatma Sultan, Bekhan Sultan and Hibetullah Sultan

Sultan Mustafa III became the new Ottoman sultan following the death of Osman III, his cousin and son of his paternal uncle. Mustafa III was very fortunate to have Koca Ragıp Pasha, a magnificent grand vizier, at his disposal. The period of peace spilled over into his reign; in fact, he pursued diplomacy of accommodation to keep the Ottoman Empire out of war while the ongoing Seven Years' War prevented Europe from attacking the Ottomans.

Sultan Mustafa III seated on the throne.
Painted by the Ottoman-Armenian painter Rafael, Topkapı Palace

After thirty years of peace with Russia following the Treaty of Belgrade in 1739, Russian ambitions against the Ottoman interests brought the two countries on the verge of war in the year 1768.

Catherine II of Russia wanted to bring Crimea and Caucasus under Russian control, and then to send the Russian fleet down to the Black Sea to obtain free passage through the Ottoman straits of Bosphorus and Dardanelles, and to expand her sphere of influence in the Balkans. She eventually made her belligerence clear when Russia interfered with the internal affairs of Poland, violating of the Treaty of Prut. The Ottomans reacted shortly after.

The Poles asked the Ottomans for help after the Russians replaced the late Polish king with a pro-Russian leader. Finally, the Ottoman Empire declared war against Russia with the overt support of the Crimean Khan and the French in 1768. When Russia laid siege to Khotyn in 1769, the Ottomans effectively fought back, which earned the sultan the title of Gazi. Nonetheless, the Ottoman army lost the following combats and the sultan, now the Gazi Sultan, fell under heavy criticism of the public.

Russia's response to the Ottoman declaration of war was swift: the Russian army penetrated into Wallachia and Moldavia, captured the ports of Kilia and Akkerman, which controlled the mouths of the Danube and Dniester, while Russian naval forces sailed all the way from the Baltic Sea through the Straits of Gibraltar down to the Mediterranean, thanks to the help of the British.

In the Mediterranean, the Russians agitated the Moreans to rebel against the Ottoman Empire. The Ottomans effectively quelled the rebellion to Russia's surprise; however, they burned down the Ottoman fleet anchored at the harbor of Çeşme on the western coast of Anatolia. The unfolding events revealed a prediction of what would happen next in 1770.

The chief commander of the Ottoman navy, *Kaptan-ı Derya* Cezayirli Hasan Pasha finally forced the Russians out of the Mediterranean and caused them to alter the course of war; Russian forces annexed Crimea. The Ottoman forces could not fight off the Russians in Crimea, and the sultan was forced to offer a truce. Meanwhile, Russian victories over the Ottomans

Laleli Mosque built by the architect Mehmet Tahir Ağa in 1764
on the orders of Sultan Mustafa III

angered and alarmed the Austrians because of their territorial intentions regarding Wallachia and Moldavia. The war resumed after the Bucharest peace meetings had proposed conditions too heavy for the sultan to accept. Russia captured Silistra and Rousse on the Danube. No good news came from the battlefields, rather more and more losses. All these cost the sultan his health. On Friday, January 21, 1774, Sultan Mustafa III passed away in the Ayasofya Mosque while listening to the *adhan*, or Islamic call to prayer, for the Friday congregational prayer.

Chronicles refer to Sultan Mustafa III as a candid, benign, gracious, philanthropic, and generous character. He was a devout Muslim; in particular, he secretly performed the *fajr*, or morning prayer, in the Ayasofya Mosque with the public. Utterly considerate of the good of the community, Mustafa III regulated the taxes levied on his subjects in a way that put them at ease. He was very organized and thrifty; he inspected all expenditures, including those of the palace in order to keep the imperial treasury full. Particularly speaking, he also took very firm measures to provide the pilgrimage route with security and re-ordered the structures of the endowments to the Haramayn. Generally speaking, his frugal policies in financial matters and strict inspections of administrative corruption yielded the result that the state income increased. *Defterdarlık*, or the Imperial Revenue Office, grew into a significant state department during his reign. Sultan Mustafa III was an impressive orator and calligrapher. He tried to master even the minute details in state affairs.

As his predecessors Mahmud I and Osman III had no children, the coming of sultan Mustafa III's first daughter Hibetullah in 1759 and his first son Selim in 1761 received a very warm

The chain mail of
Sultan Mustafa III

and happy reception. Since the Ottoman dynasty gave birth to no heirs for forty years, their births became occasions for a gala that lasted for days.

Sultan Mustafa III continued the lessons of *Huzur* (literally, presence of the heart with God), a tradition his father Sultan Ahmed III had initiated. These lessons were composed of inspiring lessons from the Holy Qur'an and held in the presence of the sultan during the month of Ramadan each year.

It is recorded that Sultan Mustafa III had roamed the capital in disguise during the Russian war, hearkening his people's ideas and wishes, and doing his best to meet their needs. He also mobilized all state resources to reconstruct the city and its vicinity when a major earthquake shook Istanbul on the last day of the Islamic Festival of Sacrifice (*Eid al-Adha*) on May 22, 1766. Sources note that the government spending on this enormous project exceeded twenty-two thousand bags of golden coins, a huge amount at the time. The earthquake inflicted extensive damage on the Fatih Mosque, Eyüp Sultan Mosque, the *Kapalı Çarşı* (Grand Bazaar), the city walls, *Kız Kulesi* (Maiden's Tower), and many other buildings. Nevertheless, the sultan would heal many wounds and construct the city *de novo* thanks to the imperial treasury filled to the brim by his frugal government spending.

Sultan Mustafa III also had two other projects. He wanted to link the Sapanca Lake, located on the east of the Gulf of Izmit, to the Black Sea as well as to open a canal in Suez. These projects never materialized primarily because of the stark opposition to them by the statesmen and broader public. Among the mosques the sultan sponsored were the Mihrişah Mosque known also as the Ayazma Mosque in Üsküdar, which served the memory of his late mother Mihrişah Emine Sultan and his older brother Süleyman. He

Üsküdar Ayazma Mosque
built by Sultan Mustafa III

شبیه سلطان والاسلطان مصطوخان الحصر ترکیان هی خوانلیه ویسط بریدر ابرام الاینکور ونشی

Gravure of Sultan Mustafa III on horseback in front of the Gate of Salutation, dated 1762. On passing through this gate,
all except for the sultan had to dismount their horses in the First Courtyard of the Topkapı Palace.

250

also constructed the Laleli mosque complex on the European side of the city in honor of Laleli Baba, a saint whom the sultan respected very much. Both the sultan and saint were buried in the courtyard of the Laleli Mosque. A fan of poetry, the sultan wrote many poems under the name "Cihangir." One famous quadrant translates as follows:

In the process of destruction the world is, suppose not we resuscitate,
On the useless the despicable world has bestowed the state,
Now are wonderers at the Happiness' Gate all false and base,
At the mercy of the Everlasting then is our fate.

An elegant wall fountain in the
Imperial Terrace of the Topkapı Palace

251

The Twenty-seventh Ottoman Sultan

Sultan Abdülhamid I

Reign: 1774—1789

Honorifics and Aliases: *Gazi* [Warrior for the Faith] and *Veli* [Friend of God]
Father's Name: Ahmed III
Mother's Name: Rabia Şermi Sultan
Place and Date of Birth: Istanbul, March 20, 1725
Age at Accession to the Throne: 49
Cause and Date of Death: Anguish, April 7, 1789
Place of Death and Burial Site: Istanbul – he was buried in a tomb under his name in Bahçekapı, Istanbul
Male Heirs: Mustafa IV, Mahmud II, Murad, Nusret, Mehmed, Ahmed, and Süleyman
Female Heirs: Esma, Emine, Rabia, Saliha, Alimşah, Dürrüşehvar, Fatma, Melikşah, and Hibetullah Zekiye

Sultan Abdülhamid I replaced his late older brother at the age of forty-nine at the time when the Ottoman Empire was undergoing many problems. When the Ottoman Empire was in dire need of a competent sultan, it was inopportune for both the empire and sultan that he was so inexperienced in running the government when he assumed the sovereignty.

The greatest challenge that Abdülhamid I faced in the beginning was the Russo-Ottoman war that broke

Sultan Abdülhamid I seated on the throne in ca. 1770. Painted by the Ottoman-Armenian painter Rafael, the Topkapı Palace Museum

out during his brother Mustafa III's reign and had been ongoing for five years. He attempted to liberate Wallachia and Moldavia from invasion, which he thought would also help to afford a lucrative treaty with the Russians. The Ottoman army, however, was defeated near Kozlica and Shumen. Hence in only the sixth month of his reign, the sultan was forced to accept the terms of a truce that the Russians would dictate. On July 21, 1774, the Russians and Ottomans signed the Treaty of Küçük Kaynarca,[36] one of the most cumbersome the Ottomans had ever agreed to. This treaty stipulated that the Ottomans would accept the nominal independence of Crimea; in this vein, the Ottomans lost their first Muslim-majority territory. Particularly, the Ottomans lost the Kabardino region, and most importantly, Azov. Furthermore, the Russians established a protectorate over the Ottoman Orthodox-Christians, which they would use to interfere with Ottoman internal affairs. They were given free-passage through the straits as well as commercial privileges identical with those given previously to the French and British.

The Ottomans, particularly Sultan Abdülhamid I, lamented the sheer fact that they lost Crimea, the land that felt like homeland to the Turks after 1,500 years of presence there. Following the Treaty of Küçük Kaynarca, the sultan suppressed several revolts in the Mediterranean, Syria, the Morea, and Egypt all with the support of the Ottoman Admiral General Gazi Hasan Pasha and Cezzar Ahmed Pasha; he also ended the troubles the *Levend*s (Ottoman marines) had caused in Anatolia. It was during this period that Wahhabism spread in the Arabian Peninsula and that Abdul-Aziz ibn Saud, the Amir of Najd, took the possession of central Arabia.

The Crimean region detached from the Ottoman domain based on the clause in the Küçük Kaynarca treaty that Crimea would be autonomous; however, the Russians waited for opportunities to capture it. The time seemed ripe for the Russians when the turmoil in the Arabian Peninsula turned out to be too overwhelming to handle swiftly. When Catherine II of Russia attempted to make Şahin Giray the new khan of Crimea, the Crimeans turned for

Detail from the Privy Chamber of Sultan Abdülhamid I in the Topkapı Palace

help to the Ottomans, with whom they were bound on the basis of Islam. The sultan knew too well that the Russians were looking for ways to invade Crimea. He gave orders to prepare the army in case of a potential Russian invasion of Crimea. Upon the reactions of local people, Şahin Giray this time wanted Selim Giray III to be the new khan. When the ongoing diplomatic disagreement was on the brink of turning into a major Russo-Ottoman war, France stepped in and mediated the belligerent parties; eventually, the parties met in the Aynalıkavak Palace for the Aynalıkavak Convention in Istanbul in 1779. The convention concluded that Crimea would remain independent, Russia would withdraw its forces from the Crimean region, and the Ottomans would approve Şahin Giray as the new Crimean khan. In addition, more liberal rights would be granted to the Christian Ottomans.

The Aynalıkavak Convention strengthened Russia's tutelary role not only in Crimea but for all the Balkan Orthodox-Christians as well. Bitterly opposed to the Russian diplomacy in Crimea, Sultan Abdülhamid I aimed to be more effective in southern Caucasus. In practice, the forts of Soğucak and Anapa were fortified. Ali Pasha, the constable of the Soğucak Fort, established relations with the Circassian tribes, and the Ottomans developed relations with the Daghestanis. Furthermore, Sultan Abdülhamid I corresponded with Ebulgazi Seyyid Muhammad Bahadır Khan, the ruler of Bukhara. He wrote Bahadır Khan a number of letters requesting his help when the Ottomans marched on Russia to liberate Crimea.

Meanwhile, the new Crimean khan, Şahin Giray used his Russian support to undertake Euro-centric reforms. The Crimeans revolted and Şahin Giray had to flee from Crimea. When this happened, the Russian Marshall Potemkin rushed into Crimea. Potemkin cruelly slayed nearly thirty thousand Crimean Muslims, and then restored Şahin Giray as the khan. Most of the remaining Muslims abandoned Crimea, and Şahin Giray repopulated the city with Russian immigrants. Potemkin returned to Crimea after a short while to annex it this time on January 9, 1784. The Ottoman Empire was not equipped to fight Russia; thus the invasion of Crimea by Russia was accepted, albeit grudgingly.

After several years without wars, Russia and Austria met up in Saint Petersburg to discuss the partitioning of the Ottoman lands. Later, Russians agitated the Circassian Mamluk (slave) *bey*s to revolt against the Ottoman authority. At this point, the Ottoman Empire first delivered an ultimatum to Russia then declared war. Another main objective of the war was to bring Crimea back to the Ottoman

Hamid-i Evvel Mosque built by Sultan Abdülhamid I in Beylerbeyi on the Asian shores of Istanbul

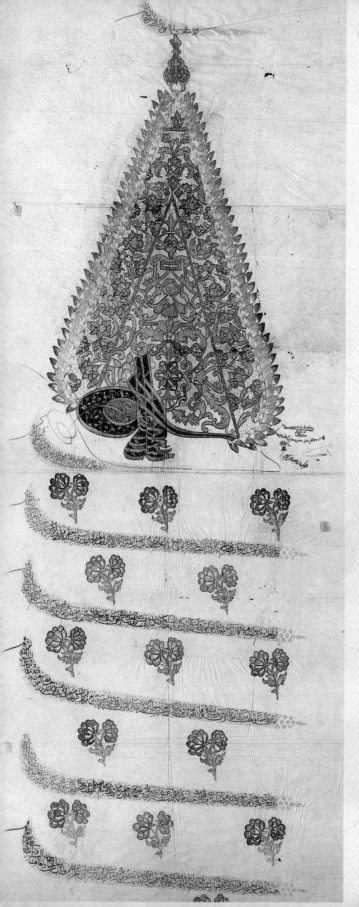

domain. The Ottomans had to fight against Russia on one front and against Austria, Russia's ally, on another. Although the Ottoman forces won against the Austrians, the Russian army eventually defeated the Ottomans. The sultan's state of health continuously worsened during the wars. The capture of Ochakiv, the fort along the Dniester, by Russians deeply affected the sultan; in fact, it paralyzed him. Finally, Sultan Abdülhamid I passed away in the Privy Chamber in the Topkapı Palace on April 7, 1789.

Chronicles emphasize that Abdülhamid I was a compassionate and good-natured man with sincerity. Abdülhamid had to grapple with unending problems both inside and outside his empire. During his reign, a variety of military reform went into practice. The reforms aimed primarily to modernize and uplift the bombardier, artillery, and Janissary corps as well as the imperial navy. In foreign affairs, Sultan Abdülhamid I established close relations with the Uzbek khanate and the Muslim states in Morocco and India.

Sultan Abdülhamid I had a building compound constructed, which consisted of an alms house, children's school, college, and a research library in Sirkeci, Istanbul. The books surviving from Abdülhamid I's reign are located today in the Süleymaniye Library. On behalf of his mother Rabia Sultan, the sultan erected a mosque along the Beylerbeyi Seaside, along with many water fountains all across Istanbul, especially in Beylerbeyi and Çamlıca on the Anatolian side of the city. It was he who ordered the establishment of the Privy Chamber, which came to be called by his name, as well as the Imperial Apartments of *Mabeyn* ("place in-between") as it is located between the living quarters and the official areas of the palace.

Sultan Abdülhamid I's edict for the renewal of the appointment bestowed onto Mrs. Hanife, the mother of Ahmed Said, as titular custodian in the Tomb of the Prophet.

Aerial view of the Topkapı Palace

The sultan undertook the reparations of the Zamzam well and waterways in Mecca. The *maqam*s (stations) of Prophet Ibrahim (Abraham) and Imam Shafi'i both underwent complete maintenance, and the two towers around Mecca, which had worn out with time, were built anew. A generous devotee to science and knowledge, Sultan Abdülhamid I opened a library in Medina, and shipped from Istanbul 1,669 units of manuscripts for use in the newly opened library in Medina. He ordered the construction of the Ajyad Fortress (which stood until 2001) on a hill overlooking the Grand Mosque with the objective of protecting it from invaders.

Following pages: General view of the Topkapı Palace on the promontory of Sarayburnu (Palace Headland), swinging around from the Golden Horn into the Bosphorus and the Marmara Sea with views of Istanbul

Sultan Selim III

Reign: 1789–1807

Honorifics and Aliases: *Cihandar, Gazi, Halim*, and *İlhami*
Father's Name: Mustafa III
Mother's Name: Mihrişah Valide Sultan
Place and Date of Birth: Istanbul, December 24, 1761
Age at Accession to the Throne: 28
Cause and Date of Death: Assassination, July 28, 1808
Place of Death and Burial Site: Istanbul – he was buried in the Tomb of Mustafa III in Laleli, Istanbul

The Ottoman dynasty reproduced no heir after 1725; therefore, the birth of Sultan Selim III became an occasion for a grand gala. Selim III was 13 years old when his father passed away. Selim received an impressive education in part because his paternal uncle Abdülhamid I allowed him to grow up in a liberal environment. He was cognizant of the global news and had an innovative mind. His rise to the throne at a young but mature age, contrary to his predecessors, would bring tidal changes in the fate of the Ottoman Empire.

Sultan Selim III painted by Kostantin of Kapıdağ, the Topkapı Palace

The wars with Russia and Austria were still on in the early years of his reign. Sultan Selim III led a number of fund-raising campaigns to meet the expenditures of the army warring on two fronts. Sweden allied with the Ottoman Empire and waged war against Russia. However, the news from the fronts of more and more territorial losses was disappointing. While Russia captured Tighina on the right bank of the Diniester, Kilia, and Akkerman, Austria took the possession of Bucharest and Belgrade.

It is recorded that Sultan Selim III, distressed by extensive territorial losses, paid a visit to the Tomb of Eyüp Sultan and recited long prayers. During this period, Prussia allied with the Ottoman Empire and mobilized some of its forces to its Austrian border. Austria worried that the ideas of the French Revolution would spread in the land; for this reason, it abolished the alliance with Russia and signed the Treaty of Svishtov with the Ottomans in 1791. The treaty stipulated that Austria would give back the territories annexed from the Ottomans during the war.

Russia continued the war for a while longer. However, something unexpected happened; for the first time in its history the Ottoman commanders at war wrote a petition to the sultan and demanded that he end the ongoing war, an act indicative of the problems within the chain of command in the army that were spoiled and turned arrogant while the army itself was exposed to misrule. By the time that the French Revolution had far-reaching ramifications throughout Europe and Sweden was bound to their alliance with the Ottoman Empire, an efficient administration of the army would promise definitive victories. Sultan Selim III, however, resolved to sign with Russians the Treaty of Jassy in 1792 and lost a bit more tracts of land. The Dniester River drew the new border between the Ottoman Empire and Russia. The most significant consequence of the treaty was that the Ottomans came to understand there was no way they would get Crimea back; the wars that the Ottomans had fought to reclaim Crimea yielded no positive results, only more territorial losses. After four consecutive years of fighting, the sultan greeted his army back in Davutpaşa.

Two main problems during this period revolved around the political and social turmoil in Anatolia and the rising wave of migration to Istanbul.

Responding to the pressure from the local notables, many peasants abandoned their lands and came to Istanbul, the capital. They caused civic unrest, a food shortage, and aided in the mounting inflation.

Sultan Selim III was very concerned with the many problems that plagued the capital, and so he embarked on a set of reforms when the course of events did not improve. Aware that the Ottoman Empire had lagged well behind Europe from the economic and military points of view, the sultan received ideas from the statesmen prior to launching his reforms. Particularly speaking, a collaborative committee led by Ebubekir Ratip Efendi, the Ottoman ambassador to Paris, Bertranaud of France, and D'Ohsson of Sweden came up with a comprehensive, 72-article report on the application of the reforms and the methods for handling problems in the capital.

In response to the obvious fact that the Ottoman army had suffered defeat after defeat, the sultan established a small corps of new troops called the *Nizam-ı Cedid* (New Order) in 1793, allocated the *İrad-ı Cedid* (New Revenue) for their expenditures, and dressed the new corps in the fashion of European armies.

Later, the *Nizam-ı Cedid* (New Order), the name previously given to the newly established military corps, would be used to broadly identify Sultan Selim III's reform movement. European experts became involved in modernizing the artillery, bombardier, and miner-sapper units. Furthermore, the Land Engineering School (a new military college) opened, and the imperial shipyards were reordered and brought under discipline. In turn they succeeded in building the modern vessels and battleships the empire desperately needed. The same year, the Ottomans instituted permanent embassies in London, Paris, Vienna, and Berlin with the purpose of tracking developments in Europe.

In order to prevent future destructive fires or to circumscribe their effects in Istanbul, Sultan Selim III published *nizamname*s (regulatory edicts) in order to standardize the positions and height of the structures.

France had invaluably benefited from its diplomatic and commercial relations with the Ottomans; in fact, the French had made a fortune out of them. For this reason, it surprised the Ottomans when the French commander Napoleon Bonaparte invaded Egypt in 1798 during Sultan Selim III's reign. Indeed, the invasion appalled the Ottoman government. The British burned down the French fleet moored at the Abukir Harbor mainly because France's

Oil painting of Sultan Selim III by the Ottoman-Greek painter Kostantin of Kapıdağ in 1803, the Topkapı Palace Museum

penetration into the Mediterranean discomforted them. Eventually, this act brought about rapprochement between Britain and the Ottoman Empire. With the support of Britain and Russia, Sultan Selim III declared war on France, its *consort ancien*.

Napoleon marched toward Syria to force the Ottomans into a truce and to buy some time to reconstruct his fleet. The *Nizam-ı Cedid* troops took its litmus test against the French. At the end of the day, the Ottomans won a definitive victory. Napoleon, the great commander of the French army, faced the defeat and evacuated Egypt in accordance with the treaty signed in Arish on the Mediterranean coast of the Sinai Peninsula in 1801.

Allied with the Ottomans during the French occupation of Egypt, Russia soon began to cause problems in the Balkans. The Ottomans retaliated by removing the *bey*s of Wallachia and Moldavia, both supporters of Russia, and by blocking Russian ships from passing through the straits. Russia wanted the *bey*s to return to their posts and moved to annex Wallachia and Moldavia. Sultan Selim III was appalled a second time after the French invasion of Egypt by the sheer fact that the Russians had ignored the recently signed alliance with the Ottomans and that Russia was still determined to do whatever it would take to invade the upper Balkans. The Ottomans engaged a new war against the Russians, one that would outlast Sultan Selim III's reign.

Ottoman scholars, merchants, minorities, Janissaries, and the broader public did not espouse Sultan Selim III's reform movement under the rubric of *Nizam-ı Cedid*. The natural disasters that hit the land in 1805 were bad signs for them, and they reacted to the fact that the sultan wanted to launch his reforms right from Rumelia. A social uprising ensued and spread; eventually, the revolt led by Kabakçı Mustafa, who worked as an apprentice at Rumelikavağı on Bosphorus, resulted in a severe chaos.

Sultan Selim III would have been able to subdue the revolt easily if he had used his new military forces, which were modernized, heavily invested, and strong enough to defeat the army of Napoleon Bonaparte. However, he chose not to employ them as he did not want to shed any more blood. Despite his humane intentions, the state of the empire was way too clear. The sultan called his nephew Şehzade Mustafa, informed him that he would relinquish the throne to him, and wished him good luck. This meant that all the reforms, for which the sultan had spent considerable time, effort, and money, were abandoned; eventually, the sultan's defeatism would precipitate the fall of the Ottoman Empire.

Oil painting of Sultan Selim III on horseback by Hippolite Bertaux, the Topkapı Palace Museum

Selimiye Mosque constructed by Sultan Selim III next to the Selimiye Barracks in Üsküdar for the soldiers to perform their daily prayers. Taken by Ali Rıza Bey.

About a year before his assassination, Sultan Selim III secluded himself in the *harem* (literally, sacred inviolable place) section of the palace, spending most of his time reading the Holy Qur'an and playing a reed flute—a wind instrument that most closely resembles the human voice and whose plaintive tunes are thought in the Sufi understanding to be an allegory for the soul's sorrow at being separated from God. Selim III had no desire to reassume the throne; however, Sultan Mustafa IV ordered the execution of the sultan and Şehzade Mahmud after one of his followers, Alemdar Mustafa Pasha of Rousse, marched his forces to Istanbul, annihilated the rebels, and besieged the Topkapı Palace. Sultan Selim III was called to come outside of his room and was assassinated. The body of the deceased Sultan was thrown out to the front of the Audience Hall in the Topkapı Palace. Alemdar Mustafa Pasha had rushed in the palace to save Selim III, the ex-sultan; instead, Alemdar would only burst into mourning when he saw Selim's dead body covered with blood. He could only save Şehzade Mahmud, the heir to the throne, with the help of Cevri Kalfa, a superintendent in the palace.

Sultan Selim III was very concerned with the reforms, the panacea for the ills of his empire. The Ottoman public knew him too well not to recognize him on visits he paid out to them, albeit as an ordinary *humbaracı* soldier *incognito*; in addition, these visits taught him what people were experiencing. Selim III wanted to solve the problems that he had observed on these visits with many regulations, like those on the use of domestic commodities, the avoidance of extravagance, the dress code for women, and provisions for the needy. His clothing was tailored with fine domestic textiles from Istanbul and Ankara, not from India or Persia. In fact, he reproached those who did not follow suit.

A man of arts, Selim III was a talented musician; he had been a great master of Turkish classical music whose compositions are still played in Turkey. At the same time, he was a renowned poet as well as an expert in Ottoman calligraphy.

His reign saw the establishment of the Üsküdar Selimiye Mosque and Selimiye Barracks, both of which are still functioning. The Eyüp Sultan Mosque, extensively damaged by the earthquake, was restructured during his reign. Selim III added to the Topkapı Palace one Privy Chamber under his name and one chamber for his mother; in addition, he shipped precious pieces of textiles to Mecca and Medina to cover and ornament the sacred prefectures and tombs that keep alive the memories of the Prophet, his family, and his Companions.

The Sofa Mosque in the Fourth Courtyard of the Topkapı Palace overlooking the Bosphorus. In the place of the mosque once stood the Arms-Bearers Pavilion where the statesmen held a meeting to dethrone Sultan Selim III after the Kabakçı Mustafa Revolt. Their decision of execution precipitated a whole course of events that ended with the murder of the sultan in the palace. The pavilion lurked in Sultan Mahmud II's mind as a reminder of what had happened to his uncle Selim III; therefore, he had it razed and erected in its stead the mosque, which is still functioning today.

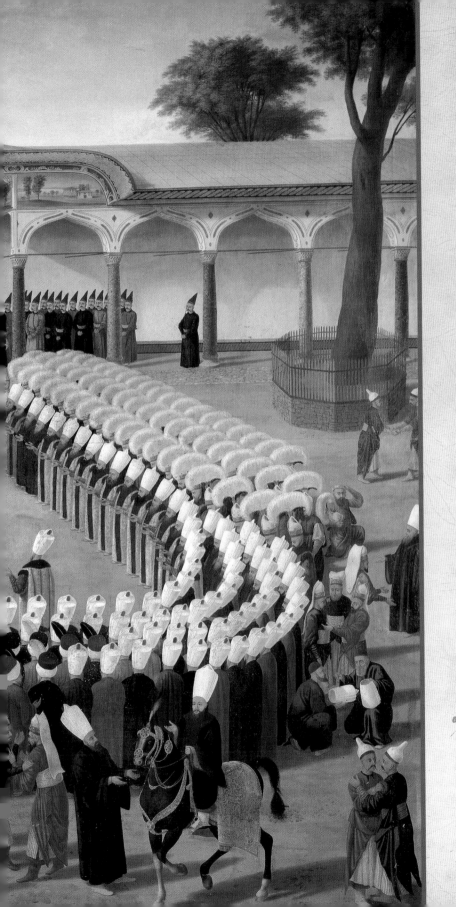

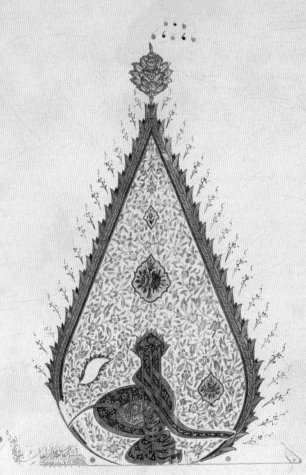

The *tughra* of Sultan Selim III

Islamic holiday reception of Sultan Selim III in front
of the Gate of Felicity in the Second Courtyard of the
Topkapı Palace by Kostantin of Kapıdağ

ATLANTIC
OCEAN

France

Austria

Galicia

Uyvar
Vienna
Zsitvatorok   Eger
Vasvár   Esztergom   Mezőkövesd
Kanizsa
Szigetvár   Mohács   Banat   Szeged
Karlowitz
Bosnia   Belgrade   Wallac
Herzegovina   Niš   Bu
Serbia   Nikopol
Kosovo
Ragusa   Montenegro   Sofia   Plo
Albania
Serres
Salonica

Venice

Genoa

Spain

I T A L Y

Dalmatia

Corsica

Rome

Sardinia

Otranto

Naupactus
Preveza

Athens

Morea

Sicily

Tunis

Algiers

Cre

T u n i s i a

Malta

A l g e r i a

M E D I T E R

Tripoli

Benghazi

B e r k a

T r i p o l i

N
W   E
S

Boundaries of the Ottoman Empire
at the beginning of the 18th century

SCALE

0   125   250   375   500 miles

The Twenty-ninth Ottoman Sultan

Sultan Mustafa IV

Reign: 1807—1808

Father's Name: Abdülhamid I
Mother's Name: Ayşe Sinerperver Valide Sultan
Place and Date of Birth: Istanbul, September 8, 1779
Age at Accession to the Throne: 28
Cause and Date of Death: Strangled, November 17, 1808
Place of Death and Burial Site: Istanbul – he was buried in
the Tomb of Hamidiye in Bahçekapı, Istanbul
Female Heir: Emine Sultan

Sultan Mustafa IV assumed the throne after the Kabakçı Revolt dethroned his uncle Selim III. Mustafa IV was afforded a convenient childhood; with his brother Mahmud II, he wandered around Istanbul in disguise while Selim III, his childless uncle, cared for them kindly and tenderly.

Sultan Mustafa IV met with the rebels shortly thereafter. When they assured him that the Janissaries would no longer interfere with the state affairs,

Gouache tableau of Sultan Mustafa IV seated on throne

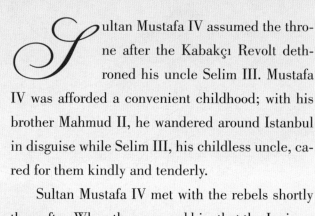

Mustafa IV promised them an amnesty they would benefit from. However, it is impossible to imagine that those having enough power to replace the sultan would step aside and not interfere with the state affairs. The political anarchy and social turmoil, which resulted from the rebels' arrogance and interference in government affairs and from the struggles between supporters and opponents of the reforms, continued during the course of Sultan Mustafa IV's reign. Finally, a sense of penitence emerged because of Selim III's replacement with Mustafa IV as the new sultan.

The anarchy spread even among the army ranks fighting Russians in the ongoing war that began during Sultan Selim III's reign; as a result, the army began to show signs of debility.

Musa Pasha—the *Sadaret Kaymakamı*, or grand vizier's representative in Istanbul while he was on campaign, and Grand Judge Ataullah Mehmed Efendi had already been involved in the Kabakçı Mustafa Revolt; therefore, they could not succeed in bringing peace and order to Istanbul.

The coming of Alemdar Mustafa Pasha and his army to Istanbul from Rousse helped restore security. Kabakçı Mustafa was executed and Ataullah Mehmed Efendi was discharged. The followers of Alemdar Mustafa Pasha had wanted to reinstate Selim III to the throne, while the followers of Mustafa IV sought a way to kill him. When the course of events came to jeopardize Selim's life, Alemdar Mustafa Pasha rushed into the *Bab-ı Ali*, or Sublime Porte,[37] arrested the grand vizier, and moved toward the palace with the intention to rethrone Selim III. After Alemdar demanded that Sultan Mustafa IV relinquish his throne and allow Selim III to return, Mustafa IV slammed the palace gates shut and ordered the execution of Selim III and Şehzade Mahmud in order to end the ongoing turmoil. Alemdar Mustafa Pasha was able to enter the palace only by force, but all that remained were the dead body of the old sultan and a wounded and trembling Şehzade Mahmud II, whom he saved and supported. Sultan Mustafa IV was dethroned and replaced by Şehzade Mahmud II, the only surviving heir to the throne in 1808. Alemdar Mustafa Pasha would be his grand vizier.

Sultan Mustafa IV's reign was one of the shortest in Ottoman history. Although Mustafa IV was confined to his chamber later, he longed to be the sultan again, and corresponded accordingly with his men on the outside. Soon after, Grand Vizier Alemdar Mustafa Pasha was assassinated during a rebel raid. The rebels wanted to move on toward the palace; therefore, the order of execution, similar to the one he gave previously to his brother Selim III, was now given to him.

Chronicles narrate that, since his *şehzade* years, Mustafa IV, and even his sister Esma Sultan, had been involved in the opposition camp that criticized and aimed to dethrone Selim III.

Many contemporary sources further employ humiliating words and sturdy accusations in their examination of Sultan Mustafa IV. However, during his reign, the Russian war continued, the ramifications of the Kabakçı Mustafa Revolt were still effective, and the political and military activities of Alemdar Mustafa Pasha were too strong to ignore. All considered, it seems that the sultan did not have enough time to carry on with the reform agenda that his uncle Selim III had initiated.

Sultan Mustafa IV was too strict in penalizing the guilty who caused turmoil or manifested debauchery in the city, even if they were Janissaries. Mustafa IV continued to use some good statesmen surviving from his uncle's time mainly because he lacked of competent men to work with. In addition, Mustafa IV drew up plans to train soldiers in the Artillery Barracks in the Taksim region of Istanbul, in a proper and modern way, and was tremendously concerned with the status of the newly established Engineering School. When put together, the evidence strongly suggests that Sultan Mustafa IV had planned to go forward with reforms his uncle had pioneered.

View of the Privy Chamber of Selim III from the marble terrace of the Pavilion of Osman III, the Topkapı Palace

The *tughra* (calligraphic imperial signature) of Sultan Mustafa IV

Sultan Mahmud II

Reign: 1808–1839

Honorifics and Aliases: *Adli* and *Büyük*
Father's Name: Abdülhamid I
Mother's Name: Nakşidil Valide Sultan
Place and Date of Birth: Istanbul, July 20, 1785
Age at Accession to the Throne: 23
Cause and Date of Death: Tuberculosis, June 28, 1839
Place of Death and Burial Site: Istanbul – he was buried in the Tomb of Mahmud II on Divan Yolu, Istanbul
Male Heirs: Abdülmecid and Abdülaziz
Female Heirs: Saliha Sultan, Atiyye Sultan, Hadice Sultan, and Adile Sultan

Sultan Mahmud II had seen his uncle Selim III dethroned in 1807 and then murdered. This was followed by the efforts of Alemdar Mustafa Pasha to dethrone his older brother and those who wanted to claim his life. Mahmud II ascended to the throne wounded and frustrated on July 28, 1808. His reign started amidst revolts and counter-revolts, went on with hard-fought struggles, and ended by having recorded many firsts in Ottoman history. Following him, Mahmud II's two sons and four grandsons assumed the throne, and the Ottoman dynasty that survives today follows his lineage. For this reason, Mahmud II is regarded as the third and last forbearer of the dynasty after Osman Gazi and Sultan İbrahim.

Painting of Sultan Mahmud II seated on throne, painter unknown

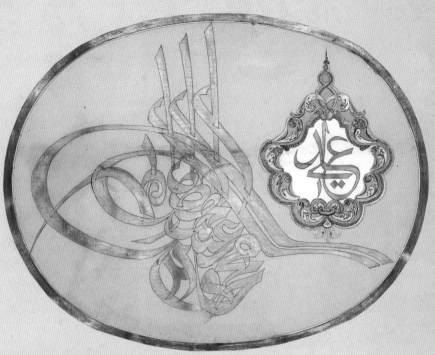

The tughra (imperial emblem) of Sultan Mahmud II

The greatest challenges Sultan Mahmud II faced included: the incessant revolts of the Janissaries, the corrupt and oppressive governors and local notables in the provinces, the Serbian and Greek revolts in the Balkans, the rebellion of Mehmed Ali Pasha in Egypt, and the long wars with Persia and Russia. Despite such overwhelming circumstances, a series of reforms, both initiated and sustained, characterized the reign of Mahmud II.

The Janissary corps revealed itself as the main catalyst for disorder and chaos in the capital. The Janissaries constantly interfered with administrative matters directly and far more than what was expected from soldiers. In fact, the Janissaries had spurred many costly and troublesome coups, at the end of which they dethroned quite a number of sultans. Sultan Mahmud II abolished the centuries-old Janissary corps, which the chronicles recorded in

Gravure of Mahmud II (Nusretiye) Mosque, Tophane, Istanbul by Thomas Allom, 1839

1826 as *Vaka–i Hayriye* (the Auspicious Incident). With this he purged the strongest opposition group against the works of recent sultans and installed his sovereignty. Until the forced disbandment of the corps, Mahmud II had to take control of both the military and intelligentsia, who strongly opposed the reforms that quarreled with their interests, as well as the pressures of local notables in the provinces.

The *Sened-i İttifak*, or the Deed of Agreement, which was signed with the rebel representatives from provincial lands during the grand vizierate of Alemdar Mustafa Pasha, affirmed the sultan's authority in the provinces; however, it also meant that the sultan from then on acknowledged the power of *ayan*s, or local notables, which culminated in popular discontent later on. Alemdar's attempt to establish a new army called the *Sekban-ı Cedid* (New Soldiers) both cost his life and caused two Janissary mutinies, which abated the new army. Sultan Mahmud II struggled with the notables following the *Sened-i İttifak* (the Deed of Agreement) and eliminated the rebellious notables like Tepedelenli Ali Pasha. After putting an end to the threats from the Janissaries and notables, he concentrated his efforts on recruiting a new army, his earliest piece of reform. In order to raise revenue for the military expenditures, the sultan worked to bring under state control the huge income of the *awqaf* (endowments), which were the most important owners of property and income. For instance, the Grand Bazaar, which was constructed by the order of Sultan Mehmed the Conqueror and vastly enlarged

Gravure of Sultan Mahmud II with his sword bearer and Harem's overseer prior to the declaration of the dress code

Cevri Kalfa, one of the heads of the palace servants, snatched Şehzade Mahmud from these narrow stone stairs near the Golden Passway when the rebels rushed in the palace to kill the şehzade; it thus saved the future sultan's life.

during the reign of Sultan Süleyman the Magnificent, became one of the largest covered markets in the world with more than sixty streets and 3,600 shops whose rent income supported the upkeep of Ayasofya as the endowment of the mosque. In 1826, the Ottoman state founded the *Evkaf-ı Hümayun Nezareti* (Ministry of Imperial Estates) to oversee such endowments.

Unlike preceding reformist sultans, Sultan Mahmud II was concerned with getting popular support for his reforms, and he used the media to reach out to the public. He had the *Takvim-i Vekayi* newspaper publish extensively on the reforms, and articles came out defending the disbandment of the Janissary corps.

The Russian war, which began during his uncle's reign in 1806, was still underway when Mahmud II became the sultan. The Ottomans were also in a state of war against Britain. When the Treaty of the Kale-i Sultaniye (also known as the Treaty of the Dardanelles) in 1806 stipulated that the Ottomans would not allow Russian battleships to pass through the straits of Dardanelles and Bosphorus, the war with Britain came to an end. When France, which recently pursued anti-Ottoman diplomacy, attacked and defeated Russian forces, the war with Russia ended, and the Treaty of Bucharest was signed with Russia in 1812. The treaty agreed that the Ottomans would lose Bessarabia but would reacquire Wallachia and Moldavia, and the Pruth River would be the border between the two countries; however, another clause in the treaty that attributed autonomy to the Serbs would be applied after 1817, one of the first steps to dissociate the minorities from the Ottoman domain.

The Greek Revolt was the first significant minority uprising against the Ottoman Empire in 1821. The Ottoman Empire failed to quell the revolt in a short time; thus, the revolt gained international coverage and concern. Europe did not give it a warm reception when Kavalalı Mehmed Ali Pasha, the governor of Egypt, came to help the Ottomans and ended the revolt; in particular, the Ottoman-Egyptian fleet anchored in Navarino was burned by an instantaneous raid in 1827. Sultan Mahmud II asked for compensation as he could not allow the fleet that he had sent to settle a domestic rebellion to be burned. The British and French broke off diplomatic relations with the Ottoman Empire; in addition, the Russians declared war against the Ottomans, justifying it with the Greek revolt, and advanced as far as Edirne. After the Ottoman army suffered defeats near the Danube and in the Caucasus, the Treaty of Edirne was signed on August 14, 1829. This treaty paved the way for the establishment of a small Greek state; it would stretch from the Morea into some Aegean islands and Athens would be its capital.

The autonomy of Serbia and independence of Greece set the pace for other Balkan Christians to rise up and revolt. The coming series of revolts received tremendous support from Christian Europe, and their increasing influence in Ottoman internal affairs with an emphasis on "Christianity" brought about widespread hatred and hostility against the Muslims and Turks. In years to come, the intervention of European great powers would help the Ottoman Christians become independent and separate from the empire.

After Egypt, the Ottoman *consort ancien* France invaded Algeria in 1830. This invasion provided an early lesson in the ways in which the colonizers would partition and dissolve the Ottoman Empire. The way this partition would occur among the Ottoman Muslims became obvious by the Mehmed Ali Pasha revolt.

Mehmed Ali Pasha was an undistinguished soldier. After effectively thwarting the rebellions and establishing order in Egypt, Mehmed Ali became the governor of Egypt and undertook French-style reforms in the land. His revolt against the Ottoman Empire was short-lived. When the Ottomans lost the Morea, which they would give to Mehmed Ali Pasha in return for his help against the Greek Revolt, Mehmed Ali requested the governorship of Syria. Following a negative response to the request, Mehmed Ali Pasha sent his forces, commanded by his son İbrahim Pasha, to Syria. İbrahim Pasha won victory after victory and advanced as far as Konya. In Konya, his army fought the Ottoman army led by Grand Vizier Reşid Mehmed Pasha, defeated the Ottomans in 1832, and moved up to Kütahya with the Ottoman grand vizier as his captive.

The wall fountain in the Privy Chamber of Abdülhamid I

281

Alongside this revolt, Sultan Mahmud II came across an even greater threat that could replace the Ottoman dynasty. When the sultan requested help from Russia as a last resort, Russian land and marine forces came to Beykoz. Another domestic revolt turned into an international crisis, especially after the British and French intervened. With the accord concluded in Kütahya, Mahmud II gave up on the lands conquered during the reign of Yavuz Sultan Selim and handed them to Mehmed Ali Pasha. He also signed the Treaty of Hünkar İskelesi with Russia, which made the two countries allies for the next eight years. Hence, Russia acquired remarkable rights to the straits. While the first stage of revolt in Egypt passed away with no strings attached, the Russian domination over the straits alarmed and panicked European powers.

The Ottomans and Egyptians had been disillusioned by the Treaty of Kütahya; after extensive preparations, they confronted each other in Nizip in southeastern Anatolia in 1839. The Ottoman army suffered another defeat; eventually, the Egyptian threat resumed in Anatolia. Sultan Mahmud II did not live long enough to receive the bad news and died on June 28, 1839.

Sultan Mahmud II is known for his undertaking of fundamental reforms. Aware of the importance of establishing central authority, the sultan eliminated those against it, particularly the Janissaries, despotic and corrupt governors, and local notables. Perhaps the only despotic governor he could not do away with was Mehmed Ali Pasha. The sultan carried out his reforms only after he established his *de facto* sovereignty. He studied well his uncle's life and times; he split the military and intelligentsia so successfully that he eventually avoided confronting concerted efforts of opposition. The sultan convinced the intelligentsia's towering figures of the need for reforms; thus, he not only received their support but forfended their opposition as well. Sultan Mahmud II chose a perfect time for the abolishment of the Janissary corps: the Janissaries failed to put down the Greek Revolt for many years, but the modern, regular Egyptian forces made it happen in a very short time. Reflecting this out to the public, he made his point and convinced the public that the Janissaries were good for nothing. Despite the failed attempt of establishing the new army of Sekban-ı Cedid, Mahmud II launched another army-establishment project; the new military corps would be called "Eşkinci Ocağı." It seems that this project materialized as a set up to agitate the Janissaries into a revolt; eventually, the last Janissary revolt followed, and the sultan abolished their corps in response.

During the reign of Sultan Mahmud II, a code of dress for men went into effect; mustaches became much shorter, beards were less than two fingers

Medallion, in the form of an oil painting of Mahmud II, on ivory after the declaration of the dress code

long, and the state officials began to wear uniforms that consisted of pants, a jacket, and a fez. The Ottoman imperial military band's house was closed as it would be reminiscent of the Janissaries. The return to playing marching songs would take place during the Second Constitutional Monarchy Period (1908–1922).

Sultan Mahmud II liked to live his everyday life simply and away from flamboyance; therefore, he did not like the Topkapı Palace and stayed instead in his humble, wooden, waterfront palace in Beşiktaş. He also did away with palace protocols. European ambassadors who met Sultan Mahmud II noted that even the mansion of any European merchant was more imposing than the sultan's waterfront palace.

During Mahmud II's reign, the Ottoman central government established new institutions to reform and facilitate state affairs; more, the *Divan-ı Humayun* (Imperial Council) was closed and replaced with *nazırlık*s (ministries). A head of ministers was assigned to organize and lead on state affairs, and the grand vizierate was terminated in 1838.

The apparent need for an educated class prompted the sultan to open new schools; in addition, the Muslims began to learn foreign languages, reflective of the attempt to challenge the monopoly of non-Muslim dragomans, or translators, mainly from the Greek quarter of Phanar in Istanbul.

Regardless of their religious affiliations, Sultan Mahmud II pursued various activities that embraced his subject people all as one. He worked very hard to relieve the discounted among them; in particular, he attempted to buy non-Muslims into the state and repaired a great number of churches. Likewise, he repaired and renovated many mosques and dervish lodges.

The sultan applied a hands-on policy in state affairs; for instance, he wrote and signed personally several official documents of importance. During the wars in which Russia advanced up to Edirne (1828–1829), the sultan occupied the Rami Barracks for over a year, wearing his colonel uniform.

Sultan Mahmud II was cool-headed and magnanimous; he was a forgiver in his personal life whereas he had acted harshly against the criminals of the state.

"The state pothers have wearied me," he once said. In reality, all the struggles in and outside the empire had collapsed his state of health. Death eventually overtook him when he was accompanied to the Çamlıca Hill on the Anatolian side of the capital to get some fresh air on June 28, 1839. In the face of the possibility that the already-disbanded Janissaries might revolt upon the news of his death, the body of the deceased sultan remained where he had died. After the precautionary military measures were taken, his dead body was buried in a funeral ceremony that Muslims and non-Muslims attended in significant numbers.

Sultan Mahmud II was committed to the holy cities of Mecca and Medina. As soon as he was told that the Haramayn required extensive maintenance (in particular some mosques and tombs in Mecca and Medina were in miserable condition), he began urgently repairing them. He restored the graves and tombs in the Jannat al-Baqi cemetery across from the Mosque of the Prophet as well as various burial places (*maqam*s) in Mecca. As caliph, Mahmud II further replaced the broken and worn-out marble floors and columns around the Ka'ba with new ones shipped from Anatolia.

Extensive renovations were undertaken on the mosques in Mina, Muzdalifa, and Arafat. In addition, Sultan Mahmud II renovated the houses of the Prophet, his Companions, and the four rightly-guided Caliphs.

Oil portrait of Sultan Mahmud II after the declaration of the dress code, painter unknown, the Topkapı Palace Museum

Sultan Mahmud II's calligraphy with the hadith in the first line: "My intercession will be for those of my community who committed great sins." In the second line the sultan begs for the intercession of the Prophet.

In Medina, Mahmud II established a library and public fountains as well as a school and the Mahmudiye College. The more than eighty precious chandeliers and *kandil*s, (traditionally bowl-shaped oil lamps) that Mahmud II sent to the holy cities symbolized his affection for them as well as his responsibility to the title "caliph" bestowed on him.

Sultan Mahmud II dispatched engineers and craftsmen from Istanbul to the Prophet's Mosque in Medina for extensive renovation and experts and construction workers from Egypt. In addition, he shipped a variety of materials and equipment from Anatolia. After long years of work, the Ottomans erected new columns around the Prophet's Mosque, and painted, embroidered, and engrained calligraphies on the mosque. Most significantly, the old and worn-out dome, which the Mamluk ruler Kayıtbay had constructed, was replaced with a new one that was made from stone, covered with lead, and painted green. This Green Dome over the

Fountain of the Holy Mantle erected by Sultan Mahmud II on the exterior wall of the Privy Chamber of the Pavilion of the Sacred Relics. The bodies of the deceased sultans were washed here.

Sultan Mahmud II's calligraphy of the Kalima at-Tawhid: *La ilaha illallah Muhammadan rasulullah*
(There is no deity other than God, and Muhammad is the Messenger of God)

Prophet's tomb (Qubbat al-Khadra), the symbol of Medina and the Prophet's Mosque today, is illustrative of Sultan Mahmud's affection and attachment to his Prophet, peace and blessings be upon him. The epigraph over the fountain outside of the Pavilion of Sacred Relics in the Topkapı Palace displays the tughra of the sultan and refers to the accomplishment of the Qubbat al-Khadra in Medina. The most important aspect of this fountain was that the bodies of the deceased sultans were washed here.

The tughra (imperial emblem) of Sultan Mahmud II
inscribed over the Gate of Felicity, the Topkapı Palace

Next page: One of the earliest photographs of the Qubbat
al-Khadra (Green Dome) over the Prophet's tomb
constructed by Sultan Mahmud II (circa 1880s)

Sultan Abdülmecid

Reign: 1839–1861

Honorifics and Aliases: *Gazi* and *Safveti*
Father's Name: Mahmud II
Mother's Name: Bezmialem Valide Sultan
Place and Date of Birth: Istanbul, April 25, 1823
Age at Accession to the Throne: 16
Cause and Date of Death: Tuberculosis, June 25, 1861
Place of Death and Burial Site: Istanbul – he was buried in his tomb at the yard of the Yavuz Sultan Selim Mosque in Fatih, Istanbul
Male Heirs: Murad V, Abdülhamid II, Mehmed V (Mehmed Reşad), Ahmed Kemaleddin, Mehmed Burhaneddin, Ahmed Nureddin, Selim Süleyman, and Mehmed Vahdeddin VI
Female Heirs: Saliha Sultan, Atiyye Sultan, Hadice Sultan, and Adile Sultan

Upon his father's death, Sultan Abdülmecid assumed the throne as the last Ottoman sultan who ascended to the throne at a young age. During his *şehzade* years, he received an impressive, Western-style education and learned French. Since he was inexperienced in administration, and internal affairs and foreign relations were overwhelmingly difficult, he assured the leading statesmen that he would esteem their proposals.

Sultan Abdülmecid tried to solve the Egyptian question by absolving Mehmed Ali Pasha; however, all his plans concerning Mehmed Ali went down the hill after the news reached the capital that the Ottoman army had suffered a defeat in Nizip. Moreover,

Portrait of Sultan Abdülmecid by Josef Manas, 1888

the fleet admiral Ahmed Fevzi Pasha handed the fleet over to Mehmed Ali Pasha in Alexandria, in retaliation for his opponent Hüsrev Pasha's becoming the new Head of Ministers by force on July 3, 1839. Now that the Ottoman Empire remained devoid of its army and fleet, the only way to handle the Egyptian question pointed to Europe for support.

Golden inner case of the Mantle of the Prophet

Mehmed Ali Pasha did not want accord with the new sultan, so the Egyptian question invited de facto the involvement of Britain, France, Russia, Austria, and Prussia.

Mustafa Reşid Pasha, the Ottoman minister of foreign affairs, had been to European capitals often to observe thoughts and advice on the coming reforms and their benefits. In Istanbul, he persuaded the young sultan that European support on the Egyptian question would come only if they prepare a fundamental reform package and put it into effect.

Recorded in history as the *Tanzimat Fermanı* (Edict of Reorganization), this reform program was proclaimed out to the public in the Gülhane Park, Istanbul, where a huge gathering including the sultan and foreign ambassadors had occasioned on November 3, 1839. This very important document, which started the Era of Tanzimat (1839–1876), promised more civil liberties and regulations, including educational, cultural, legal, conscription, and taxation reforms.

The Tanzimat reforms helped to work out the Egyptian question, which had already become an international issue. Britain took the lead, and at the London Conference, which France did not attend as it supported Egypt, four great powers of Europe (Britain, Russia, Austria, and Prussia) unanimously signed a treaty on July 15, 1840. The Egyptian question was solved with the following terms: The Mehmed Ali Pasha dynasty would keep the governorship of Egypt by succession; Egypt would keep allegiance to the Ottoman sultan and send to Istanbul one-fourth of the total taxes collected per annum.

Mehmed Ali Pasha did not readily acquiesce, but he was forced to accept the decision when Britain and Austria landed their forces in Beirut. The following year, the same countries met at the Straits Convention in London upon the expiration of the eight-year Treaty of Hünkar İskelesi signed with the Russians in 1833, and agreed that the authority of the straits belonged to the Ottoman Empire and warships could not pass through.

During the European Revolutions of 1848 with a series of political upheavals throughout Europe, Hungarians had lost against the forces of Austria and Russia that marched into Hungary while they were at war with Austria to gain their independence; therefore, some Hungarians took refuge with the Ottomans. This severed the relations between the Ottoman Empire and Austria, and Russia. All Austrian and Russian diplomatic pressures and threats of war notwithstanding, Sultan Abdülmecid made it clear that he would not return the refugees who ended up in the Ottoman lands. For the first time, his humanitarian attitude changed popular feelings in Europe from hatred to sympathy. As a matter of fact, this change of the Ottoman image in Europe would facilitate the Ottoman search for allies later during the Crimean War.

The earliest war photos in history were shot during the Crimean War (1853–1856). The photo illustrates İsmail Paşa and his attendants.

When the Revolutions of 1848 spread over the *memleketeyn*, or "the two valued countries" of Wallachia and Moldavia, Russians signed the Treaty of Baltalimanı with the Ottomans in 1849, which provided short-term solutions for the matter. The next issue on the foreign relations agenda was "the Question of Holy Land." After France applied for a protectorate over the Catholics in Jerusalem, Russians delivered a note to the Sublime Porte, the Ottoman government, demanding that more rights be given to the Orthodox citizens of the Ottoman Empire and Russia establish over them a protectorate. Following the negative answer from the Ottoman government, Russians invaded Wallachia and Moldavia; soon after, Sultan Abdülmecid declared war on Russia in 1853. Recorded in history as the Crimean War as most of the conflict took place in Crimea, this Russo-Ottoman war began with the burning of the Ottoman fleet by Russians in Sinop on the south of the Black Sea. Britain, France, and the Kingdom of Sardinia allied with the Ottoman Empire

Qur'anic calligraphy of Sultan Abdülmecid from the Surah Yusuf reads:
"God is the best to take care; and He is the Most Merciful of those who show mercy" (12:64).

whereas Austria and Prussia, Russia's potential allies, decided to remain neutral. At the end of the day, Russia suffered a crushing defeat.

Prior to the Congress of Paris, which would mark the end of the war, the Ottoman allies requested that Sultan Abdülmecid execute another edict that would confirm and extend the rights proclaimed in the Tanzimat Decree. In line with the request, the grand vizier, grand judge, and British and French ambassadors prepared the *Islahat Fermanı* (Reform Decree), proclaimed the decree on February 18, 1856 before the congress started. The decree not only extended the rights given in the Tanzimat but also gave other rights to non-Muslims far bolder than Russia had desired, which would later let Western powers intervene more in Ottoman internal affairs. The Treaty of Paris signed on March 30, 1856 at the Congress of Paris after the Crimean War referred to this decree. According to the articles of the treaty, the Ottoman Empire was a European country and European countries had to secure its territorial integrity. Considering the Ottoman Empire was the winning side, the stipulation that closed the Black Sea to all warships whatsoever casted a long shadow on the fairness of the treaty as the Ottoman fleet also had to leave the Black Sea. The decrees proclaimed by Sultan Abdülmecid emanated from his efforts to unify his subjects under the idea of "Ottomanness," which saw all the subjects as equal, regardless of their religious beliefs. However, new privileges granted to the non-Muslims

contributed to, rather than halting, the nationalist movements that proliferated day by day within the Ottoman domains. The Ottoman multi-national structure, provoked by the Westerners, turned out to be impossible to hold together.

The *Islahat Fermanı* (Reform Decree) had given the European countries a blank check to intervene in Ottoman internal affairs; soon after, Britain, France, Austria, Prussia, and Russia claimed that the reforms promised in the decree did not go into effect and sent a diplomatic note to the Ottoman government in 1859. Provoked by Britain and France, the struggle between the Druzes and Maronites emerged again. This time civil turmoil expanded up to Damascus. Europe continued to pressure the sultan and Ottoman government. The course of events dramatically changed when France landed its forces in Beirut. As a result of talks with Europe, a semi-autonomous administration, called *Mutasarrıflık*, was set up in Mount Lebanon, and the region was left to the administration of a Christian governor in 1861.

Like his father, Sultan Abdülmecid suffered from tuberculosis and passed away in his 39th year in the Ihlamur (Linden) Pavilion in Beşiktaş, Istanbul on June 25, 1861.

Sultan Abdülmecid resembled his predecessors in recognizing the authority of religion above his; the reforms he enacted were fed by Islamic laws. He committed himself to bringing the Western modernization into the Ottoman lands, beginning with the railroads.

The sultan paid visits to observe public needs on the spot. He changed ambassadorial admission procedures and began to see ambassadors in person; moreover, he visited the French embassy and even attended a French ball once. Whereas former Ottoman sultans had given medals of distinction to foreigners but accepted no returns, Sultan Abdülmecid abrogated this imperial tradition by accepting a medal from the French Emperor Napoleon III.

Sultan Abdülmecid terminated the post called the *başvekillik* (head of ministries) and brought the grand vizierate back; in addition, he supplemented the assembly and ministries instituted during his father's reign with new ones.

During the years that followed the Tanzimat, the sultan sometimes made decisions based on suggestions from his wives, children, and sons-in-law. Bitter enough, British and French ambassadors also vied to mentor the sultan; thereby, their stance polarized the Ottoman statesmen into two opposing camps, one in favor of the British and the other in favor of the French.

Important steps were taken in reforming education; for instance, elementary school education became obligatory. The first private newspaper *Ceride-i Havadis* (News Journal) began

Sultan Abdülmecid had the Mecidiye Mosque built in Ortaköy on the European shore of the Bosphorus.

to be printed by a publisher of British origin. For the first time in Ottoman history, the first Ottoman banknotes of *kaime* (substitute) were stamped, and external debt was withdrawn from Britain to pay the military expenditures during the Crimean War. During Sultan Abdülmecid's reign, foreign indebtedness increased, and important revenue sources were mortgaged at each of the four occurrences.

Financial difficulties and non-Muslims' extended rights brought about discontent in Ottoman society and caused much turmoil. European intervention in these events on the basis of their interests forced Ottoman statesmen to yield to the Westerners, which Sultan Abdülmecid could not stave off.

During the last years of the sultan, the foreign debts put a great burden on the imperial treasury; particularly, the debts obtained from the non-Muslim money-lenders of Beyoğlu, Istanbul accumulated into a huge sum total. The jewels and checks that were given to the lenders as collateral could not be retrieved.

At a time when the empire was tumbling into acute financial crisis and borrowing large sums of foreign debts, it is odd that Sultan Abdülmecid constructed the Dolmabahçe Palace on the European side of the Bosphorus, the Beykoz and Küçüksu mansions on the Asian side as well as the Mediciye Pavilion in the Topkapı Palace.

The Mecidiye and Teşvikiye mosques and the Galata Bridge that spans the Golden Horn were also established during Sultan Abdülmecid's reign. Sultan Abdülmecid further ran the

most extensive reparations in the Prophet's Mosque in Medina. After Sheikh Davud Pasha of Medina sent a letter to the sultan and informed him of the fact that the mosque had not for long gone under a thorough maintenance, the sultan got personally involved in the matter. He first received a detailed report on the mosque's present condition, and was then determined to conduct an extensive construction and renovation work there. Finally, he assigned the famous architect Abdulhalim Efendi as the project coordinator.

Sultan Abdülmecid held a calligraphy contest in the palace; the winner, Abdullah Zühdü Efendi was given the responsibility for the calligraphy of the Prophet's Mosque. Although Abdulhalim Efendi took his construction team to Medina, he passed away

Funeral procession of Sultan Abdülmecid by Henri Pierre Blanchard Montani, 1861. The public accompanies the deceased sultan to the grave while his coffin was carried through the Gate of Salutation in the Topkapı Palace.

in Mecca during his pilgrimage the same year. In his place, the sultan assigned Mehmed Raif Pasha. After ten years of work, the Prophet's Mosque took its marvelous shape in 1861. In his travelogue, Sayfu'd-Dawla, the Persian traveler to Medina, said that "the reparations ended up being sultanly, indeed." In addition, Aminu'd-Dawla, another traveler, commented that, "Indeed, Sultan Abdülmecid Khan put a great sense of gratitude in the hearts of Muslims toward him. The spirit of this sacred mosque praised by God does not assume any better meaning in any other place of worship." The sultan also constructed a library next to the Ka'ba and an alms house for the poor pilgrims who came to visit Mecca.

Sultan Abdülaziz

Reign: 1861–1876

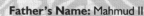

Father's Name: Mahmud II
Mother's Name: Pertevniyal Valide Sultan
Place and Date of Birth: Istanbul, February 8, 1830
Age at Accession to the Throne: 31
Cause and Date of Death: Assassination, June 4, 1876
Place of Death and Burial Site: Istanbul – he was buried in the Tomb of Mahmud II on the Divanyolu, Istanbul
Male Heirs: Yusuf Izzeddin, Mahmud Celaleddin, Mehmed Selim, Mehmed Şevket, Abdülmecid (the last caliph), and Seyfeddin
Female Heirs: Saliha Sultan, Nazime Sultan, Esma Sultan, and Emine Sultan

Sultan Abdülaziz lived comfortably during the reign of Abdülmecid, his older brother. During his *şehzade* years, the Ottomans came to know him by his equanimity and striking appearance; later on, he would be seen by people as their way out of the despair cast by Abdülmecid's obsession with modernization that came down to imitating the West. Seen as a latter-day Sultan Selim I, Sultan Abdülaziz succeeded his late older brother to the throne only to find the empire at a difficult juncture, the imperial treasury immersed in debt, and an Ottoman social landscape still simmering but well ready to boil over.

The sultan announced that he would join in the process of economization, a necessity induced by the ongoing finan-

Oil portrait of Sultan Abdülaziz, by Pierre Désiré Guillemet, 1873

Emerald pendant

cial crisis. He first downsized the state officials in both the palace and other administrative offices, starting from those who were paid well despite the fact that they did not fulfill their duties. Setting an example, he also curtailed the general palace spending and gave up on one-third of his personal income. Although not unable to disentangle the financial crisis, the measures he put in effect seem to have given partial relief and recovery.

Sultan Abdülaziz followed an active policy of developing relations within and without his empire. After Sultan Selim I, Sultan Abdülaziz became the first sultan to visit Egypt on April 3, 1863. His visit received a very warm welcome by Egyptians; the sultan's objective in his visit was to reinforce the allegiance to the Ottoman Empire to these lands that had come to be known for their rebellions against the empire. Ismail Pasha, the governor of Egypt, benefited from the sultan's visit; in particular, the title of *Khedive* (Lord) began to be used for Ismail Pasha and his successors from the same family as the Ottoman viceroys governing Egypt.

Sultan Abdülaziz went to France at the invitation of Napoleon III of France, which made him the first Ottoman sultan to go abroad for the sake of diplomacy and, in fact, the first caliph to visit the Christian world. He departed Paris for London after the queen of the Great Britain invited him. His travel to Europe, which started on June 21, 1867, included visits to Belgium, Prussia, and Austria, and ended on August 7, 1867. Although the sultan's travel contributed positively to the diplomatic relations, his frugal worldview and stance against extravagance began to change after the travel.

Along with the financial crisis, the greatest challenge for Sultan Abdülaziz was the internal revolts agitated by foreign interventions. The apparent reason for the revolts was that the non-Muslims had been unhappy with the rights the imperial edicts had granted to them. European great powers fully exploited this discontent as a way to intervene in Ottoman domestic affairs.

After the Greeks in the Crete Island revolted under the banner of integration with Greece, European pressure forced the sultan to issue a code of rules, called *nizamname*, which legitimized the establishment of a special administration in the island in 1867.

Pan-Slavism, invented by the Russians as a political tool to control the Orthodox Slavs, had led to turbulent events in the Balkans. The first rebellion that Russians heavily invested on and triggered in the Balkans erupted among the Christian population in Bosnia-Herzegovina and was followed by the Bulgarian Revolt. While the Ottoman Empire was

Sultan Abdülaziz posing at his work desk, the Yitik Hazine Archives

occupied with silencing these revolts, Serbians and Montenegrins were provoked by Russia to revolt like others; however, the revolts were suppressed in a relatively short time. Interestingly, the revolts that the Ottoman Empire contained in its own lands were transmitted to Europe in a purposeful way that led Europeans to believe "the Ottomans raided and massacred Christian peoples."

In Istanbul, Midhat Pasha and former Serasker (the vizier commander of the army) Hüseyin Avni Pasha, whom Sultan Abdülaziz had removed from their posts because they were seen as dangerous to the state interests, sought ways to dethrone the sultan. The first step was agitating college students in Istanbul to revolt.

At the second stage of their plot, Mütercim (Interpreter) Rüşdü, Hüseyin Avni and Midhat pashas planned how they would dethrone Sultan Abdülaziz. They received a religious permission from the grand judge to execute the sultan under the pretext of destroying the state and property, and wasting the Muslims' treasury. Soon after, the Dolmabahçe Palace was under siege on land by the students of Military Academy commanded by Süleyman Pasha, and at sea by the warships of the Ottoman fleet, which the sultan had invested in and was committed to establishing.

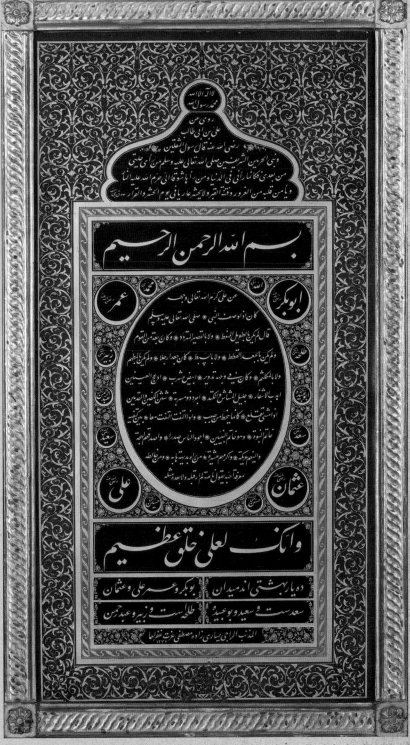

Hilye-i Şerif (Verbal portrait of the Prophet) by Yesarîzâde Mustafa İzzet Ketebeli, dated 1822

Sultan Abdülaziz during the later years of his reign. Taken by the Abdullah Brothers

Serasker Hüseyin Avni Pasha brought the sultan's nephew Şehzade Murad to the *Bab-ı Seraskeriye*, the Military Headquarters of the Ministry of War, and organized his ceremony of accession to the throne. Sultan Abdülaziz and his family were taken to the Topkapı Palace, which was in a miserable condition for it had not been used for years when the Ottoman seat of government moved to the Dolmabahçe Palace during the reign of his elder brother Sultan Abdülmecid. After this relocation under the rain, which did not befit the sultan's honor, he was voluntarily removed to the Fer'iye Palace in Istanbul. Worried for two days that he would be murdered there, the sultan used most of his time reading the Qur'an. He got even more anxious when his sword was taken away from him. On June 4, 1876, he was found in the Fer'iye Palace, the vessels on both his wrists had been cut. On the table in front of him was the Holy Qur'an open to the *Surah Yusuf*. After a general inspection on the body, Hüseyin Avni Pasha did not allow intensive treatment. Pointing to the scissors in the room, the doctor's report noted that the death of Abdülaziz was suicidal.

Eleven days after the death of the sultan, the Major Çerkez Hasan, the brother of sultan's wife Neş'erek Kadın, killed Hüseyin Avni Pasha and Raşid Pasha, the Minister of Foreign Affairs, who he was sure had murdered Abdülaziz. This issue would come to the fore once again during the reign of Abdülhamid II. The Yıldız Court then ruled that the old sultan had been murdered, and the guilty were punished.

The Sultan Abdülaziz era can be studied two ways in terms of the grand viziers in power. The period of Ali and Fuad pashas was very much distinct in character from the period of Mahmud Nedim and Midhat pashas. In general, the sultan's first period was more successful in terms of reforms and foreign diplomacy.

In spite of the financial crisis, the sultan heavily invested in and opened new military colleges as well as established the third largest naval fleet in the world.

The Beylerbeyi Palace at the Asian shore of the Bosphorus, situated just north of the Bosphorus Bridge today

The length of railroad lines expanded from 280 to 835 miles. The railroad tracks began to be constructed between Istanbul and Paris. When the sultan was informed that the tracks could pass through the yard of the Topkapı Palace, he quipped that "the rails can pass over my shoulders if they have to," representative of the importance he attributed to the railroads and rail transport.

As the most significant tool of correspondence, the telegram spread across the land to all state departments even in smaller districts. In addition to the compulsory primary education for all, new state and arts schools opened for boys and girls.

In response to increasing pressure of the Western countries, Sultan Abdülaziz applied another innovative policy that granted the right of property to foreigners; eventually all foreigners obtained the right of estate within the Ottoman borders, except the sacred Hijaz region.

The Çırağan and Beylerbeyi Palaces on the Bosphorus were constructed during Abdülaziz's reign, attracting lots of public reaction. The sultan's mother Pertevniyal Valide Sultan sponsored the construction of the Valide Mosque in Aksaray, Istanbul, and the sultan rebuilt in Kasımpaşa the Cami-i Kebir (the Big Mosque), which had burned down.

Sultan Abdülaziz was a master calligrapher, a successful composer, *ney* (an end-blown reed flute) player, and expert in Turkish music; a number of his compositions have survived

The *tughra* (imperial emblem) of Sultan Abdülaziz on top of the Gate of Salutation, the Topkapı Palace

to this day. In addition, he was very interested in *Karakucak* wrestling; indeed, this traditional Turkish wrestling was particularly frequented during his reign.

Abdülaziz regarded the lifestyle symbolized with the concept *A-la-franga* ("in the European style") as a sign of impiety; he had taken to reading the Holy Qur'an each and every morning. The broader public really admired his simplicity and attitude; for instance, he greeted, like anybody else, the passers-by at a local coffee shop.

The fifth minaret of the Prophet's Mosque, which does not exist today, was constructed during his reign and thereby called "the Aziziye Minaret." The sultan constructed a mosque on the Mount of Nur (Light) in Mecca and entrusted an engineer, minister of water, and supplier with facilitating the water distribution in the Holy Cities of Islam.

Sultan Abdülaziz conducted extensive reparations in hospitals for the needy in Mecca and Medina and expanded them with additional buildings. The sultan's mother Pertevniyal Valide Sultan paid the expenditures to employ a medical crew of competent doctors, pharmacists, and surgeons in these hospitals. In addition, the fortresses and city walls in Medina were repaired, and the city hall, two rose chambers, and a military barrack were also constructed in the city. The fortress of Ta'if was reconstructed during Abdülaziz's reign as well.

The Crystal Staircase (also known as the Sultanate Staircase), the Dolmabahçe Palace.
The Dolmabahçe Palace served as the main administrative center of the Ottoman Empire from 1856–1922.

Sultan Murad V

Reign: 1876

Father's Name: Abdülmecid
Mother's Name: Şevkefza Kadınefendi
Place and Date of Birth: Istanbul, September 22, 1840
Age at Accession to the Throne: 36
Cause and Date of Death: Diabetes, August 29, 1904
Place of Death and Burial Site: Istanbul – he was buried in a tomb under his name in the Yeni (New) Mosque, Istanbul
Male Heirs: Süleyman Efendi, Seyfeddin Efendi, and Mehmed Selahaddin Efendi
Female Heirs: Hadice Sultan, Fehime Sultan, Fatma Sultan, and Aliye Sultan

Oil portrait of Sultan Murad V

Sultan Murad V, whose birth-name was Mehmed Murad, was raised with great care by his father during his *şehzade* years. He was the sultan whose reign lasted the shortest in Ottoman history. As the future sultan, he received an impressive education and occupied leading positions in imperial ceremonies. He accompanied his uncle on travels to Egypt and Europe, and kept in touch with the Young Ottomans—a group of intellectuals that were influenced by the Western thinkers and the French Revolution and who defended the constitutional monarchy as the ideal form of government. He met up with Şinasi, Namık Kemal, and Ziya Pasha and received their conspicuous support. Once, the Young Ottomans, who left the theater after watching Namık Kemal's play of *Vatan Yahut Silistre* (Homeland, or Silistra) gathered up in front of Namık Kemal's house for pro-test, using punning slogans like "What is your *Murad*? (both the name of Şehzade Murad and the word 'wish'). This is our *Murad*. May God give us our *murad* ('wish')," illustrative of their espousal of Murad IV.

Sultan Murad V's piano

During Sultan Abdülaziz's reign, the tumultuous events in Salonica that cost the lives of two ambassadors the-re had given Europeans an incentive to intervene in the Ottoman internal affairs; furthermore, the sultan's adversaries dethroned Sultan Abdülaziz and replaced him with Murad V. Unlike his predecessors, Murad V's as-suming the throne was not celebrated by an accession ceremony or the procession to gird on his sword in the Eyüp Sultan Mosque.

Under rainfall, Sultan Murad V was brought hurriedly to the Porte of the Commander General's Office (the main gate of the present-day Istanbul University), and the leading statesmen paid homage to him as the new sultan. The same homage ceremony recurred in the Dolmabahçe Palace.

Meanwhile, a bitter conflict arose among those who had brought Murad V to the throne; in particular, the libertarian ideas of Midhat Pasha did not attract others' attention and concerns.

Commander General Hüseyin Avni Pasha, who helped Sultan Murad V ascend to the thro-ne, dictated that he was going to vigilantly select those who would see the sultan in person.

While having his breakfast on the fifth day of his sultanate, Sultan Murad V received the breaking news that the ex-Sultan Abdülaziz was found dead in his room at the Fer'iye Palace; all of a sudden, he fainted in a fury of shock. Eleven days later, the Senior Major Çerkez Hasan Bey, the brother-in-law of the ex-Sultan, raided a meeting of *Meclis-i Vükela* (Cabinet of Ministers) and murdered Hüseyin Avni Pasha for the suspected murder of his sister's husband.

Sultan Murad V by the Abdullah Brothers

An already ill Sultan Murad V was deeply touched and finally distressed by the recent events. When visited by his brothers, the sultan revealed to them that his state of health was bad, and complained about terrible headaches he had recently begun to have.

The way Sultan Murad V acted during his first Friday prayer ceremony showed that he had lost his consciousness. Although the sultan had been transferred to the Yıldız Palace, Istanbul in line with the doctors' advice, he had once thrown himself into the pool in a moment of madness. Soon after, it became obvious that he had lost his mental health. After this he stopped attending the Friday prayer ceremonies nor would he meet with anyone from then on.

Although the government wanted to cover the truth, the word of mouth already spread that the sultan had gone mad; in addition, the public criticized Grand Vizier Rüşdü Pasha for trying to govern the Ottoman Empire in the absence of a sultan.

On the day after he returned from a salutation ceremony, the sultan smashed a glass window in the palace and attempted to kill himself. The doctors came in and examined him; however, they unanimously agreed that his chance of recovery was very slim. Midhat Pasha went to see Abdülhamid II, the *de facto* heir of the sultan, and told him that they would proclaim him the new sultan on condition that he would pronounce the new constitution, called *Kanun-i Esasi* (Fundamental Law) written by members of the Young Ottomans, particularly Midhat Pasha.

Following the religious executive order from the grand judge on August 30, 1876, the parliament ruled to dethrone Sultan Murad V and replace him with Abdülhamid II.

An original composition of Sultan Murad V

Murad V's sultanate that began *fait accompli* ended after ninety-three days.

During the reign of Sultan Abdülhamid II, Murad V and his family were relocated to the Çırağan Palace, and his medical treatment carried on there.

Because the Masonic lodge and a number of dissenting groups pursued propaganda that the ex-sultan was healthy but caught by injustice and corruption, Sultan Abdülhamid II had his brother examined by a medical committee of native and foreign doctors. The committee underscored the fact that the ex-sultan was still mentally impaired, and his treatment was not within the limits of possibility.

Dissenting groups including the masons dared to abduct the ex-sultan three times; eventually, they were always caught and punished. These attempts of abduction bothered Murad V and

Ottoman postcard of a view of the Dolmabahçe Palace from the Bosphorus

his family most. He had to live the life of a prisoner for his remaining twenty-eight years, for he had to be protected from abductors under heavy surveillance.

The shortest-staying guest of the Ottoman throne, Sultan Murad V was very interested in painting, carpentry, and architecture. He was a genius composer; he wrote more than 550 compositions in the European style, called *a-la-franga*. The piano he used while composing has survived to this day. His character and image were quite different than his brothers in the way that he had championed an *a-la-franga* lifestyle since his *şehzade* years. He became a member of the Masonic lodge as he thought that state politics would benefit from it; however, Murad V seemed that he regarded the lodge as a sports club without knowing what the organization of this secret society was really about.

The Sultanate Gate of the Dolmabahçe Palace

Sultan Abdülhamid II

Reign: 1876-1909

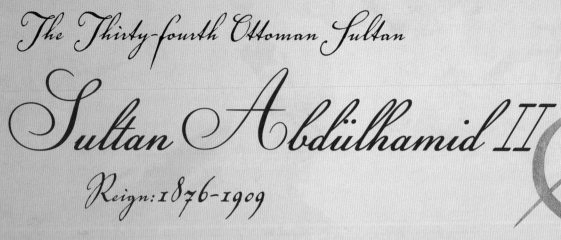

Father's Name: Abdülmecid
Mother's Name: Tirimujgan Kadınefendi
Place and Date of Birth: Istanbul, September 21, 1842
Age at Accession to the Throne: 34
Cause and Date of Death: Cardiac arrest, February 10, 1918
Place of Death and Burial Site: Istanbul – he was buried in the tomb of Mahmud II on the Divanyolu, Istanbul
Male Heirs: Mehmed Selim, Ahmed Nuri, Mehmed Abdulkadir, Mehmed Burhaneddin, Abdurrahim Hayri, Ahmed Nureddin, and Mehmed Abid
Female Heirs: Zekiye Sultan, Naime Sultan, Naile Sultan, Şadiye Sultan, Ayşe Sultan, and Refia Sultan

Although it was unlikely that Abdülhamid II would be a sultan, the execution of his uncle Abdülaziz and the dethronement of his older brother Murad V led him to be the thirty-fourth guest to the Ottoman throne.

The loss of his mother when he was eleven left an indelible mark in Abdülhamid's mind. Moreover, he learned to cope with solitude specifically after his father Sultan Abdülmecid had shown more interest in his older brother Murad V rather than in him. The palace staff did not give him due respect as well, primarily because no one predicted him to be a sultan one day. Neither had he enjoyed the palace life, nor liked the palace staff, this introvert *şehzade*.

Oil portrait of Sultan Abdülhamid II, painter unknown

Abdülhamid II was nineteen years old when his father died. As a child, he received lessons in Turkish, Arabic, Persian, and French. His uncle Sultan Abdülaziz was the first to realize his superior intellect and administrative talents. Abdülaziz let him grow up in a comfortable environment and took him on his travels abroad. Whereas his older brother Murad V demonstrated a cool and relaxed personality, Abdülhamid II, the younger *şehzade*, preferred to sit in a corner, away from the social scene. The railroads he excitingly observed in Britain illuminated him to a great extent. He did not take pleasure living in the palace; besides, he toiled the land on his farm in Maslak, Istanbul, raised sheep, mined ceruse minerals, and exchanged bonds in the stock market. It seems that had he not be a sultan, the personal wealth, over 100,000 golden coins that he had accumulated by hard-work, could have provided him with a comfortable standard of life.

After his accession to the throne, Sultan Abdülhamid II donated his personal assets to the army. Interestingly enough, because he had been away from the palace and in the public and quite involved in the economy during his *şehzade* years, he had been raised the way the old *şehzades* were raised with firsthand administrative experience in the provinces as a governor prior to assuming the throne.

During the period of Sultan Abdülhamid II, Midhat Pasha and his friends endeavored to affect the establishment of a constitutional monarchy, which they could not do in the course of Murad V's reign. In fact, Abdülhamid's word on it had them pronounce him as the new sultan on August 31, 1876.

Abdülhamid II assumed the throne during the turbulent years of the Ottoman Empire; he had to grapple with the Balkan revolts, the Russian-oriented "Eastern Question," and European banks' unwillingness to lend money to the Ottomans. Financial impossibilities delayed suppressing the revolts.

Sultan Abdülhamid II visited and dined with the soldiers at their barracks and with mariners in their shipyards; he treated the scholars, commanders, and soldiers to *iftar*s—the dinners for breaking the fast of Ramadan. He prayed in different mosques amongst the public, and he visited in hospitals the veteran soldiers wounded in the Balkan wars. In particular, he gifted soldiers who had lost their feet with walking sticks of his own make. All of these small but soulful gestures made the army and public feel much affection for the new sultan, the army boosted its morale, and the public rekindled their candles of hope.

The Ottomans won wars against the Serbs in the Balkans; however, they agreed to sign a three-month truce with the Serbs as a result of tremendous pressure from Russians. Furthermore, a conference was scheduled to take place in Istanbul. Under the leadership of Britain, the participating countries would discuss ways to appease the turbulent events in the Balkans and ameliorate the Russo-Ottoman relations.

Meanwhile, a gang against the peace with Serbia framed a plot to assassinate Midhat Pasha and his men and dethrone the sultan, but their plan was discovered soon enough and the culprits arrested.

The first constitution in Turkish history was to be legislated; for this purpose, a commission of Muslims and non-Muslims was founded. In particular, Midhat Pasha became the new grand vizier to replace the recent retiree Rüşdü Pasha.

The first day of the Istanbul Conference focused on the political situation of the Balkans, and the constitution, *Kanun-i Esasi* (Fundamental Law), was proclaimed on December 23, 1876. Henceforth, the First Constitutional Monarchy Era commenced.

The constitution had been announced hurriedly in the Istanbul Conference mainly because the Ottomans thought the Western countries would see the constitution and refrain from making great demands. Nevertheless, it did not interest them. The Europeans prepared in the Russian embassy a list of requests as follows: Bosnia and Bulgaria should be independent, the Ottoman army had to leave Serbia and Montenegro, and scores of reforms had to be carried out in the Balkans. The Ottoman general assembly met under the sultan's order, discussed the contents of the list, and declined the requests unanimously on the basis that the clauses on the list would violate Ottoman domestic sovereignty. Britain moved on to organize another conference in London this time. On April 12, 1877, the Ottoman general assembly once more denied the decisions made in London simply because the clauses were in direct violation of the Ottoman sovereign rights.

Midhat Pasha, the real force who brought Sultan Abdülhamid II to the throne, put constant pressure on him. In line with his war-mongering, Midhat Pasha attempted to recruit an army called the *Millet Askeri* (the Army of Nation) to be commanded by him. Later he added a cross-sign on the Turkish flag in Bosnia Herzegovina and had an army consisting of Mus-

The Mahmil-i Şerif, the leading camel litter of the Imperial Gifts Caravan with the sultan's yearly offering for sacred uses to Mecca and Medina, is carried out of the Yıldız Palace before the caravan sets out for the Haramayn.

lims and Christians parade in Istanbul, carrying the same flag. Moreover, he said in drinking parties that he would repeal the Ottoman dynasty and establish a Midhatian dynasty. All put together, he attracted quite a reaction. Midhat Pasha had succeeded in enacting the law of exile, which authorized sending certain criminals on exile; oddly enough, he became the first to be exiled based on this law.

Soon after the Ottoman government pronounced that it would not recognize the resolution of the London Conference, Russia got the opportunity it had been waiting for and declared war on the Ottoman Empire on April 24, 1877. Romanians, Serbians, Montenegrins, and Bulgarians allied with Russia. The Ottoman military and finance were in a bad situation; worse, the Ottoman Empire failed to receive any outside help. The heroic resistance of Gazi Osman Pasha in Pleven in Rumelia and Gazi Ahmed Muhtar Pasha in Erzurum in Anatolia against the invaders could not change the inevitable ending. The Ottoman army, helpless in

An Ottoman train going all the way to Medina on the Hijaz Railroad, regarded by Sultan Abdülhamid II as his magnum opus

both the East and West, had to retreat desperately. Another drama following the losing streak of wars was experienced by thousands of Muslims who had been living on recently invaded territories. These Muslims became emigrants and fled to Anatolia, particularly Istanbul.

While the Ottoman Empire went through a turbulent period because of intricate results of a great war with the Russians, the representatives from different ethnic backgrounds occupied themselves with a different agenda in the parliamentary assembly, the empire's main executive body. Instead of making decisions on the Russo-Turkish War (1877–1878), the assembly overwhelmingly discussed the independence movements of minorities along with the desire that their languages be given an official status, which upset the sultan to some degree.

Medina Train Station, the last stop on the Hijaz Railroad

The Ottomans signed an armistice agreement with Russians in Edirne. In the palace meeting during which peace terms would be negotiated, the Astarcılar Kethudası (commander of cloth-liners) Ahmed Efendi, one of the attendee representatives, spoke out that not the assembly but the sultan was responsible for the regressing course of events. In response to this offbeat incrimination, Sultan Abdülhamid II emphasized that he was not guilty for he had done the best he could in his capacity. When Ahmed Efendi turned up his accusatory tone, the sultan made it clear that he was ready to keep fighting Russia for the rest of his life if he had to and entrusted the assembly to put Ahmed Efendi in his place for his scornful behavior against the sultan's authority.

The sultan would not hand the sovereignty over to the statesmen who were clearly acting in their own interests. His very words, "I am now obliged to follow in Sultan Mahmud's tracks" heralded what was to happen. On the basis of authority conferred on him by the constitution, Sultan Abdülhamid II dissolved the assembly on February 13, 1878 just like his grandfather Sultan Mahmud II disbanded the long-dead Janissary corps.

Following the Russo-Turkish War of 1877–1878, the Ottomans signed the Treaty of San Stefano, known also as the Yeşilköy Treaty, with Russia. Britain and other European countries raised their dissenting voices after they found out that Russia determined to partition the Ottoman lands (known

Sultan Abdülhamid II attends a public ceremony after the Friday Prayer in the Hamidiye Mosque. Taken by the Abdullah Brothers

as the "Eastern Question" in European history) simply on its own. Eventually, all concerned wanted to discuss the matters further and scheduled a conference to be held in Berlin. Meanwhile, on June 4, 1878 Britain signed a secret agreement with Russia while it also acquired the administration of Cyprus from the Ottoman Empire with the promise that it would help out the Ottomans during the negotiations. Sultan Abdülhamid II did not want to endorse that treaty, which the British already had the Ottoman government sign *fait accompli*; nevertheless, military coercions compelled him to do so.

The Ottoman government had given up Cyprus, supposing that Britain would back them up in the Berlin Conference; however, that did not happen. Sultan Abdülhamid II was well-aware of the fact that the conference was held with the purpose of partitioning the Ottoman lands. The Treaty of Berlin on July 13, 1878 conceded independence to Serbia, Romania, and Montenegro; forced Russia to pay a war indemnity; seceded the cities of Kars, Ardahan, and Batum to Russia; divided Bulgaria into three spheres; and attached Bosnia-Herzegovina to Austria. In 1881, France invaded Tunis, Britain occupied Egypt in 1882, and Bulgaria marched on eastern Rumelia in 1885.

When Sultan Abdülhamid II became the sultan, he had found an empire at war on several fronts. Within a matter of months, his empire began to suffer tremendous losses. Eventually, the sultan committed his focus to international politics and worked to pursue an informed and consistent foreign policy. The fact that the Ottoman Empire had been subject to humiliation and defamation at the Tersane (Shipyard) Conference in Istanbul and at the Berlin Conference required the sultan to apply a solid, self-respecting, and honorable diplomacy.

For the first time in its history, the Ottoman Empire came to pursue engaging and involving foreign policies during Sultan Abdülhamid II's reign. The sultan effectively devised a balance-of-power strategy, played on the conflict of interests between ruthlessly competitive European countries, and consequently safeguarded his empire in a competitive world.

Abdülhamid II during his şehzade years

Sirkeci Train Station in Eminönü, Istanbul by the Abdullah Brothers

The sultan, hence, established in the palace an intelligence center, a type of foreign relations department whose staff collected and analyzed international publications and ambassadorial reports. He met foreign and native scholars and discussed with them foreign diplomacy. The rationale behind his balance-of-power policy was apparently simple, based on taking advantage of the conflict-of-interests among countries; however, it was quite difficult and complicated when put into practice. The main actor in his policy was Britain, which he detested and never confided in. Russia stood against Britain according to his policy, and the sultan got closer to Russia against Britain when needed. When Britain occupied Egypt, he turned to France. Later on, he contributed to the Franco-Italian confrontation in North Africa. As a matter of fact, Sultan Abdülhamid II did not have any long-term alliance or agreement with any of these countries.

The sultan applied a similar policy in the Balkans; in particular, he set the Balkan states at loggerheads and prevented them from unifying against the Ottoman Empire. In addition, he appeased the visiting ambassadors using the caliphate, and sent photographs and images to great powers to show off that his empire was doing fine. It turned out that these practices were masterfully devised and effectively worked.

The sultan discharged many corrupt statesmen who had accustomed themselves to receiving orders and gifts from foreign embassies, and gave more responsibilities to his trusted men such as Gazi Osman Pasha and Cevdet Pasha against the treacherous members of the government. He always used caution, predicting that he would follow the path of his uncle and older brother, who both dearly suffered the consequences of not doing so.

Influential cabals had wanted to bring Murad V back to the throne simply for their own interests and tried abducting him from the Çırağan Palace several times. Coups d'état and revolts had been attempted in the past quite a number of times, and foreign countries had employed several plots. As a result of these, the sultan felt forced to establish a bureau of investigations and ordered top-level attention to foreign publications in order to avert domestic sedition they might instigate.

Sultan Abdülhamid II thought that the empire needed time for recovery; for this reason, he determinedly endeavored to keep it away from wars. The only war that the pacifist sultan engaged in was fought against the Greeks on the Island of Crete. After the revolt in Crete proved impossible to suppress and Greece declared that it had annexed the island, the sultan declared war on Greece on April 18, 1897. The Ottoman forces crushed the Greek army in Larissa and at the pitched battle in Domokos. These victories were the first military achievements of Abdülhamid II; eventually, the Greeks submitted and asked for a truce. The Ottoman flag waved in Crete for another ten years, but Crete would be integrated into Greece during the convoluted years that followed the declaration of the Second Constitutional Monarchy.

The sultan understood that the Ottoman Empire had lost its reputation in the West on account of its accumulated debts to European countries and that the repayments of these debts and interests constituted more than half of the empire's annual revenues. Therefore, he proclaimed to the creditor countries a decree called *Muharrem Kararnamesi* on December 20, 1881. Founded by this decree, the Ottoman Public Debt Administration relegated, to a degree, the control of the Ottoman economy to the foreign countries to which it was indebted. Foreign credits, albeit in small amounts, were withdrawn during this period; however, the aggregate foreign debts remarkably dwindled away for an amount greater than the recently borrowed had been repaid.

322

One of the earliest photos of the Ka'ba in Sultan Abdülhamid II's Yıldız Photo Albums. Taken by Albay Sadık Bey

Sultan Abdülhamid II was the most modest and unostentatious of all the Ottoman sultans in his way of living and dress. He dropped down the palace spending, shortened the palace food menu, and reduced the number of palace staff. The foreigners' commercial competitions in the Ottoman lands materialized during his reign as well. The Germans won the first round and obtained the contract of a great railroad project. The extension of the tracks between Haydarpaşa-İzmit down to Ankara and the construction of new Baghdad-railroad were given to the Germans.

Among the Ottoman sultans, Sultan Abdülhamid II was the first to actually put his caliphate power in practice. In his view, the Muslim subjects always came first. Against the British-oriented sedition in the Muslim lands that the caliphate could not belong to the Ottomans, the sultan consulted and received the approval of Muslim scholars. In fact, Islamic

Clock Tower of Jaffa on the Mediterranean Sea constructed by Sultan Abdülhamid II

thinkers put forward a wealth of religious and historical proofs that the caliphate had nothing to do with race or ethnicity.

British agents did not stop there; they announced the Khedive of Egypt as the new caliph with the objective of weakening the sultan's power in the region. To counter this British scheme, the sultan gave importance to Pan-Islamism. The sultan did not want to see the foreigners growing the seeds of discord sowed by the British, so he collected a group of religious leaders and tribal chiefs and sent them to reach out to the broader public. He dispatched his most trusted competent governors to administer in Muslim-majority provinces. In addition, he sponsored Islamic scholars to spread Islam in the countries as far away as South Africa and Japan. His influence in China was tremendous; in particular, a university of Islam opened in Beijing with an Ottoman flag waving on top of its main gate.

In September, 1900, Sultan Abdülhamid II launched the construction of the Hijaz railroad between Damascus and Mecca, what he referred to as his "magnum opus." Despite all the obstructions of the European powers, continuous Bedouin attacks, many misfortunes, and climatic hardships, the rail tracks reached all the way to Medina on October 1, 1908.

Apprehensive of the course of events in the region, the powers of Europe (especially Britain and France) exerted heavier pressure on the

Ottoman Empire by continuing to claim that the Ottoman government subjected non-Muslims to prejudice and inequality. These pressures caused Sultan Abdülhamid II to step back on some issues. However, he preserved his integrity and defense against the Armenian Question until the end of his reign; in particular, he resisted to the pressure which forced him to conduct reforms in the lands the Armenians inhabited, which an article in the Treaty of Berlin had stipulated. Aware of the fact that this particular pressure would lead to granting autonomy to the Armenians, the sultan made no concessions in the face of the pressure tactics of and threats from the West.

Sultan Abdülhamid II maintained that there was no province in which there lived more Armenians than the Turks; therefore, he would not undertake Armeno-centric reforms. Sullying the sultan's name, the Armenians started calling him as "the Red Sultan." For the first time in Ottoman history, Armenian terrorists attempted to assassinate the sultan with a time bomb on July 21, 1905.

According to the plan, a 220-pound [100-kilo] time-bomb would explode following the Friday prayers and kill the sultan and statesmen, and then terror would reign in Istanbul with a series of bombings at critical spots. Quite unexpectedly, the grand judge halted and discussed some issues with the sultan on his way out from the Hamidiye Mosque; his several-minutes en retard saved his life. A terrible explosion cost 26 lives, wounded

Clock Tower of İzmir on the Aegean Sea constructed by Sultan Abdülhamid II

Inner dome of the Hamidiye Mosque built by Sultan Abdülhamid II

58, and killed 20 horses. It seemed that the only one calm in these panic-stricken moments was the sultan; he got on the horse cart as if nothing had happened, bridled his horses, and drove away to the palace. When the brain-trust behind the plot was captured, the sultan said he had forgiven them. Later on, he had them work for the empire.

For a long time, the Zionists had been working to establish a Jewish state on "the Promised Land" in Palestine. They approached Abdülhamid II and told him that they would scratch out the empire's entire debt only if he permitted them to settle in Palestine. The sultan not only declined their generous offer but also took measures to avoid their settlement in Palestine.

Because of financial setbacks, Sultan Abdülhamid II later dismissed his policy of detachment but still refrained from long-term alliances. For instance, he set up a commercial alliance with Germany for a variety of reasons: unlike other European countries, Germany had not attempted to occupy Muslim lands, had supported the Ottoman stance on the Armenian Question, and Abdülhamid II really appreciated Germans' work ethics and discipline.

The sultan knew that a balance-of-power policy could not sustain the Ottoman sovereignty in the long run; in fact, his main objective in applying that policy was to buy some time to fortify his empire. Nonetheless, the foreign debts that accumulated during the Tanzimat (Reorganization) Era, the domination of the Public Debt Administration in many branches of economy, and spending hard-saved imperial capital to suppress domestic revolts all hindered Abdülhamid II's broader plans of extensive reforms. Despite all, important reform steps were taken especially in education.

Sultan Abdülhamid II was very concerned with colleges that schooled statesmen and military personnel. He opened schools for girls as well as increased the number of primary and elementary schools. The most eminent politicians and military commanders of the future such as Mustafa Kemal, the founder of the Republic of Turkey, would be educated in the schools founded by Abdulhamid II.

Whereas the sultan intensely censored many venues of publications, he helped the publishing sector grow and expand; in particular, numerous books, booklets, journals, and newspapers published in his time survive to this day.

The sultan had a great passion for photography; he had photographers take pictures of the Ottoman lands across the board mainly because he lacked the chance to visit the public

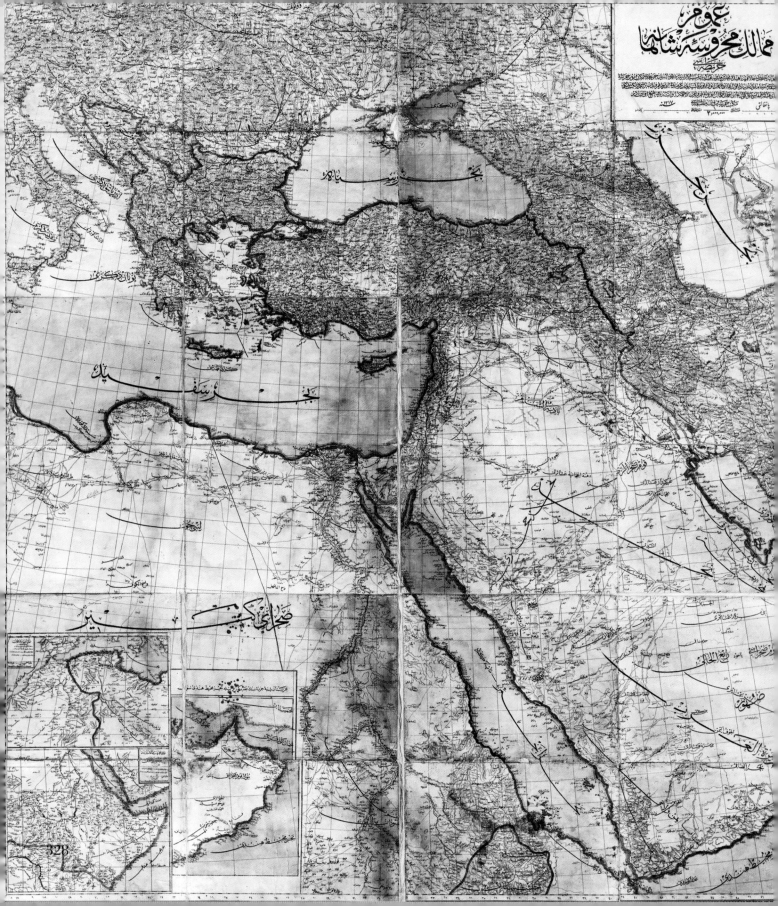

and supervise the ongoing projects in the field. Abdülhamid II prepared 911 photo-albums, collectively known as the Yıldız Albums that are made up of approximately 36,000 photos taken from hundreds of cities throughout the Ottoman lands, portraying various scenes and events of his time, including the recently-opened schools, hospitals, railroads, and bridges as well as the statesmen on duty, field-exercises in military colleges, students, the Holy Lands, as well as ranches raising livestock. Sultan Abdülhamid II was a great patron of photography, and his Yıldız Albums are one of the world's largest photo collections, contributing a unique archival documentation of the time.

The sultan paid for the construction of the Children's Hospital and the *Darülâceze*—a charitable housing for the seniors and the needy in the Şişli district of Istanbul from his personal savings.

Railroad networks were on top of the sultan's agenda. He completed the Anatolian, Rumelian, and Baghdad railways. About half the railroads in Turkey today were constructed during Abdülhamid II's time. In addition, the railroad infrastructure set back then is still being used in Turkey. Furthermore, he significantly laid out an extensive telegram network along with the railroads.

The sultan attached importance to developing relations with the Turkish peoples. He contacted the Turks in Central Asia through Sheikh Süleyman Efendi of Bukhara. Süleyman Efendi also represented the sultan in the Turan (Turkic peoples) Congress held in Pest.

Meanwhile, an opposition camp bubbled up, challenging the sultan. Led by the Committee of Union and Progress (*İttihat ve Terakki Komitesi*), which thought the declaration of the constitutional monarchy was the panacea for the empire's stagnation inside and in the international arena, this camp received the support of non-Muslim committee members and revolted in Rumelia. Eventually, the sultan declared the Constitution once again on July, 23, 1908; thus, the Era of the Second Constitutional Monarchy began. In the long run, the constitutional government did not avert the empire's stagnation; to the contrary, it expedited the process of demise. Austria-Hungary occupied Bosnia-Herzegovina to avoid Bosnian representatives being sent to the new parliament on October 5, 1908. Bulgaria declared its independence, and Crete pronounced its association with Greece.

Following the elections, the new parliament received the newly elected representatives; oddly enough, Turks became minority. What the sultan had been afraid was coming true.

An Ottoman map showing the borders of the empire during the reign of Sultan Abdülhamid II.

Reckless operations of the Unionist government augmented domestic discontent, and various factions were formed within the army. Meanwhile, a counter-committee was founded against the Unionists. The opponents of the Unionists garnered up in what was termed the Society of Islamic Unity (*İttihad-ı Muhammedi Cemiyeti*). They published provocative articles in Volkan and Mizan, their two major newspapers, defended physical violence, and called for the parliament to be suspended. Amidst all the tension, a pervasive rebellion broke out in Istanbul. Called the "Counter-revolution of March 31," this rebellious event had caused bloodshed on April 13, 1909—the day corresponding to March 31st on the Julian calendar in use at the time.

Meanwhile, Armenians rose in a huge rebellion and slaughtered many Muslims in Adana on April 14, 1909. The turbulent events in Istanbul came to an end when the *Hareket Ordusu* (Operation Army) came near Yeşilköy in Istanbul all the way from Salonica—the base of the Committee of Union and Progress. Some parliament members paid visits to the army.

Rumors spread that the sultan caused the rebellion to break up and therefore should be dethroned. In return, the sultan told Grand Vizier Tevfik Pasha that he could relinquish the throne but would like it to be revealed whether he played any role in the rebellion. Hearing about it, Said Pasha rejected the sultan's inquiry and remonstrated, "what would come of us if he became clean?"

Sultan Abdülhamid II was informed that the loyal First Army was waiting for his orders to counter the Operation Army; however, the sultan said that he was the caliph of Muslims and would not let Muslims kill Muslims. The First Army commander promised him that they would not bear their arms against the Operation Army.

The Operation Army led by Mahmud Şevket Pasha entered Istanbul and occupied the city. Soon after, martial courts opened, gibbets were set up. Many innocents, not involved in the rebellion, were gibbeted. A wind of violence blew in the air of Istanbul, thanks to the Union and Progress. The First Army was exiled to Rumelia, and the press was placed under extreme censorship. In theory, there was a parliament; in reality, the administration rested on absolutism, not constitutional monarchy.

A *fatwa*, religious executive, was issued against Sultan Abdülhamid II based on false accusations directed at his character and administration. The sultan was accused instigating the Thirty-First of March Incident, distorting and burning religious books, and consuming the imperial treasury.

A scene from the Ottoman Parliament while a member of the Parliament reads the message of Sultan Abdülhamid II to the Parliament

Said Pasha, the chair of the parliament, turned against the sultan, who had assigned him as grand vizier seven times and guarded him many times. He issued with the rule of majority an order from the parliament to dethrone the sultan.

A delegate consisting of Armenian Aram, Georgian Arif Hikmet the Mariner (one of the sultan's former aides), Jewish Emanuel Karasu, the Salonika representative in the parliament, and Albanian Esad Toptani came to the palace to inform the sultan of the parliament's final decision. Reputedly, Sultan Abdülhamid II greeted them, and said "Couldn't the parliament find any better messengers than a Jew, an Armenian, an Albanian, and an ungrateful one to convey the note of execution to a sultan of Turks and caliph of all Muslims?" The delegate responded to him with silence.

The sultan wanted to reside in the Çırağan Palace after his forced retirement; however, Mahmud Şevket Pasha, the draconian commander of the Operation Army, packed him and his family and railroaded them headfirst to Salonica. For the first time in Ottoman history, a dethroned sultan was exiled outside of Istanbul.

In Salonica, the sultan busied himself with carpentry and ironworking, ignorant of the fact that the fine diplomatic balance he carefully tuned in the Balkans had awkwardly disintegrated. A law enacted by the Union and Progress dissolved the controversial views of the Balkan peoples; soon after, the Balkan states constituted a unified front to confront the Ottoman Empire in what were called the Balkan Wars. The sultan urgently departed Salonika, for his life would be in danger there. The sultan boldly expressed that he did not want to leave Salonica and could bear his arms and fight if he had to. When the conditions escalated to the brink of war, the sultan was brought back to Istanbul and settled in the Beylerbeyi Palace on November 1, 1912.

The sultan spent the last years of his life watching from afar the greatest trouble the Ottoman Empire was going through. The sultan passed away in the Beylerbeyi Palace on February 10, 1918. He would not see the many miseries to come or the consequences of the First World War. The body of the deceased sultan was buried in the Tomb of his grandfather Mahmud II on the Divanyolu in Istanbul.

The real worth of Sultan Abdülhamid II was better understood during the recent turbulent years of the empire, and his absence was conspicuously felt. Those who had staunchly opposed him during his reign came to their senses, albeit too late. Had Sultan Abdülhamid II not been dethroned by a multinational setup, it was very likely that the Balkan Wars would not have broken out, and the sultan would have spared his subjects from the First World War. In this vein, today's Republic of Turkey would have span over larger territories.

One of the most extraordinary sultans in Ottoman history, Sultan Abdülhamid II was cool-headed but a bit skeptic. The kindness that he showed to his addressees and the smiling face that he gave even those he detested were among his striking features. He was impressively smart; in human relations, he intuitively predicted the ideas and emotions of his addressees by closely examining their mimics and body language. It is recorded that his memory was outstanding, for he never forgot familiar faces.

Sultan Abdülhamid II abstained from debauchery; he ate and dressed simply and lived quite an ordinary life. He was very interested in sports. His swordsmanship was remarkable, and he made precise shots with his gun. He listened to Western music, went to theaters, and most importantly did carpentry in an effort to release the stress-filled years of his reign. Arguably, he was a genius master of carpentry; many of his well-crafted works endured up to now.

The Gureba Hospital built during the reign of Sultan Abdülhamid II in Bursa

Sultan Abdülhamid II comported himself with the elevated dignity expected from a caliph. He was a devout Muslim and keen on charity works. He perceived the caliphate not only as a political duty but also a tremendous responsibility; in particular, he pursued a series of beneficial activities in the Holy Cities, which can be elucidated under seventy-seven headings. The sultan undertook in the Holy Cities the following extensive construction projects: the construction of a city hall, police headquarters, a fort for Mecca's defense, the reparations of the tombs of the Companions and the following Muslim generations, waterways, a significant guesthouse for the poor pilgrims, a telegram network, and a provision of labor and military services to the military barracks located there. All these projects strongly suggest that the sultan followed the suite of his predecessors and turned out to be a real "Servant of the Holy Cities." The chronicles state that, after the period of the Four Rightly-Guided Caliphs and Umar ibn Abdulaziz, there had been no other country than the Ottoman Empire which committed itself this much to the service of the Holy Cities. In addition, the pictures of Mecca and Medina taken by the Colonel Sadık Bey were added to Sultan Abdülhamid II's photo albums.

Sultan Abdülhamid II was a peace-lover. He detested wars and blood-shed. Nevertheless, he dared to engage war when necessary, like in Greece, over which the Ottomans eventually triumphed. He was so appreciative of merits that he allocated salaries for his aggressive opponents sent abroad on exile.

Thanks to the Hamidiye Hijaz Railroad, which was completed during Sultan Abdülhamid II's reign, the pilgrims set out on their sacred journey of pilgrimage far more cheaply, comfortably, and safely. The railroads further provided faster mobilization for the army toward Yemen and the broader Arabian Peninsula. Although short-lived, the Hijaz Railroad showcased the caliphate's un-ignorable power to the whole world. Significantly enough, this giant project was made possible by the donations from the Muslims around the world.

Muslims from India to the United States, Persia to Algeria, and Sudan to Russia doggedly contributed to the project in spite of all distractions, restrictions, and other obstacles; eventually, they made it happen. Many European statesmen had mocked the sultan for his pipedream project and impeded it in numerous ways right when it began to materialize.

At the end of the day, the 800-mile rail tracks were laid out and opened to traffic, indicative of the Muslims' honor and dignity. Indeed it coincided with Sultan Abdülhamid II's reign that the Muslims of the entire world came together for the same goal.

Sultan Abdülhamid II attends a public ceremony after the Friday Prayer in the Mecidiye Mosque on the European side of Istanbul with the Beylerbeyi Palace and the Çamlıca Hill in the background on the other side of the Bosphorus.

Sultan Mehmed V

Reign: 1909–1918

Honorific: *Gazi*
Father's Name: Abdülmecid
Mother's Name: Gülcemal Kadınefendi
Place and Date of Birth: Istanbul, November 2, 1844
Age at Accession to the Throne: 65
Cause and Date of Death: Cardiac arrest, July 4, 1918
Place of Death and Burial Site: Istanbul – he was buried in the tomb under his name in Eyüp, Istanbul
Male Heirs: Mehmed Ziyaedin, Mahmud Necmeddin, and Ömer Hilmi

Like his older brothers, Sultan Mehmed Reşad was throned following a coup. Whereas Sultan Mehmed IV, one of his great grandfathers, was, at seven years old, the youngest sultan in the history of the Ottoman dynasty to ascend to the throne, Mehmed Reşad was the oldest.

Subsequent to the Counter-Revolution of March 31, the parliament under the control of the Committee of Union and Progress decided to dethrone Abdülhamid II and bring his heir Mehmed Reşad to the throne. The Operation Army's arrival in Istanbul and its quench of the Counter-Revolution of March 31 were regarded as the second conquest of Istanbul by Union and Progress members. In addition, they titled Mehmed Reşad as Sultan Mehmed V while the public would know the sultan more popularly as Sultan Reşad.

Oil portrait of Sultan Mehmed Reşad by Antranik

The sultan assumed the throne at a very old age. Had it been up to him, he would have stayed away from throne and committed himself to prayers. Turbulent years exhausted the inexperienced and already-aged sultan. The government's main agent was the grand vizier, for the system was still constitutional monarchy. The sultan had the authority to appoint the grand vizier, but he did not have the permission to make sovereign decisions. Thus the impact of the sultan on the administration was reduced significantly, and *de facto* control of the administration went to the Union and Progress, the grand vizier, and the government. This he learned only several days after his older brother Abdülhamid II had been carried away to Salonica by Mahmud Şevket Pasha, the draconian commander of the Operation Army.

Sultan Mehmed Reşad wanted to know more about the Ottoman lands and paid visits to cities in Anatolia. The Union and Progress Party, which had proclaimed the constitutional monarchy and had become very influential in the central administration, was not ready and too inexperienced to run the empire. There were also those within the party who exploited the constitution for their own interests. Their close connections to the *de facto* government heralded the iniquitous and unstable days of rule to come.

The interference of the Union and Progress into all administrative branches and the replacement of the existing anti-Unionist officials with new pro-Unionist ones caused administrative departments to fall into the hands of an amateur, unlearned, inexperienced, and partisan group.

Many rebellions followed the Unionists' strange and inconsistent political operations. Coercive methods went into practice while queilling the rebellion in Albania. Eventually the government's violent behavior aggravated popular discontent. "The Church Question" still prevailed in the Balkans. The Unionists issued a new executive law to settle the matter. Abdülhamid II had continuously worked to avert the unification of the Balkan states against the Ottoman Empire, but Sultan Mehmed Reşad failed to take into account the informed warnings of the Greek Patriarch of Istanbul and approved the law.

It did not take long for the Balkan states to come together against the Ottoman Empire. At the same time, the sultan's travel to Rumelia could not alleviate the disturbances in the region.

Hakkı Pasha, the head of the government and former Ottoman ambassador to Rome, transferred the Ottoman troops, which Abdülhamid II had deployed to buffer possible Italian

Sultan Mehmed Reşad's declaration of "Greater Jihad"
was announced in the Fatih Mosque, from the Navy Journal

Ottoman trenches in Gallipoli during the Battle of Gallipoli, 1915

attacks, from Tripoli and Benghazi to other regions. Soon after, Italian forces mobilized. Italy wanted Tripoli to be delivered and declared war on the Ottoman Empire on September 29, 1911.

Meanwhile, a new party called Freedom and Unity (*Hürriyet ve İtilaf*) Party was formed in opposition to the Union and Progress Party. Tough bi-partisan struggles broke out in the parliament. At this moment, the parliament was terminated with the approval of the Senate, or *Meclis-i Ayan* (Selected Delegation), on January 18, 1912. Later, the Freedom and Unity Party was eliminated at the elections held under the control of the Union and Progress Party. The new parliament was dominantly composed of the Unionists, with the exception of fifteen delegates.

While the elections for the parliament and constitutional changes were underway, Italians occupied the Dodecanese Islands in the southeast Aegean Sea. In addition, Italian forces bombed the Dardanelles and advanced near Istanbul while continuing to fight the Ottoman forces in Tripoli. Some Unionist army officers went to Tripoli and started a local resistance movement. The resistance effectively held the Italian advance along the bay for a while but failed to fight them out of the region.

In Rumelia, the newly-established small Balkan states were preparing for war against the Ottoman Empire. Interestingly enough, some officers of the army, which had moved to the Balkans to suppress the Albanian Revolt, revolted themselves against the Unionist government. Calling themselves the *Halaskaran* (Saviors), these commissioned officers did exactly the same to the Unionist government what the Unionists had once done to the Ottoman authority. Their demands were met, following the warning note they gave to the government. With the resignation of Grand Vizier Said Pasha, the Union and Progress Party was no longer in power.

Sultan Reşad announced that the involvement of the armed forces in politics was treacherous and on July 22, 1912, appointed as grand vizier Gazi Ahmed Muhtar Pasha, who was also popular among the soldiers. An odd structure was formed within the Ottoman government; while the cabinet consisted of neutral ministers, the Union and Progress Party dominated in the parliament in strong opposition to the cabinet. This duality destabilized the political foundation of administration. Upon the new grand vizier's request, Sultan Mehmed Reşad abolished the parliament.

In the Balkans, Russia's clandestine agents functioned effectively; Greece, Bulgaria, Serbia, and Montenegro combined their forces against the Ottoman Empire, their one common enemy. The First Balkan War erupted when Montenegro declared war on the empire, the others following suite on October 8, 1912. For the Ottoman army, it proved impossible to keep fighting in the Tripoli War while they had to mobilize in the Balkans as well. While a far better agreement could be concluded in the absence of the Balkan War, the Ottomans submitted

Jewelry chest, the Dolmabahçe Palace

Picture of the Ottoman ships and rowing boats in the Bosphorus with a view of the Galata region in the background

and subsequently signed the Treaty of Ouchy with Italy on October 18, 1912. The treaty gave Tripoli and Benghazi to Italy. In addition, the Dodecanese Islands temporarily stayed in the possession of Italians, and they would not reintegrate into the Ottoman lands.

The army was unusually involved in politics and was swarmed with partisanship. Moreover, the struggle between the educated and rank-and-file officers created havoc within the divisions of the army. Eventually, the hierarchical order in the army grudgingly shattered, and the Ottoman forces suffered a crushing defeat from the Balkan peoples, who had lived under the Ottoman rule for many ages. The Ottoman Empire lost all of its Balkan territories; Grand Vizier Gazi Ahmed Muhtar Pasha resigned and was replaced by Kamil Pasha of Cyprus. Muslims deported from the lost lands in the Balkans began to flow toward Anatolia. The main objective of the new grand vizier was to minimize the cost of the war. A group of Unionists led by a young Enver Pasha spread the rumor that the grand vizier would give Edirne to Bulgarians, and marched toward the Sublime Porte, the Ottoman government. They engaged in a coup, killed many along the way, and secured a note of resignation from Grand Vizier Kamil Pasha on January 23, 1913. They lobbied and convinced the sultan to appoint Mahmud Şevket Pasha as the new grand vizier. Called "the Sublime Porte Coup," this rebellion symbolized the first coup to overthrow the grand vizier and the government, contrary to traditional ones against the sultan.

The Unionists overthrew the grand vizier with the pretext that Edirne would be sacrificed soon; however, they signed the Treaty of London on May 30, 1913 when they came to power, surrendering the entire Rumelia region, including the former capital of Edirne. The loss of territories in Rumelia, which had been part of the Ottoman heartland for ages, caused a wave of indignation among the public. In the ensuing civil turmoil, Mahmud Şevket Pasha, who had played an important role in ending the reign of Sultan Abdülhamid II, was assassinated: The draconian commander of the Operation Army and the exiler of Abdülhamid II, Mahmud Şevket Pasha died in Istanbul.

The Unionists used Mahmud Şevket Pasha's assassination as an excuse to terrorize Istanbul: in a matter of days, hundreds of people were arrested and twenty-nine of them were hanged. Salih Pasha, the husband of the sultan's niece Munire Sultan was one of them; the sultan could not use his right to grant amnesty to him mainly because he shunned the villainy of the Unionists.

The Bulgarians came out of the First Balkan War as the largest Balkan state, so the other Balkan states unified their forces against Bulgaria this time. The Ottoman Empire exploited this opportunity to reclaim Edirne on July 21, 1913. Lieutenant Colonel Enver became the new minister of war, Cemal Pasha the minister of the navy, and Talat Pasha the minister of internal affairs. The Enver-Cemal-Talat triumvirate formed the only agency to keep in touch with the sultan and the government.

Grand Vizier Said Halim Pasha had long lost his means and authority. On August 2, 1914, the triumvirate above signed a secret agreement with the Germans, supposing that the Ottomans could win back the territories lost in the Balkans in a potential war, which they thought the Germans would certainly win. The agreement had been signed when the parliament was in recess. Four months later on November 11, 1914, the Ottoman Empire found itself at war, which would be its final. Aware of neither the irreversible agreement with the Germans nor of the ensuing war, Sultan Reşad was forced to declare war, *fait accompli*, on the Allies (Britain, Russia, and France). As the caliph of all Muslims, he urged his subjects to join in the war effort, for the Ottoman army was fighting "the Great War" (*Jihad al-Akbar*).

Pleased with the victories that the Ottoman army accomplished in the Dardanelles and Iraq, the sultan had given a speech of hope at the inauguration of the parliament in 1916.

He further penned an optimistic poem published in the *Harb Mecmuası* (the War Journal). However, he discontinued referring to the victories after the ensuing losing streak of battles. Meanwhile, Yusuf İzzeddin Efendi, Sultan Abdülaziz's son and heir to the throne, was found dead. The record read that he committed a suicide; however, his death remained mysterious like that of his father, the case closed.

Upon the resignation of Said Halim Pasha, whose relationship with the Unionists had become strained, Talat Pasha, the minister of internal affairs became the new grand vizier on February 3, 1917.

Carried away by the heavy consequences of the First World War, the sultan became distressed by the news of continuous defeats and retired to his palace. He also showed up in the imperial ceremonies to greet the German and Austria-Hungarian emperors.

The aged, diabetic sultan, who had been exhausted by the protocol in honor of the Austrian emperor, barely completed his visit to the Holy Mantle of the Prophet in the month of Ramadan. Three days after this visit, the old sultan met his destiny at the dawn of *Laylat al-Qadr* (the Night of Power, the most blessed night of the year) on July 3, 1918.

Sultan Abdülhamid II and Sultan Mehmed Reşad had seen the defeats of the Ottoman army in the latest war, but both died, without seeing the ramifications of the Treaty of Montreaux, in the same year, only five months apart.

Sultan Reşad had ordered the architect Kemaleddin Bey to construct his tomb in Eyüp before his death. The sultan was the only sultan to be buried in Istanbul outside of the city walls, and perhaps also the only one to assume the throne reluctantly. Had it been up to him, most probably he would have committed himself to prayers and would not have spent his remaining years as the sultan. Sources refer to him as a devout Muslim and a gracious and kind sultan.

At a young age, the sultan became a member of the Mevlevi Sufi order and read over and over Rumi's *Mathnawi* during his long *şehzade* years. Fascinated by Ottoman history, the sultan visited the Tombs of Sultan Mehmed the Conqueror and Sultan Selim I whenever he had the chance to do so. He was also concerned with Sufism and literature. He constructed a mosque in Karapınar, Konya, under his name.

Mehmed Reşad's sultanate was circumscribed by the activities of the Union and Progress Party, which interpreted the constitution in a way so that the sultan should not interfere with state affairs. The sultan detested the partisanship and the Unionists, but there was not much

Funeral procession of Sultan Mehmed Reshad, from the War Journal

he could do. It seems that his calm and cold-headed character averted severe clashes with his opponents, and thus avoided potential strife within the state. He was thrifty; it was only in the living quarters of the palace and the *Haramayn* that he made munificent spending.

The Ottoman Empire drifted into the First World War during Sultan Reşad's reign. For the empire, the war meant to live or die, and the second would happen. Despite that, significant reforms undertaken during this period would provide a springboard to the foundation of the Republic of Turkey.

Sultan Mehmed VI

Reign: 1918-1922

Father's Name: Abdülmecid
Mother's Name: Gülüstu Kadınefendi
Place and Date of Birth: Istanbul, January 4, 1861
Age at Accession to the Throne: 57
Cause and Date of Death: Paralysis, May 16, 1926
Place of Death and Burial Site: Sanremo, Italy – his tomb is located in the garden of the Süleyman Shah Mosque built by Sultan Süleyman the Magnificent in Damascus
Male Heirs: Şehzade Ertuğrul Mehmed Efendi
Female Heirs: Münire Sultan, Fatma Ulviye Sultan, and Rukiye Sabiha Sultan

Mehmed Vahdeddin,[38] the last Ottoman sultan, rose to the throne quite unexpectedly like his three older brothers before him. Vahdeddin became the heir to the throne after the sudden death of Şehzade Yusuf İzzeddin Efendi, the eldest son of Sultan Abdülaziz on February 1, 1916, and after the death of his brother Sultan Reşad, he became the new sultan.

Mehmed Vahdeddin lost his mother when he was only sixth months old, and his father when he was four. His brother Sultan Abdülhamid II (nineteen years the elder) took care of him; in fact, Abdülhamid II turned out to be his father figure. He was a good composer and played the piano and *qanun*—a descendant of ancient Egyptian harp. By the time Sultan Vahdeddin emerged as the heir to the throne, the

Sultan Vahdeddin by Sébah and Joaillier

First World War had already broken out and the Ottoman Empire had drifted into the war. Vahdeddin Efendi, the heir to the throne, made an official trip to Germany between December 15, 1917 and January 4, 1918. Mustafa Kemal, the founder of the future Republic of Turkey, accompanied him as his aide during his stay there.

Sultan Vahdeddin's sultanate took place in the worst of times. The news coming from the battlefields were all defeats and losses. The Ottomans lost Palestine and Syria; even Anatolia was under enemy threat. The sultan summarized the fallacy of compelling the empire into war when he said, "the government's imprudence drifted us into this quagmire and made us fall." Eventually, he had to suffer the consequences of a war that he had not wished to enter in the first place.

An Ottoman commission headed by the minister of navy Rauf Orbay Bey signed the Armistice of Moudros in the Moudros harbor on the northern Aegean island of Lemnos on October 30, 1918.

In less than four months on the throne, Sultan Vahdeddin had seen the signing of the Moudros, which dictated extremely severe sanctions and consequently paralyzed the Ottoman Empire. The sultan thought that the empire and its army could rally only if he could buy some time. He believed that a peace agreement would not result in dire conditions with the support of Britain and France.

Meanwhile, the leading members of the Union and Progress Party secretly fled the country on November 2–3, 1918. Ten days later, the Allies' navy consisting of sixty battleships moored along the shores of Istanbul on November 13, 1918.

The sultan pronounced that the responsibility for the losing war rested solely on the Union and Progress Party, and he would endeavor to maintain close relations with Britain. As the government and parliament fall into a bitter conflict over trying the Unionists, Sultan Vahdeddin used his constitutional executive authority and terminated the parliament on December 21, 1918.

The sultan tried to save his empire and maintain Istanbul by seeking the support of Britain. Britain and France pressured the Ottoman government to hand over the Unionists to them; Tevfik Pasha could not withstand this coercion and resigned. The sultan replaced him with Damad Ferid Pasha as the new grand vizier. The Unionists began to be arrested and punished.

The Greek invasion of the city of İzmir on the western coast of Anatolia caused civil havoc on May 15, 1919. Damad Ferid submitted his resignation to the sultan upon the invasion; however, the sultan kept him at his post.

The sultan appointed Mustafa Kemal Pasha, his former aide, as an officer-in-charge to inspect the Pontus-Greek Rebellion in the Black Sea region. Confirmed also by British archival documents, this appointment had followed a meeting between the sultan and Mustafa Kemal during which the sultan told him he could save the fatherland. Mustafa Kemal was bestowed with an extraordinary authority of giving orders to military, judicial, and administrative bodies in the entire Anatolia, Eventually he debarked in the city of Samsun on the north coast of Anatolia.

The sultan met with the Council of the Sultanate on May 26, 1919; the council agreed on the principle of unilateral independence and decided that a national council had to be established immediately to let the nation determine its own fate. The Allies reacted vigorously to these activities.

Sultan Vahdeddin did not trust Damad Ferid Pasha; therefore, he took Tevfik Pasha to the Ottoman delegation that would represent the Ottoman Empire in the Paris Peace Conference, the major platform to conclude the details of the armistice.

In greater parts of Anatolia, the Ottomans began to conduct armed resistance against the ongoing invasions, particularly the Greek invasion of İzmir. The British were pressuring on the sultan and the government to recall Mustafa Kemal Pasha, who had played a profo-

Accession ceremony of Sultan Vahdeddin, the last accession ceremony in Ottoman history

und role in broader resistance movements in Anatolia. The sultan remained aloof in face of pressures. Although the government issued a circular note that Mustafa Kemal had been discharged, it was generally kept silent. Mustafa Kemal Pasha telegraphed to the sultan his complaints about the government's hostile attitude and told him that he would resign if he had to do so, but he would carry on his struggle in the spirit of the nation. The sultan's response was sympathetic; he did not want him to return to Istanbul or resign from his post. He only recommended that he take a two-month break and rest a while until things clear up.

The British announced that the sultan and his government were behind the resistance movement in Anatolia; furthermore, they issued an official notice to the sultan, requesting him to arrest and bring Mustafa Kemal back to Istanbul. The sultan wired Mustafa Kemal Pasha on July 9, 1919 in Erzurum, and told him that he was dismissed from his post and that the British wanted him to return to Istanbul immediately. In order not to cause any trouble for Sultan Vahdeddin and the government, he resigned from his official duty and continued to work individually for the sultan and state.

Gold ceremonial throne

Sultan Mehmed Vahdeddin made it clear to Britain that he had nothing to do with the resistance. He further informed them that, since his army was disbanded, he could not suppress the civil turmoil, which all started with the Greek oppression of the natives in the land, and that it would be impossible to put the people in Anatolia on hold, had the Greek-mania not come to an end.

The Erzurum Congress met up under the leadership of Mustafa Kemal Pasha on July 23, 1919. The correspondence of the congress that was held in Erzurum in eastern Anatolia showed manifest allegiance to the sultan and reaction to the government. When the British requested the government to treat Mustafa Kemal as a rebel, the government urged to bring Mustafa Kemal Pasha and Rauf Bey to Istanbul for arrest. The patriot ministers, who criticized the government on this matter and in fact supported the National Struggle, resigned from the government. The Sivas Congress followed the course of these events and was held in Sivas in central Anatolia on September 4, 1919. The government prevented Mustafa Kemal Pasha and the sultan from communicating by telegraph. When the pasha sent a letter to the sultan and asked for the establishment of a national government, Sultan Mehmed Vahdeddin demanded the resignation of the current government and appointed Ali Rıza Pasha as the new grand vizier.

Mehmed Vahdeddin during his şehzade years

The new government supported the *Kuvayı Milliye*, or the National Forces. Furthermore, they met up with Mustafa Kemal in the city of Amasya, reached a total agreement, and signed a protocol with him on October 22, 1919.

Following the elections, the new parliament opened in Istanbul on January 12, 1922. British intelligence reported that the sultan first had seen Kara Vasıf, an agent working for Mustafa Kemal, and then ordered the inauguration of the parliament, but did not attend the ceremony in person in order for it not to be closed down by the British. The sultan announced that his illness did not allow him to attend the inauguration; Mustafa Kemal Pasha could not come to the first meeting of the parliament either because of the warrant for his arrest. The pasha telegraphed the sultan with best wishes, and the sultan replied to him with greetings.

Mazhar Müfit Kansu met up with the sultan on behalf of the Committee of Representatives. He reported that the sultan asked about Mustafa Kemal, whom the sultan metaphorically likened to the gems on top his crown, and that the sultan had really missed conversing with him.

The sultan also admitted a delegation from the parliament. He recommended that they watch their words as British were cold-blooded manipulators and might use their words against them. When the representatives told the sultan that the nation always kept its allegiance to the sultan and the British could do nothing to change this, the sultan responded to them that the British could advance as far as Ankara within a day if they wanted to do so.

The Allies put the sultan in the Yıldız Palace under heavy surveillance because they were worried about the resistance movement in Anatolia; this way they aimed to protect him against a coup and also to prevent him from moving to Anatolia to join the resistance.

The last Ottoman parliament acknowledged the *Misak-ı Milli*, the National Pact, on February 17, 1919. With this pact, the parliament declared its position on state borders, minority rights, and the status of Muslims and of the straits. In their view, the borders prior to the Armistice of Moudros were *de facto* state borders. The Allies showed an aggressive reaction to the National Pact; they officially occupied Istanbul and usurped all official institutions with the objective of maneuvering the sultan in a corner on March 16, 1920. The sultan was notified that the occupation was temporary, but its duration could change given that a civil turmoil plagued Anatolia. Many patriots were arrested and sent into exile.

The occupation disconnected Istanbul from Anatolia. Reappointed as the grand vizier and pressured by British, Damad Ferid ordered judges to issue *fatwa*s, legitimizing and orde-

The Yeni (New) Mosque in Eminönü, by Abdullah Brothers

Detail from the Prayer Hall of the Dolmabahçe Palace

ring the killings of the nationalists as treacherous infidels. The issues were printed on paper, and the British planes dropped them down to the public. Following the occupation, Sultan Mehmed Vahdeddin reclosed the parliament.

After the parliament was dismissed in Istanbul, the Committee of Representatives opened the Turkish Grand National Assembly (TGNA) on April 23, 1920 on Friday following the Friday prayer. This assembly began to effectively reinforce national unity and to lead the National Struggle. TGNA cabled a note of loyalty to the sultan and explained that the National Struggle was fighting to emancipate the sultan.

At the end of the First World War, the Ottoman Empire was forced to sign the Treaty of Sevres on August 10, 1920, which put forward unacceptable terms and conditions for the Ottomans. Prior to the treaty, the sultan regarded the terms of the treaty as "the compilation of evils." The Council of the Sultanate met up to discuss the terms and conditions of the treaty. Although the council signed the treaty in fear of a Greek occupation of Istanbul had they not done so and recognized the treaty with the rule of majority, the sultan never ratified the treaty.

The greatest reaction to the signing of the Treaty of Sevres came from TGNA in Ankara.

The Allies knew that the application of the Sevres would be too difficult in the face of an extensive resistance in Anatolia; therefore, they asked the sultan to establish a government that could come to terms with Anatolia. The sultan made Tevfik Pasha the grand vizier again. The new government had meetings in Ankara. Around this time, right after the Turks crushed the Greek forces in the Battle of İnönü near Eskişehir on January 10, 1921, the Allies invited the Istanbul government and TGNA to review the articles of the Treaty of Sevres at the London Conference; the conference did not generate any tangible results.

Detail from the Yıldız Palace, the late 19th century residence of the Ottoman sultans

Following the achievements of the National Struggle and the signing of the Mudanya Armistice on October 11, 1922, Refet Pasha came to Istanbul on behalf of TGNA and met up with Sultan Vahdeddin. Refet Pasha requested that the sultan not send a delegation from Istanbul to the coming peace conference, to dismiss the Istanbul government, and issue an official notice that he acknowledged TGNA. The sultan told Refet Pasha that the *de facto* representative of the throne was the Ottoman government; he was the sultan of the constitutional monarchy and could not dismiss the government. He rejected Refet Pasha's offer.

When the Istanbul government announced that it would attend the Lausanne Conference in November, TGNA abolished the sultanate on November 1, 1922 and declared that TGNA would appoint the caliph. In addition, November the 2nd was agreed to be celebrated as a national holiday. The sultan reacted to the idea and said that the caliphate was identical with the sultanate. The members of the Ottoman dynasty supported him.

TGNA decided that the sultan should be tried. The media was publishing news about the "traitor" sultan, and there were protests against him. Tevfik Pasha resigned on November 4, 1922, explaining that the sultan had a right to defend himself before the nation. The sultan would later say that Tevfik Pasha resigned and left him alone in his most difficult days.

Meanwhile, the lynching of the author and journalist Ali Kemal, a former minister of internal affairs and one of the leading opponents of the National Struggle, on his way from Ankara to İzmit caught Istanbul by surprise. Those with travel visas fled and others took refuge with British soldiers. The fact that those lacking money to escape came to the sultan and asked him to help them out frustrated the sultan.

After the abolishment of the sultanate, the sultan showed up in his first *Cuma selamlığı*—the ceremony held among public on every Friday. It was the first time that the name of the sultan was not mentioned in the *khutba*, or Friday sermon. Sultan Mehmed Vahdeddin contemplated the case of late Ali Kemal, his being left alone in the crowded Friday prayer ceremony, the daily digests in the newspapers against him, and the strong possibility that his life was in danger. Finally, he decided to leave Istanbul. He sent his personal aide Colonel Zeki Bey to General Harrington to carry him his message that he saw his life under threat, and he expected Britain to protect him on the condition that he would maintain all his rights to the sultanate and caliphate. He signed the written request not as the sultan but as "Mehmed Vahdeddin, the Caliph of Muslims."

The sultan packed up only his personal belongings from the palace. When someone recommended he take the sacred trusts of Islam with him, the sultan kindly declined, saying that they are gifts to the Turkish nation from his ancestors. The sultan was picked up from the Yıldız Palace and sent off with a ceremony by the British troops. His ship departed Istanbul for Malta.

British newspapers wrote that Sultan Vahdeddin was reasonable and cool-headedly completed the last Friday prayers alone in spite of the demonstrations against him, but he had to escape as he would be assassinated in the next ceremony on November 17, 1922. The executive order called the "Betrayal of the Nation" issued by TGNA was given as another reason for his departure.

In his memoirs, Sultan Mehmed Vahdeddin wrote the following: "I was left to have to accept or reject a caliphate without sultanate. I was unable to challenge that. I was surrounded by the blind and ungrateful, so I decided to leave off until things cleared up. I did not escape but emigrated. I came to choose Malta as the less unpleasant choice from which to set out on the journey to the Holy Lands. I tracked the footsteps of the Prophet. I never renounced my right to the sultanate and caliphate inherited from my ancestors."

The Süleymaniye (a.k.a. Süleyman Shah) Mosque built by Süleyman the Magnificent in Damascus

TGNA proclaimed on November 19, 1922 that Abdülmecid Efendi, the heir and son of Sultan Abdülaziz, was the caliph-elect. The new caliph accused Vahdeddin of betraying his country and blemishing the honor of the Ottoman dynasty.

Sherif Husain, the Ottoman governor of Mecca, invited the old sultan to the Hijaz. He informed British that he did not go to the Hijaz upon Sherif Husain's invitation but as the caliph of the Prophet and with the belief that spiritual goodness was awaiting him there.

Mehmed Vahdeddin journeyed from Malta to Mecca. Although he said that he wanted to go to Cyprus or Haifa, the British instructions given to She-

Sultan Vahdeddin is the only Ottoman sultan who was buried outside the borders of present-day Turkey. His tomb is in the garden of the Süleymaniye Mosque, Damascus

rif Husain ordered that he should reside in Ta'if. And so he went to Ta'if. The statement he made there was censored by Sherif Husain but contemporary media became very interested in it and published it. The former sultan explained the reason of his departure as follows: "The reason for my relinquishing the sultanate and leaving my homeland was not the fear of responsibility before those who themselves needed to be tried for what they had done after the World War, especially in its aftermath. To the contrary, I left in order to abstain from submitting my life into the hands of those who were lawless, ruthless, and deprived of even the virtue of acknowledging the right to defend." Since he understood that he could not stay in Hijaz for long, he wanted to go up to Palestine; however, British declined his wish. His request to go to Cyprus was rejected as well. The British had wanted him to go to Switzerland with the travel expenses to be paid by him, but the Lausanne Conference was going on and his presence in Switzerland might be misinterpreted. Eventually, British offered him Italy as his best option.

Mehmed Vahdeddin settled in Villa Magnolia, Sanremo, his consecutive applications to Britain to go to a Muslim land such as Cyprus or Haifa were answered negative, mainly because British thought that the ex-sultan's persistent emphasis on his being the caliph would cause trouble if he lived in a Muslim land. Furthermore, his demand to be given passports for him and 12 others in his family was rejected on account that the passports could be granted only to British citizens or those under British protection.

The sultan lived alone for sixteen months; the only family member with him was Şehzade Mehmed Ertuğrul Efendi. It was only after TGNA agreed on March 3, 1924, when all the members of the Ottoman dynasty had to be deported, that the last sultan was reunited with his family. The conglomeration of the deported dynasty members particularly in Sanremo caused Vahdeddin, already suffering financial difficulties, to use up all his savings.

After the abolishment of caliphate on March 3, 1924, Mehmed Vahdeddin found out that a caliphate congress would be held in Egypt. He wrote a letter to the Sheikh of Al-Azhar in Cairo and said that he was alive and did not renounce his right to caliphate. He further requested the sheikh to find a residence to the already-existing caliph in a Muslim country instead of looking for a new one. He sent a manifesto to the steering committee of the caliphate congress and protested their preparations. He once more made it clear that he did not and would never renounce his right to sultanate and caliphate. It was during the days the congress was held that the last Ottoman sultan passed away on May 16, 1926.

The sultan had left Istanbul with 20,000 British pounds; this amount enabled him to live sufficiently for three years. However, he underwent financial difficulty especially after his family came to Sanremo. In a short while, Vahdeddin began to sell all of his belongings; eventually, he even put his golden sultanate badge up for sale. He soon found out that the medal had been fake and became very upset, remembering those who could have done that to him.

After the death of Mehmed Vahdeddin, the merchants of Sanremo applied to sequestrate the debts he left behind in the amount of 200,000 francs. The sequestration officers came to his house, locked all the property and the embalmed body of the deceased sultan together in a room, and sealed off the house. The Italians did not allow a funeral ceremony until all his debts were paid off and gave the dead body back only a month later.

Meanwhile, the Süleyman Shah Mosque in Damascus, a Muslim land, was chosen as the burial place for the sultan. Under the supervision of Şehzade Ömer Faruk Efendi, his corpse sailed on a ship to Beirut, railroaded from there to Damascus, and reached its final destination on July 3, 1926, 48 days after his death.

Sultan Mehmed Vahdeddin spent his years of reign suffering the bitter consequences of WWI, which he had always said was a cathedral mistake for the Ottomans to participate in in the first place. The last Ottoman sultan thought that he could save his empire by a pro-British diplomacy at a time when the Ottoman Empire was invaded and torn apart, its armies dispersed, the labor force dramatically diminished, and the people impoverished and exhausted from the ongoing wars.

Sultan Mehmed Vahdeddin was middle-sized, slim, light-skinned, and pale-faced. He was smart; he had very good comprehension. His disposition was natural and his emotions were candid. He had a gentle and patient character. He detested gossip and did not let it happen around him; he did not speak much, preferring to listen. His visible facial image was reflective of a set of frowning brows, and hard and serious facial expressions.

List of the Heads of the House of Osman Gazi
from the Abolishment of Sultanate to Today

Sultan Mehmed Vahdeddin, the last Sultan	March, 3, 1924 – May 16, 1926
Abdülmecid Efendi, last Caliph	May 16, 1926 – August 23, 1944
Ahmed Nihad Efendi	August 23, 1944 – June 4, 1954
Osman Fuad Efendi	June 4, 1954 – May 19, 1975
Mehmed Abdülaziz Efendi	May 19, 1975 – January 19, 1977
Ali Vâsıb Efendi	January 19, 1977 – December 9, 1983
Mehmed Orhan Efendi	December 9, 1983 – March 12, 1994
Osman Ertuğrul Efendi	March 12, 1994 – September 23, 2009
Osman Bayezid Efendi	September 23, 2009 – present

Endnotes

1. *Gazi* [or *Ghazi* in Arabic] is a warrior for the faith who takes part in a *gaza*, or campaign for the cause of Islam. *Gaza* [or *ghazah*] is originally an Arabic term referring to the campaigns in which the Prophet participated. In line with the Islamic concept of the sultan as a *gazi* leader, Ottoman sultans remained *gazi* sultans and attached great importance to the *gaza* tradition from the very beginning of the state. The honorific title of *gazi* was assumed by Osman Gazi and many of the following Ottoman Sultans, like other Muslim rulers, who struggled for the preservation and expansion of Islam. The honorific was also used in the Ottoman state for the military officers who distinguished themselves in the battlefield against the enemy.

2. The Ottoman Empire was named after the name of its founder, Osman (Othman or Uthman in Arabic), from which the name "Osmanlı" in Turkish (or "Ottoman" in English) derives. The dynasty Osman Gazi established ruled over the Ottomans throughout its history.

3. Levni (d.1732) was the Ottoman court painter under Sultan Mustafa II (reigned 1695–1703) and Ahmed III (reigned 1703–1730). Levni's miniature portraits of the Ottoman sultans presented in this book, from Osman Gazi to Sultan Ahmed III, are from his *Kebir Musavver Silsilenâme* ("The Great Envisaged Portraiture Geneology") in the Topkapı Palace Museum archives.

4. The Seljuk Turks' defeat of the Byzantine army at the Battle of Manzikert in 1071 marked the beginning of the Turkic power in Anatolia. They established the Anatolian Seljuk State in 1075 and ruled Asia Minor from the eleventh to the beginning of the fourteenth centuries.

5. *Bey* is a Turkish title assumed by the rulers of an independent principality.

6. Janissary [or *Yeniçeri* in Turkish] literally means "New Force." The Janissaries were the sultan's standing elite infantry corps.

7. *Sipahi*s [or *Tımarlı Sipahi*s] were the cavalry corps composed of cavalry-men who were given fiefs called *tımar* in the provinces.

8. The soldiers of Turkish origin served as *Mamluks* (literally "owned," soldiers of slave status) for the Abbasids. In time these Turkic *Mamluks* became a powerful military caste and seized power for themselves, for example, ruling Egypt in the Mamluk Sultanate from 1250–1517.

9. During the early years of the fourteenth century, most of the Anatolian Peninsula was ruled by Turkish principalities which had been founded after the destruction of the Anatolian Seljuk state (1075–1318) by the invading of Mongols.

10. While the male heirs of the Ottoman sultans who legally had a claim to the throne were called *şehzade*s, their daughters were called *sultan*, such as Fatma Sultan and Ayşe Sultan.

11. *Akıncı*s were the frontline cavalry units of the Ottoman army and were known for their mobility and prowess in battle.

12. *Beylerbeyi*, literally "*bey* of the *bey*s" is the Ottoman title used for the highest rank in the hierarchy of provincial administrators.

13. *Tacü't-Tevarih* [or *Taju't-Tawarikh*, literally, "The Crown of Histories"] is one of the most brilliant examples of the 16th century Ottoman Turkish. Hoca Saadeddin—the author of this prime example of high-style Ottoman prose, provides a detailed history of the Ottoman Dynasty from its foundation to the death of Sultan Selim I, emphasizing the lives and careers of the leading political and learned men in each reign.

14. Calligraphy, the Islamic art of elegant handwriting, was originally used to adorn religious texts, specifically Qur'an manuscripts. Since pictorial ornaments are prohibited in Islam and since Qur'anic calligraphy has played an important role in the development of this Islamic art, a sense of sacredness always hovered in the background of calligraphy.

     Calligraphy—an art greatly loved and respected by the Ottoman sultans, is more than beautiful handwriting as its purpose is both aesthetic and functional. It engages the eye, mind, and soul while communicating meaning. The art of calligraphy flourished particularly in Istanbul after its conquest in 1453 as it was in the new Ottoman capital that the finest and most mature works were produced. Ottoman sultans, some of whom were themselves accomplished in this art, gave their full support to the calligraphers. During the Ottoman times, the Qur'an manuscripts continued to be copied as the most common sources for the art of calligraphy. Later, the calligraphy of the Qur'anic verses with splendid repetitive geometric shapes was written, tiled, stone- or wood-carved on walls, doors, and ceilings inside and outside of mosques throughout the empire—the Grand Mosque in Mecca and the Prophet's Mosque in Medina in the first place, as well as the Ottoman palaces, mansions and pavilions.

15. The Grand Vizier was the sultan's chief minister presiding over the imperial council.

16. The Fourth Crusade (1201–1204) was undertaken at the behest of Pope Innocent III to restore Jerusalem to Christian control. It veered off course, and finally landed in Constantinople. On April 13, 1204 the Crusaders broke through the Byzantine walls, sacking the city with looting and violence against local Christians. The Latin State was then set up in Constantinople by the Crusaders in 1204 and lasted until 1261. There had been violent mutual antipathy and animosity between the Latin settlers and the local Greeks throughout the Latin rule. The Byzantine's regaining the control of Constantinople from the Latins could not restore the once splendid city to its former glory.

17. Ottoman society was composed of an extraordinary mixture of peoples of various ethnicities and a multitude of languages. Each of the multireligious and multiethnic communities, called *millet*s, was given the freedom to practice their religion without restriction and retained under the protection of the sultan their own cultures, traditions, languages, educational institutions as well as their own courts responsible not only for religous laws but also for civil laws in such matters of personal status as marriage, divorce, and property inheritance.

18. *Balyos* is the term used during the Ottoman times for the Venetian ambassador in Istanbul—in Italian "bailo" means diplomatic or consular agent. Venice had the privilege of having commercial links with the Ottoman Empire through their *balyos* Bartelemi Marcello, the first residential ambassador arriving in the Ottoman capital a year after the 1453 conquest of Istanbul. Much later arrived the residential ambassador of France in 1535, England in 1583, and the Netherlands in 1612. As the relations with the Sublime Porte, the Ottoman government, were particularly important to these countries, they competed with each other to prevent the coming of new residential ambassadors in Istanbul. When William Harborne of England was recognized as the residential representative of English merchants in the Ottoman lands, the Venetian *balyos* cooperated with the French ambassador in Istanbul to attempt to prevent his accreditation by the sultan.

19. Fractricide was indeed an old practice in the world before the time of Sultan Mehmed the Conqueror. It was, for instance, referred to as an established rule by the Byzantine Emperor John VI Cantacuzenus, who died in 1383. In Ottoman history, the rivalry of *şehzade*s sometimes resulted in civil strife with detrimental effect on the state. For instance, the region was torn by civil strife between Bayezid's sons, each hoping to succeed the Ottoman throne for nearly a decade after the defeat of Sultan Bayezid I by the armies of Tamerlane at Ankara in 1402. Sometimes defeated claimant *şehzade*s fled to the domains of Christian or Muslim rulers hostile to the Ottomans, thereby becoming rallying points for military campaigns against the Ottomans. For example, Cem, the son of Sultan Mehmed the Conqueror and the brother of Sultan Bayezid II, fled to Europe where for fourteen years until his death in 1495 his presence acted as a constraint on the Ottoman government, which feared he could make a bid for power supported by a European coalition. Naturally, the Ottoman throne witnessed the contests for the succession among brothers as there was no law regulating succession to the throne. Therefore, the *şehzade*s who were sent out into the provinces as the governors attempted to secure governorship close to the capital, while their father was still alive, and to secure the empire's capital by winning the support of the palace officials, the *ulema*, or Islamic scholars, and the janissaries. The particular experience of Mehmed III (ruled 1585–1603), who carried out the execution of the other *şehzade*s upon his accession to the throne, attracted tremendous public reaction; it was after his reign that the new succession system of seniority (*ekberiyet*) was established in the Ottoman Empire. Therefore, from the early 1600s onwards, we see that a deceased sultan was rarely succeeded by his own son, but usually by a senior member of the dynasty, the elder brother or uncle.

20. The Spanish Inquisition, which coerced the Muslims and Jews of the Andulus State (711–1492) to adapt the Christian religion, was not definitively abolished until 1834 and resulted in the expulsion of all Muslims and Jews from Spain.

21. Silk Road is an interconnected series of ancient trade routes connecting Asia Minor with various regions of the Asian continent up to Chang'an in China in the east.

22. The Grand Vizier was the highest ranking vizier ("minister") of the sultan with absolute power of attorney and could convene all other viziers to attend to affairs of the state at the *Kubbealtı*—the Imperial Council.

23. The Danube, which is the second longest river in Europe, originates in the Black Forest in the northwest, passes through the Hungarian plain and several Central and Eastern European capitals, including Vienna, Budapest and Belgrade, and falls into the Black Sea in the east.

24. Buda is the western part of present-day Budapest on the west bank of the Danube.

25. *Ehl-i Hiref* in Turkish and *Ahl al-Hiraf* in Arabic, from the plural of *hirfa*, meaning "metier."

26. The battle was so named as it took place at night under the light of torches.

27. A recurrent theme in the sources on his life describe Sultan Mehmed III immediately standing up, out of respect, each time he heard Muhammad, his holy Prophet's name.

28. The *Devşirme* was an Ottoman unit composed of recruited boys, predominantly from the rural Christian population of Rumelia. After growing up and being taught the beliefs and practices of Islam and thoroughly educated in various fields, including the law, sciences, sports, and administrative skills, they took on all kinds of roles in the empire, especially in the military and royal institutions to become court officials. The brightest of the newly-enrolled boys were given a thorough education for long years in accordance with the rigorous academic standards in the palace institution of *Enderun* (the inner section of the sultan's palace) within the Topkapı Palace, where the most able could aspire to attain the highest office of state, that of the sultan's Grand Vizier, such as Baltacı Mehmed Pasha, Kara Davud Pasha, and Sinan Pasha. Those enrolled in the military would also go through a training period under strict discipline in the *acemi oğlan* (cadet) schools. After they were given a rigorous military education, they would become the sultan's standing elite infantry corps, called the Janissaries. The Janissaries, who were paid a regular salary, enjoyed a high living standard and respected social status. But in the 17th century, as a result of their growing corruption, the *devşirme* system gradually lost its functions. It became less effective on the battlefield as a fighting force, engaged in mutiny, and hindered efforts to modernize the army structure.

29. The *divani* script, among various calligraphic scripts, is a cursive style of calligraphy that was used in Ottoman documents, mainly in the Ottoman *divan* (council of state) as well as *ahdname*s (imperial decrees) and *vakfiye*s (endowment deeds). The *divani* script became popular during the reign of Sultan Süleyman the Magnificent and reached its peak at the end of the nineteenth century. As decorative as it was communicative, the *divani* was distinguished by the complexity of the line within the letter and the close juxtaposition of the letters within the word. A variation of the *divani*, the *cel'i divani* script is characterized by its abundance of diacritical and ornamental marks.

30. The renowned Ottoman Poet Nef'i (1572–1635) rhapsodized the names of these horses in an ode entitled *Kaside-i Rahsiyye*.

31. *Makam* roughly corresponds to "mode," such as major and minor in Western music.

32. The *takbiru't-tashriq* is the expression recited in congregation laudly during the Islamic Feast of the Sacrifice as a declaration of God's immeasurably and incomparably greatness.

33. The plain of Arafat is where the "standing" (*wuquf*) of several millions of pilgrims takes place on the eve of the *Eid al-Adha*—the central rite of the *hajj* worship.

34. The Imperial Council included the top ranks of the various branches of officialdom along with the viziers.

35. The Ottomans coined many official epithets for their capital, including *Bab-ı Ali* ("The Sublime Porte" or simple "The Porte" as was broadly used in Western diplomacy), *Asitane* ("The Doorstep of the Sultan/Government"), *Payitaht* ("The Seat of the Throne"), *Mahruse* ("the Capital"), and *Dersaadet* ("Place of Felicity").

36. Also spelled Kuchuk Kainarji.

37. *Bab-ı Ali*, literally the Sublime Porte, was used to refer to the Ottoman capital, government and the building for the high governmental body within the palace where Ottoman governmental policies were established.

38. The sultan's name was originally *Wahiduddin*, meaning "the Unity of Religion" but is usually transliterated as Vahdeddin in modern Turkish orthography.

Sources

Abdurrahman Şeref Efendi. *Osmanlı Devleti Tarihi* (History of the Ottoman State). Vol. I. İzmir, 1995.

Aktepe, Münir. "Ahmed III." *TDV İslâm Ansiklopedisi* (The Turkish Religious Foundation's Encyclopedia of Islam). Vol. II. Istanbul, 1989.
——. "Abdülhamid I." Vol. I. Istanbul, 1988.

Atsız, Nihal, (ed.) *Aşıkpaşaoğlu Tarihi* (Ottoman History by Aşıkpaşaoğlu). Originally published in Ottoman Turkish as *Tevârîh-i Al-i Osman* (Histories of the House of Osman). Ankara, 1985.
——. (ed.) *Oruç Beğ Tarihi* (Ottoman History by Oruç Beğ). Undated.

Beydilli, Kemal. "Mustafa III." *TDV İslâm Ansiklopedisi* (The Turkish Religious Foundation's Encyclopedia of Islam). Vol. XXXI. Istanbul, 2006.
——. "Mustafa IV." Vol. XXXI. Istanbul, 2006.
——. "Osmanlılar." Vol. I. Istanbul, 2007.
——. "Mahmud II." Vol. XXVII. Istanbul, 2003.

Çağlar, Yusuf and Salih Gülen. *Dersaadet'ten Haremeyn'e Surre-i Hümayun* (Ottoman Imperial Gifts to the Haramayn from the Place of Felicity). Istanbul, 2008.

Dördüncü, Mehmed Bahadır. *The Yıldız Albums of Sultan Abdülhamid II, Mecca–Medina.* Istanbul, 2006.
——. *II. Abdülhamid Devri Osmanlı Coğrafyası* (Ottoman Geography during the Reign of Abdülhamid II). Istanbul, 2007.

Dânişmend, İsmail Hâmi. *İzahlı Osmanlı Tarihi Kronolojisi* (An Annotated Chronology of Ottoman History). Vols. 1–6. Istanbul, 1972.

Eldem, Edhem. *İstanbul'da Ölüm* (Death in Istanbul). Istanbul, 2005.

Emecen, Feridun. "Osmanlılar." *TDV İslâm Ansiklopedisi* (The Turkish Religious Foundation's Encyclopedia of Islam). Vol. I. Istanbul, 2007.
——. "Osman II." Vol. XXXIII. Istanbul, 2007.
——. "Mehmed III." Vol. XXVIII. Ankara, 2003.
——. "Mustafa I." Vol. XXXI. Istanbul, 2006.

Es'ad Efendi. *Teşrifât-ı Kadime, Osmanlılarda Töre ve Törenler* (Ottoman Ceremonies and Traditions). Istanbul, 1979.

Eyüp Sabri Pasha. *Miratü'l Haremeyn* (Mirror of the Haramayn), Vols. I-V. Istanbul, A.H. 1306 [CE 1889].

Halaçoğlu, Yusuf. *XIV-XVII. Yüzyıllarda Osmanlılarda Devlet Teşkilâtı ve Sosyal Yapı*

(State Organization and Social Structure of the Ottomans between the 14th and 17th Centuries). Ankara, 2003.

Bilkan, A. Fuat and Ömer Çakır, (eds.) *Harp Mecmuası* (Journal of War). Istanbul, 2005.

Hoca Sadeddin Efendi. *Tâcü't-Tevârîh* (The Crown of Histories), Vols. I–V. (edition critique by İsmet Parmaksızoğlu). Ankara, 1992.

Hülagü, Metin. *Panİslamizm Osmanlının Son Umudu* (Pan-Islamism: the Last Hope of the Ottomans). Istanbul, 2006.
——. *Osmanlı Yunan Harbi Abdülhamid'in Zaferi* (The Ottoman-Greek War: the Victory of Abdülhamid II). Istanbul, 2008.
——. *Bir Umudun İnşası Hicaz Demiryolu* (Building Hope: the Hijaz Railway). Istanbul, 2008.
——. *Yurtsuz İmparator Vahdeddin* (The Stateless Emperor Vahdeddin). Istanbul, 2008.

İbrahim Rifat Paşa. *Miratü'l Haremeyn* (Mirror of the Haramayn). Undated.

İlgürel, Mücteba. "Ahmed I." *TDV İslâm Ansiklopedisi* (The Turkish Religious Foundation's Encyclopedia of Islam).Vol. II. Istanbul, 1989.
——. "Ahmed III." Vol. II. Istanbul, 1989.

İhsanoğlu, E. (ed.) *Osmanlı Devleti Tarihi* (Ottoman History). Istanbul, 1999.

İnalcık, Halil. "Bayezid I." *TDV İslâm Ansiklopedisi* (The Turkish Religious Foundation's Encyclopedia of Islam). Vol. 5. Istanbul, 1992.
——. "Mehmed I." Vol. XXVIII. Ankara, 2003.
——. "Mehmed II." Vol. XXVIII. Ankara, 2003.
——. "Murad I." Vol. XXVIII. Istanbul, 2006.
——. "Murad II." Vol. XXVIII. Istanbul, 2006.
——. "Osman I." Vol. XXXIII. Istanbul, 2007.
——. "Orhan." Vol. XXXIII. Istanbul, 2007.
——. *Fatih Devri Üzerine Tetkikler ve Vesikalar* (Historic Documents and the Analysis of the Era of the Conqueror). Ankara, 1987.
——. *Osmanlı İmparatorluğu Klasik Çağ* (The Classical Age of the Ottoman Empire). Istanbul, 2003.

İnalcık, Halil and Günsel Renda. *Osmanlı Uygarlığı* (Ottoman Civilization). Ankara, 2003.

İnalcık, Halil and Mevlüd Oğuz. *Gazavât-ı Sultân Murâd b. Mehemmed Hân* (The Battles of Sultan Murad, the Son of Mehmed Khan). Ankara, 1989.

Kafesoğlu, İbrahim. *Türk Milli Kültürü, Boğaziçi* (Turkish National History and the Bosphorus). Istanbul, 1991.

Kazancıgil, Aykut. *Osmanlılarda Bilim ve Teknoloji* (Science and Technology in the Ottoman Era). Istanbul, 2000.

Kinross, P. Balfour. *Osmanlı Tarihi* (Turkish translation of *Ottoman Centuries: the Rise and Fall of the Turkish Empire*). 1979.

Kurşun, Zekeriya. *Necid ve Ahsa'da Osmanlı Hâkimiyeti* (Ottoman Rule in Najd and Ahsa). Ankara, 1998.

Küçük, Cevdet. "Abdülaziz." *TDV İslâm Ansiklopedisi* (The Turkish Religious Foundation's Encyclopedia of Islam). Vol. I. Istanbul, 1988.
———. " Abdülhamid II." Vol. I. Istanbul, 1988.
———. "Abdülmecid." Vol. I. Istanbul, 1988.
———. "Mehmed V."Vol. XXVIII. Ankara, 2003.
———. "Mehmed VI." Vol. XXVIII. Ankara, 2003.

Kütükoğlu, Bekir. "Murad III." *TDV İslâm Ansiklopedisi* (The Turkish Religious Foundation's Encyclopedia of Islam). Vol. XXXI. Istanbul, 2006.

Mustafa Nuri Paşa. *Netayic ül-Vukuat* (Consequences of Incidents). Edition critique by N. Çağatay. Ankara, 1979–1980.

Neşrî. *Kitab-ı Cihan-Nüma* (Book of the Global Geography). Vols. I–II. Eds. Faik Reşit Unat and Mehmet Altay Köymen. Ankara, 1987.

Ortaylı, İlber. *İstanbul'dan Sayfalar* (Pages from Istanbul). Istanbul, 2003.
———. *Osmanlı İmparatorluğunda İktisadi ve Sosyal Değişim Makaleler* (Essays on Economic and Social Change in the Ottoman Empire). Vol. I. Ankara, 2000.
———. *Osmanlı Sarayında Hayat* (Life in the Ottoman Palace). Istanbul, 2008.
———. *Topkapı Palace, Milestones in the Ottoman History*. 2008.

Osmanoğlu, Osman Selaheddin; *Ali Vâsıb Efendi Bir Şehzadenin Hâtırâtı* (Memoirs of an Ottoman Şehzade: Ali Vasıb Efendi). Istanbul, 2005.
———. *Osmanlı Hanedanı* (The Ottoman Dynasty). Istanbul, 1999.

Ottoman Imperial Edicts. Başbakanlık Osmanlı Arşivleri (Turkish premiership of Ottoman Archieves). Ankara, 2003.

Öke, M. Kemal.*Hilafet Hareketleri* (Caliphate Movements). Ankara, 1991.

Öz, Tahsin. *İstanbul Camileri* (Mosques of Istanbul). Ankara, 1997.

Özcan, Abdülkadir. "Mahmud I." *TDV İslâm Ansiklopedisi* (The Turkish Religious Foundation's Encyclopedia of Islam). Vol. XXVII. Ankara, 2003.
———."Mehmed IV." Vol. XXVIII. Ankara, 2003.
———. "Mustafa II." Vol. XXXI. Istanbul, 2006.

Özdemir, Hüseyin. *Osmanlı Yönetiminin Dinî Temelleri Kılıç Kalem ve İlim* (Religious Foundations of the Ottoman Governance: Power, Knowledge, and Science). Istanbul, 2006.

Pakalın, M.Zeki. *Osmanlı Tarih Deyimleri ve Terimleri Sözlüğü* (Ottoman Turkish Dictionary of Historical Terms and Idioms). Ankara, 1971.

Sakaoğlu, Necdet. *Saray-ı Hümâyûn Topkapı Sarayı* (The Imperial Court: Topkapı Palace). Istanbul, 2002.
———. *Bu Mülkün Sultanları*. Istanbul, 2004.

Sarıcaoğlu, Fikret. "Osman III." *TDV İslâm Ansiklopedisi* (The Turkish Religious Foundation's Encyclopedia of Islam). Vol. XXXIII. Istanbul, 2007.

Sarıyıldız, Gülden. *Hicaz Karantina Teşkilatı* (The Hijaz Quarantine Organization). Ankara, 1996.

Silâhdar Mehmed Ağa. *Silâhdar Tarihi XVII. Asır Saray Hayatı* (Ottoman Palace Life in the 17th Century). Edition critique by M. N. Özen. Ankara.

Sözen, Metin. *Devletin Evi Saray* (The Imperial Palace, the Ottoman Seat of Government). Istanbul, 1990.

Sülün, Murat. *San'at Eserine Vurulan Kur'an Mührü* (The Qur'anic Seal Stamped on Works of Arts). Istanbul, 2006.

Turan, Osman. *Türk Cihan Hakimiyeti Mefkûresi Tarihi* (The History of the Turkish Ideal of Global Supremacy). Istanbul, 2003.

Turan, Şerafettin. "Beyazid II." *TDV İslâm Ansiklopedisi* (The Turkish Religious Foundation's Encyclopedia of Islam). Vol. V. Istanbul, 1992.

Uluçay, Çağatay. *Padişahların Kadınları ve Kızları* (The Daughters and Wives of Ottoman Sultans). Ankara, 2001.
———. *Harem* (Living Quarters of the Imperial Palace), Vol. II.

Uzunçarşılı, İsmail Hakkı. *Osmanlı Tarihi* (Ottoman History). Vols. I–V. Ankara, 1988.
———. *Osmanlı Devletinin Saray Teşkilatı* (Palace Organization of the Ottoman State). Ankara, 1945.
———. *Osmanlı Devleti'nin Merkez ve Bahriye Teşkilatı* (Central and Naval Organizations of the Ottoman State). Ankara, 1988.
———. *Osmanlı Devletinin İlmiye Teşkilatı* (Legal and Scientific Organizations of the Ottoman State). Ankara, 1988.

Yılmazer, Ziya. "Murad IV." *TDV İslâm Ansiklopedisi* (The Turkish Religious Foundation's Encyclopedia of Islam). Vol. XXXI. Istanbul, 2006.

Yücel Yaşar. *Kanuni İle 46 Yıl* (Forty-Six Years with the Magnificent). Ankara, 1991.

Recommended Readings

Ágoston, Gábor and Bruce Masters. *Encyclopedia of the Ottoman Empire.*Facts on File, 2009.

Aksan, Virginia H. *Ottoman Wars 1700–1870: An Empire Besieged.* Harlow, England: Longman/Pearson, 2007.

Finkel, Caroline. *Osman's Dream: The Story of the Ottoman Empire, 1300–1923.* New York: Basic Books, 2006.

Hanioğlu, M. Şükrü. *A Brief History of the Late Ottoman Empire.* Princeton: Princeton University Press, 2008.

İnalcık, Halil and Donald Quataert. *An Economic and Social history of the Ottoman Empire, 1300–1914.* Cambridge, New York: Cambridge University Press, 1994.

Kafadar, Cemal. *Between Two Worlds: the Construction of the Ottoman State.* Berkeley: University of California Press, 1995.

Lewis, Bernard. *Istanbul and the Civilization of the Ottoman Empire.* Norman: University of Oklahoma Press, 1963.

Shaw, Stanford Jay.*History of the Ottoman Empire and Modern Turkey*, 2 vols., Cambridge: Cambridge University Press, 1976–1977.